HOW TO GET TAX AMNESTY

A Guide to the Forgiveness of IRS Debt
Including Penalties and Interest

Daniel J. Pilla

WINNING Publications, Inc.
St. Paul, Minnesota

WINNING Publications, Inc.
2372 Leibel Street
White Bear Lake, Minnesota 55110

www.taxhelponline.com

First Edition, September, 1992

Seventh Edition, January, 1998

Printed in the United States of America

Library of Congress Catalog Card Number: 92-96839

ISBN: 0-9617124-9-X

Notice from the Author and Publisher

This book is designed to provide the author's findings and
opinions based on research, analysis and experience with the subject
matter covered. This information is not provided for purposes of
rendering legal, accounting or other professional advice. It is intended
purely for educational purposes.

The author and the publisher disclaim any responsibility for
any liability or loss incurred as a consequence of the use and
application, either directly or indirectly, of any information presented
herein.

Because the United States currently operates under an
evolutionary legal system, the reader bears the burden of assuring that
the principles of law stated in this work are current and binding at the
time of any intended use or application. Caution: The law in this
country is subject to change arbitrarily and without prior notice.

Dedication

To Honor the Memory of Frederick Joseph

To Commemorate the Birth of Nathan Frederick Joseph

For with thee is the foundation of life;
in thy light do we see light.

- Psalm 35:9

TABLE OF CONTENTS

TABLE OF ABBREVIATIONS

ACS--Automated Collection Site
BMF--Business Master File
CID--Criminal Investigation Division
CSED--Collection Statute Expiration Date
DIF--Discriminate Function System
ERISA--Employees' Retirement Income Security Act
FICA--Federal Insurance Contributions Act-Social Security
FMV--Fair Market Value
FOIA--Freedom of Information Act
FUTA--Federal Unemployment Tax Act
GAO--General Accounting Office
IMF--Individual Master File
IRA--Individual Retirement Arrangement
IRC--Internal Revenue Code
IRM--Internal Revenue Manual
IRS--Internal Revenue Service
LS--Local Standards
NS--National Standards
OIC--Offer in Compromise
PRO--Problems Resolution Office
PRP--Problems Resolution Program
QSV--Quick Sale Value
RA--Revenue Agent
RO--Revenue Officer
SFR--Substitute for Return
TA--Taxpayer Advocate
TAO--Taxpayer Assistance Order
TBRA--Taxpayers' Bill of Rights Act 1988
TBR2--Taxpayers' Bill of Rights Act 2 1996
TC--Transaction Code TDA--Tax Delinquency Account
TDI--Tax Delinquency Inquiry
USC--United States Code
USTC--United States Tax Cases

About the Author . . .

For the past twenty-one years, Dan Pilla has been tremendously successful in his negotiations with the IRS. Nationally regarded as an expert in IRS procedures, Dan provides people across the country with sound solutions to tax-related financial difficulties.

In 1992, Dan uncovered and subsequently publicized tax forgiveness programs instituted by Congress but deliberately kept quiet by the IRS. Through Dan's three thousand media appearances and the sale of more than 150,000 copies of his book, *How to Get Tax Amnesty,* better than three million people have found relief from a tax debt they were unable to pay.

While Dan's book, *How to Get Tax Amnesty* continues to liberate Americans from a tax debt they cannot afford to pay, his recent release, *IRS, Taxes and the Beast,* offers us the only workable defense against the present new-age IRS audit invasion.

Dan's work has been recognized by the likes of CNN, CNBC and the USA Radio Network. His books have been recommended by leading magazines and financial journals such as *Money Magazine, Family Circle, Wall Street Journal, Investors Business Daily* and many others. Dan has contributed to major articles for *Reader's Digest, National Review* and *Reason* magazine. His policy analysis for the prestigious Cato Institute entitled, *"Why You Can't Trust the IRS,"* has been discussed in newspapers across the nation.

Additionally, Dan is an official tax consultant to the National Commission on Re-structuring the IRS, the US Taxpayer's Party, the National Taxpayer's Union and many other taxpayers' groups.

Before Reading Further . . .

Throughout the course of this text, I discuss several IRS forms and publications. They are listed below. Many of them are necessary to carry out the tax amnesty plan. I strongly suggest you gather these forms and publications and have them available while you read this treatise. By having them in front of you while you read, it is easier to comprehend the points I make about completing and using them.

Forms and publications are available from the IRS by calling your local office. Or, Winning Publications has a Forms Kit that includes all the forms discussed in this book plus many of those discussed in my other books. The Forms Kit is available for just $5 by call Winning Publications at 800-346-6829. We make this available because too often, the IRS fails or refuses to release some of the forms you need.

Forms

> 433-A--Collection Information Statement (Individual)
> 433-B--Collection Information Statement (Business)
> 656--Offer in Compromise
> 911--Application for Taxpayer Assistance Order
> 1127--Application for Extension of Time to Pay
> 4180--Interview to Determine Liability for Trust Fund Recovery Penalty
> 8379--Injured Spouse Claim and Allocation
> 9423--Collection Appeal Request
> 9465--Installment Agreement Request

Publications

> 1--Your Rights as a Taxpayer
> 5--Preparation of Protests in Unagreed Cases
> 783--Instructions on How to Apply for Certificate of Discharge of Property from Federal Tax Lien
> 784--How to Apply for Application for Certificate of Subordination of Federal Tax Lien
> 1450--How to Request Release of Federal Tax Lien
> 1660--Collection Appeal Rights

CHAPTER ONE
Promises of Hope

am-nes-ty am-ne-ste *n. the act of an authority (as a government) by which pardon is granted to a large group of individuals.*

Webster's Ninth New Collegiate Dictionary, 1983

In the same breath with the term *amnesty*, we call to mind the terms leniency, forgiveness and fresh start. The proposition of amnesty is kind of a welcome home. It embodies the notion of coming in from the cold. It means wiping the slate clean and dropping the sins and transgressions of the past into the sea of forgetfulness.

In the past, however, there has been no such thing as *tax amnesty*. In fact, as long as I have studied the tax laws and the IRS, the attitude of the system has been precisely the opposite. Rather than encourage non-compliant citizens to come in from the cold, the IRS' enforced collection practices often drive them further from the gates of forgiveness, further down the path of lost hope.

While many states have entertained some type of amnesty program, the IRS dutifully rejected the idea for fear it would weaken its iron grip on the throats of society. The IRS regularly goes to great lengths to publicize its enforcement activity. This is to ensure the masses remain in lock step with all administrative and congressional edicts. Historically, any departure therefrom is met with the full brunt of the agency's enforcement arsenal.

If that is the case, why do murmurs of amnesty enter any discussion of income taxes? Why the book, *How to Get Tax Amnesty?*

In early 1992, the media released a spattering of stories suggesting the IRS softened its enforcement touch. The stories originated with statements from former IRS Commissioner Shirley Peterson. And while she never used the word "amnesty," her statements led many to the conclusion that the IRS adopted an amnesty program.

One such statement appeared in *Forbes Magazine* in March, 1992. There, Mrs. Peterson declared, "you can't get blood out of a turnip and if we're dealing with turnips, then we're better off cutting our losses and moving on."

The old saying, "you can't get blood out of a turnip," is the ultimate justification for debt forgiveness. After all, why not forgive when you cannot extract anything of value anyway? What else is left but to forgive?

The news reports and Mrs. Peterson's statement notwithstanding, the IRS has not and I suspect, will not, implement a *formal* amnesty program. If amnesty is to be had, it will be accomplished at the behest of the citizen. Offers of forgiveness will not pour forth from the agency.

As this book progresses, you will learn that the vehicles by which to obtain forgiveness and release of debt from the IRS have always existed. It's just that historically, it did not serve the agency's purposes to discuss them.

Why does the IRS now mention the means by which to obtain release of debt? I believe there are four very important reasons and I address each in turn.

The IRS - A Kinder and Gentler Agency?

Several programs were undertaken or broadened by the IRS in 1992. They are designed to bring delinquent citizens in from the cold. The chief program began in the IRS' Phoenix office. The idea is to assist delinquent taxpayers with arranging repayment terms which, in the description of one IRS official, "will not tear them apart." This alone is quite a departure from the usual payment terms traditionally required by Collection personnel.

Historically, the delinquent citizen could expect to pay the IRS such a substantial amount that even a subsistence level of existence was difficult. In the worst case, the IRS levies all or nearly all one's pay, forcing him to live financially underground.

The program that began in Phoenix spread to Kansas City, St. Louis, Wichita and eventually, throughout the nation. Under the program operated in Missouri, the IRS utilized consumer credit counseling agencies to negotiate repayment terms based on *realistic* financial considerations.

Does this program constitute amnesty? Does it offer relief from the crippling enforcement habits that usually attend unpaid tax bills? Based on this, can it be said that the IRS is a kinder and gentler agency?

Hardly. According to IRS collection officials in the Kansas City office, the program "will not cut anyone's tax bill. It also will not offer easier payment terms than taxpayers can negotiate individually."

What kind of amnesty program is that? If there is no forgiveness and there are no terms offered to soften the blow, what is the benefit? Under the IRS' description, there appears to be no benefit.

At the same time, the IRS makes it clear that if one does not step forward, the ax will fall! A statement appearing in the April 29, 1992, issue of the *Wall Street Journal*, directed to the estimated *seven to ten million* annual individual and business tax return non-filers, plainly indicates if these citizens are "caught," they face higher penalties for late filing and late payment and possible criminal charges. I present more on this in chapter three, *Am I Going to Jail?*

In the March, 1992, issue of *Forbes Magazine*, the program was summed up by saying, "don't confuse this with leniency, since the IRS still wants, before it will settle, what it could get by liquidating a taxpayer, *and then some.*" Emphasis added.

Not exactly a forgiving attitude. Not exactly a kinder and gentler agency. But because the IRS' accounts receivable continue to rise and the underground economy continues to expand, the agency is forced to talk in terms of amnesty to bring the malefactors to the fore.

While the IRS is not a kinder and gentler agency, it has recognized that its system must change. The points to follow plainly indicate why, for *selfish reasons,* the IRS is prepared to acknowledge rights which citizens have always enjoyed.

Economic Realities Force IRS to Reexamine its Policies

The one thing the IRS has most in common with other government agencies is its bureaucratic tunnel vision. It is amazingly incapable of seeing the whole picture. Thus, when it comes to collecting overdue accounts, the agency cannot comprehend that while a citizen may very well *owe* the money, his inability to *pay* renders the amount of the debt a moot point.

I have been involved in thousands of negotiations with revenue officers (RO), IRS employees who collect taxes. The negotiations usually involve original tax liabilities, repayment terms, personal expenses, installment payments, filing deadlines, penalty assessments, property values, etc.

Often, disputes arise in one or more of these areas. When they do, the RO invariably attempts to justify unreasonable demands by retorting, "Your client wouldn't have this problem if he would have just paid his taxes in the first place!"

What a stupid thing to say!

If my client *had the money* in the first place, he *would have* paid the tax!

Rather than attempt to work out a reasonable solution, the RO trods along wearing his bureaucratic blinders to the economic realities. Often, the reality is the citizen did not have the money at a time when all he owed *was* the tax. How can he be expected to regurgitate the money later, when the bill has doubled or tripled (or worse) because of interest and penalties!?

Despite the economic realities, demands for payment in full spring forth unabated. With each bill, the IRS adds more interest and penalties. It reaches a point where many people just throw up their hands in desperate futility. The result is citizens are driven underground just to survive and the IRS ends up accumulating accounts receivable which will never be paid.

Writing for the IRS' Collection Division in April, 1992, then Assistant IRS Commissioner for Collection explained that these economic realities must be taken into consideration. In an internal memorandum directed to all Collection Field Function Personnel, the deputy chief tax collector explained,

> A collection of $1,000 today is equal to almost $1,500 collected five years from now (present value). Additionally, the $1,000 is real, and the $1,500 is speculative.

As we examine in detail later, the IRS Collection Division is under "orders" to consider the economic realities of delinquent citizens. As pointed out in the memorandum, by taking a lesser amount now, the agency receives money which it might "never collect" in the future.

Accepting economic realities does not involve implementing a new program. As I already pointed out, the programs for achieving forgiveness *always existed*. In the past, the IRS simply chose to ignore them. It often attempted to mislead citizens in favor of squeezing the life out of them.

Political Realities Force IRS to More Honest Approach

The tax gap is perennially a major debate and concern of Congress. The tax gap is defined by the IRS as the difference between the tax *owed* and that which is *paid* without the need of enforcement action. The tax gap increases year after year. Tax gap estimates are all over the lot as nobody really knows who owes what. Estimates put the figure well above $100 billion.

Given Congress' wild, uncontrolled spending habits, you can well imagine why the tax gap is a serious concern. Congress needs money desperately. And knowing of Congress' propensity to chase dollars to fund its spending spree, each year, IRS officials ask for more money, more manpower and more equipment. With more money, manpower and equipment, it argues, it can reduce the tax gap by X billion per year. "If you give us more computers, we can do computerized audits and catch cheaters. If you give us more revenue officers, we can chase the deadbeats and make 'em pay. And if you give us more money, we can accomplish a myriad of goals hitherto only dreamed of by political oppressors of yore."

Historically, Congress was only too happy to oblige its faithful servants. By 1992, the IRS' budget ascended to over $7 billion annually and by 1998, it has topped $8 billion. It employs some 110,000 people worldwide. Before it's over, the IRS intends to spend countless billions to revamp its entire computer system.

In addition, Congress handed the IRS every information gathering tool, information reporting tool, audit tool, enforced collection tool and criminal prosecution tool it ever sought. For decades, virtually nothing on the IRS' legislative or resource wish list was turned down.

Despite the landslide of financial and legal support, the tax gap continues to increase. Why do you suppose that is? More importantly, do you not think Congress is also beginning to ask questions? The answer to the second question is simple. Congress *is* indeed beginning to ask questions.

The answer to the first question, however, is a bit more complicated. Why does the tax gap increase in the face of all this collection power? The answer evades the agency because it searches in all the wrong places. I have pointed out the obvious time and again. And events of the past several years lead me to believe the agency is finally listening.

The traditional view of why the tax gap increases is simply *not valid*. The traditional view suggests the increase occurs because more citizens cheat. That is *absolutely not true*. In fact, precious few citizens cheat. Thanks to IRS propaganda, most people believe the penalties are simply too great. And indeed, they *are* too great!

The tax gap marches on because tax liabilities accrue interest and penalties at an astronomical rate! In the best case, they double a tax bill and in the worst case, triple, quadruple it, or even worse. Interest is charged at prevailing rates but it is subject to change twice per year. Moreover, interest is charged on the combination of tax, penalty and *previously assessed interest and* is *compounded daily* on the entire unpaid balance.

In addition, IRS tacks on a penalty of up to one percent per month. This brings the total hit to a rate equal to 20 to 24 percent annually! Those are *loan shark rates* and that is what the public is forced to contend with.

For example, suppose you owe the IRS $15,000. Suppose further you agree to pay the IRS $150 per month. At the rate of 24 percent per year, your penalty and interest assessments build at the rate of about $300 per month. Consequently, you must pay $150 per month for the *rest of your life* and will owe more when you are dead than you did when the payments began! All the while, IRS carries the growing balance on its books and it is accounted for in the agency's tax gap pronouncements. No *matter what the IRS does,* it cannot reduce the gap because of penalty and interest accumulations.

In the IRS memorandum I referred to earlier, the Assistant Commissioner conceded that this is exactly what is happening. This is one of the events leading me to believe the IRS is listening. In lamenting the uselessness of many installment agreements, the Assistant Commissioner states, "In many cases, the taxpayer is not paying enough to cover the accruals [interest and penalties] and will *never satisfy* the liability." Emphasis added. A copy of the memorandum appears on the next two pages as Exhibit 1-1.

Consistent with the "new attitude," the IRS rewrote the book on penalty assessments and abatements. I accused the IRS many times of being trigger happy with penalties. As we explore in chapter nine, the agency made drastic changes in its approach to penalties. It is required to take a more cautious approach with assessments and a more reasonable approach to abatements.

Exhibit 1-1

Internal Revenue Service
memorandum

·date: APR 13 1992

to: All Collection Field Function Personnel

from: Assistant Commissioner (Collection)   CO *[signature]*

subject: New Policy on Offers in Compromise

Recently I approved a new Policy Statement on offers in compromise. It states clearly that we will accept an offer if the amount offered reasonably reflects collection potential. I know this policy is a significant change in the Service's philosophy and culture at all levels. Therefore, I would like to explain the reason for the policy and how all of us are responsible for implementing both its spirit and intent.

The driving force behind the policy is the recognition that reporting accounts as currently not collectible (CNC) or entering into extended installment agreements (IA) is not always the most effective way of bringing taxpayers into compliance with the tax laws. In reporting cases as currently not collectible, we have traditionally taken the view that because of the 10-year statute, the Federal tax lien and offset authority, there is always a possibility that some payment could be received. Far too often, however, this simply does not happen. We also enter into installment agreements which require payments over extraordinarily long periods of time. In many of these cases, the taxpayer is not paying enough to cover the accruals and will never satisfy the liability.

I believe that there are many cases where we should be discussing the possibility of an offer in compromise with taxpayers. As the result of an offer, we will get money now that we might never collect, or get money that is worth more today than in the future. A collection of $1,000 today is equal to almost $1,500 collected five years from now (present value). Additionally, the $1,000 is real and the $1,500 is speculative. We believe that taxpayers will respond favorably when they recognize the long term benefits from a compromise. In many cases they may be able to utilize third party sources that would be unavailable for any enforced collection action. However, if, after taking into consideration "present value" we know that more can be collected than is offered, the offer should not be accepted.

Exhibit 1-1 (continued)

-2-

All Collection Field Function Personnel

This policy is not intended to allow taxpayers to avoid liabilities which they can pay. The policy is simply an expression of reality; it is sometimes in the best interests of both the Government and the taxpayer to resolve tax delinquencies on terms that benefit both sides as early as possible.

I know that there is some concern that the same taxpayers may repeatedly attempt to go through the offer process to reduce their tax liabilities. We have dealt with this potential by including in the Form 656, Offer in Compromise, a requirement for full tax compliance for five years. If the taxpayer fails to comply after an offer is accepted, the compromised liability may be re-established. Resolving past delinquencies and ensuring future voluntary compliance is the essence of the Service's Compliance 2000 Strategy.

As you have always done in the past, I know everyone will implement this policy in both its spirit and intent. If we take the approach that we are in the business of collection, we will look at cases in a way that makes the most business sense. In many cases, the correct course of action will be an offer in compromise.

In sum, I believe the IRS came to grips with the political reality that it cannot continue to seek more money, manpower and equipment from Congress without showing some positive results from its efforts.

The Education Factor

Since my first book was released in October, 1986, I made thousands of appearances on radio and television, in newspapers, magazines and newsletters. I shout from the rooftops the fact that citizens have rights and the IRS has limitations. Often it is frustrating because there are so many citizens in need of this priceless information and at times it seems as though I reach so few.

At other times there are signs this work is paying great dividends. The signs come in the form of the hundreds of letters I receive from grateful citizens. The letters explain how my books helped them solve seemingly hopeless tax problems. The letters tell stories of those who saved two hundred dollars or two hundred thousand dollars by following my simple tips and procedures. Throughout this book, I share some of those letters. More than anything, they prove that there really is no such thing as a hopeless tax case.

Most incredible, however, is the evidence that the system is indeed changing. Since 1992, much pressure has been placed on the IRS to stop its abusive tactics and in 1997, there was even talk of a formal amnesty program. And while there is yet no *formal* amnesty program, the programs that are available have always been there. It is just that the IRS never bothered to say anything about them. Why are they now coming to the fore?

In addition to what I already said, I truly believe one reason is *The Education Factor*. In my thousands of radio interviews, I explain to countless desperate citizens how to solve their problems. I explain that all IRS penalties can be abated, in many cases, with nothing more than a simple letter. I explain that the law allows the IRS to forgive uncollectible taxes when the citizen can demonstrate he cannot pay. I explain that when the decision of a tax auditor is challenged, the citizen wins his case between 60 to 90 percent of the time.

Perhaps the factor most dispositive in forcing the policy changes is that I disclosed in 1988 the fact that federal income taxes are fully dischargeable in bankruptcy. Prior to that revelation, this was the best kept legal secret in the nation. Since 1988, my attorneys and I have discharged millions of dollars in taxes that could never be paid. And while there remains a dearth of knowledge on the subject, more and more attorneys are realizing the truth of this apparently unbelievable claim.

As if this were not enough, the information I broadcast on penalty abatements led to reduced penalty collections to the tune of $1.1 billion in just one year. In 1989, the IRS assessed nearly thirty million penalties against individuals and businesses. In 1990, the agency assessed a nearly identical number but the revenue *decreased* by $1.1 billion. The reason is because citizens successfully used their abatement rights.

We do not see a change in the IRS' hard fisted attitude because its leaders "got religion." We see change because the IRS got a billion dollar legal education stuffed down its throat a nickel at a time by those who know their rights and stood tall in the face of improper challenges. These people deserve the credit for paving the way for tax amnesty.

What "Tax Amnesty" Really Is

If the IRS is not offering tax amnesty through a formal program, you must then be wondering who is offering amnesty and what it really is.

In answer to the first question, I am offering tax amnesty by exposing IRS policy changes which allow for the forgiveness of all or part of your tax debt. The hopeless citizen burdened with unmanageable debts is entitled to drink from the cup of relief. My years of labor in the vineyard of pressure and proclamation have produced results. The IRS may not be offering any amnesty but it realizes the political and economic necessity to provide relief. But *you* must ask, for it is written, "Ask, and it will be given you; seek, and you will find; knock, and it will be opened to you."

As to the question, what is tax amnesty?, the answer is simple. It is freedom from the oppression of debt, freedom from the pressure of relentless collection efforts, freedom from hiding and running, freedom to once again be a productive citizen.

In 1990, I received a letter from Jon of West Virginia. He told the story of how he and his friend Gene were burdened with taxes they believed they could never pay. Here Jon explains what tax amnesty really is.

In 1970 I met Gene, a person who taught me a lot about the art of selling. We were working for a company as direct, self-employed commissioned salesmen. Gene had just gone broke. As an officer of a corporation he had been assessed for employment taxes, etc. The amount was staggering. All his "advisors" (bookkeepers, lawyers, etc.) told him that he couldn't bankrupt, couldn't own property and he would owe these taxes for the rest of his life if he didn't pay them. I heard him lament for years, "I'll take it to my grave."

From 1970 to 1978 I worked on commission for companies who did not withhold taxes. I was very young and not too bright, obviously, because I did not file taxes or set the money aside so, one day, I turned myself in. The amount of the assessment was fair, around $10,000. The IRS collector said he could put me in jail and talked to me in a manner that honestly sent me into a deep despair. Depression set in.

I couldn't plan my life because of what seemed to be a huge debt. "I'll take it to my grave," I found myself saying for years.

My logic was skewed. So I went on working commissioned jobs, filing late and not paying taxes. Why pay if you'll never get even?

Now, back to Gene. Gene kept working and hiding. Selling carpet in rented garages in back allies. Forced into hiding because of a debt that he'll "take to my grave." He would buy a house and put in his child's name. Hiding. Hide the carpet, hide the car . . .

But all this stopped. It changed in 1986.

I don't remember where I ordered *The Naked Truth* but it came in the mail. In it, Dan Pilla told me about the "statute of limitations on collections." I couldn't believe it! I called Gene! "I'll be right there," he said.

At this point I cannot find adequate words. Excited? Relieved? It was like serving many years of a life sentence and having a guard open the cell door and say, "You have been pardoned. You are free to go."

Gene immediately went from a "shady black marketeer" to now the largest carpet warehouse in our city. From hiding to high profile. Rags to riches. Failure to success. The credit must go to Daniel Pilla and publisher David Engstrom [Winning Publications, Inc., St. Paul, MN]. The IRS didn't give Gene his rights...Dan and Dave did.

Although I am still in a mess I feel there is hope. I hate to bankrupt but I owe about $30,000 in back taxes and with the help of Dan Pilla and David Engstrom, I too am going to be set free!

Thank you!

Signed: Jon - West Virginia

Now that is what I call relief!

"Come to me, all who labor and are heavy laden, and I will give you rest. Take my yoke upon you, and learn from me; for I am gentle and lowly in heart, and you will find rest for your souls. For my yoke is easy and my burden is light."

Matthew 11:28-30

CHAPTER TWO
How do I owe Thee?
Let Me Count the Ways!

"The rich rules over the poor, and the Borrower is Slave to the Lender."

Proverbs 22:7

He who owes another is, in a very real way, enslaved. This is particularly true when you examine modern lending practices which include detailed financial statements, lengthy mortgage documents, liens creating public records of debt and, of course, interest that sometimes borders on usurious. This does not even consider foreclosures which dispossess people of property and can destroy the will to go on.

Excessive debt saps the borrower's strength. Over time, he loses the will to work. As a lender's demands increase, the debtor's ability to be productive, provide for himself and his family and service the debt greatly diminish. As he falls further behind, the demoralized feelings of helplessness and hopelessness escalate. Eventually, he may become wholly disheartened and entirely unproductive, running from the very world in which he lives.

Another terrible aspect of debt is that it often inextricably binds one to the mistakes of the past. Debt is continuing evidence of one's past poor judgment. Bad business decisions or unsound personal choices follow you like a ball and chain, keeping you from moving ahead. Recall the words Jon used to describe the effect of his IRS debt. He said, "I couldn't plan my life..."

Because of the "huge debt," it seemed Jon was hopelessly bound to the foolish mistakes of his youth. Because of debt, Jon believed he was unable to forge a new life with any hope for the future. Jon caught himself saying, "I'll take it to my grave."

That kind of desperation is not uncommon when the subject is tax debt. With every other type of debt, there seems to be at least *some* sprinkle of hope. After all, one can possibly negotiate with creditors for more acceptable terms. Maybe he can liquidate property to pay claims. In the worst case, he can turn to the bankruptcy court and stake a legal claim to a fresh start.

Unfortunately, most people do not ascribe the same potential remedies to tax debts. The IRS goes to great lengths to persuade the public that it does not negotiate tax bills. Often, property cannot be liquidated due to oppressive tax liens. Most of all, because the IRS lied to the public for twenty-two years about taxes and bankruptcy, too many people believe taxes are not dischargeable.

Given these facts, most live the ungodly nightmare of tax debt, believing they must take the debt to their graves. According to 1997 IRS data, there are more than *twenty million citizens* in the United States currently bearing this horrible cross. It is reported that between seven to ten million individuals and businesses failed to file required tax returns and over thirteen million owe back taxes they cannot pay.

The IRS confirms that the reasons for non-filing, in most cases, are as I have said all along. Most cannot pay or skipped filing before and now fear the IRS. In her testimony to the House Government Operations Committee in June, 1992, former IRS Commissioner Shirley Peterson stated, "Many taxpayers may want to comply, but cannot because they don't have the money to pay the tax due. When this happens, they often decide not to file a return. They may eventually drop out of the system altogether." Mrs. Peterson also correctly observed that "a good part of what we call noncompliance with the tax laws is caused by taxpayers' lack of understanding of what is required in the first place."

In this chapter, I provide the profile of what the IRS calls the "non-compliant taxpayer." In an effort to make this book as comprehensive as possible, I describe in detail the most common ways one finds himself a delinquent taxpayer. What you are about to read constitutes the seven most devastating tax collection problems in America. If you find yourself identifying with one or more of these seven problems, indeed, amnesty can be yours.

Failure to File a Tax Return

Next to outright tax fraud or deliberate evasion, failure to file a tax return is considered by the IRS to be the most "egregious form of non-compliance." Year after year, however, a cadre of citizens fail to file for a host of reasons. There seem to be two general reasons why this occurs. The first, most common reason is financial. The second, much broader in scope, encompasses numerous specific causes not necessarily related merely to dollars and cents. I address each group in turn.

Financially Induced Failure to File

Please recall the letter from Jon that we read in the opening chapter. Jon earned income as an independent salesman. Because he was *not treated* as an employee, deductions for federal and state income taxes were not taken from his pay. Jon failed to file his return because he knew he did not have the money to pay. In Jon's case, his failure was due primarily (by his own admission) to his ignorance and the "mistakes of his youth." This is entirely consistent with Mrs. Peterson's statement to Congress in June, 1992.

There are many citizens who, due to sluggish economic conditions, are forced to choose between paying their taxes and feeding their families. In that situation, one always chooses to feed the family. That creates a problem come tax time since no money is available to pay the tax man. The fear and uncertainty of dealing with the IRS leads many to avoid filing a return altogether.

In many cases, the IRS is directly responsible for exacerbating the situation. Many of these people would not avoid filing if the IRS told the truth. For years, the IRS falsely informed citizens they have no right to obtain an extension of time to pay taxes. I speak personally with hundreds of citizens who tell me they called the IRS seeking advice on what to do when they do not have the money to pay. Time and again the IRS explains there is no right to obtain an extension of time to pay. If you cannot pay the tax, IRS advises you to simply file and "hope for the best."

Unfortunately, most citizens are well aware of the IRS' capacity to inflict harm. Thus, they are unwilling to just "hope for the best." The result is, rather than file the return without the money, they file no return at all.

This particular non-filing problem would be greatly reduced if the IRS just told the truth about Form 1127. Form 1127 is the Application for Extension of Time to Pay Tax. If the form is filed on or before

April 15, one can potentially win an extension of up to six months to pay. Not only would the non-filing problem be mitigated, but the public would save more than $600 million in failure to pay penalties and an equal amount of interest. See chapter eight of my book, *41 Ways to Lick the IRS with a Postage Stamp*, for more on Form 1127. A copy of Form 1127 is provided in our Forms Kit.

Once the first return goes unfiled, a dangerous pattern begins. The citizen tells himself, "I'll just get the money in the next few months and file late." Sometimes he files an extension of time to file the return (Form 4868), sometimes not. Inevitably, however, financial hardships continue and he never finds the tax money. Before long, he faces the requirement to file his next return and has yet to file the previous return.

Now, fear sets in. In some cases, financial problems spill from one year to the next. In other cases, the fear of exposure immobilizes the citizen. In either case, one unfiled return becomes two, then three. Before you know it, one is mired in a pattern of delinquency and facing huge tax and penalty bites with no hope of solving the problem.

Unusual Circumstances Cause Failure to File

Not all failures to file are due exclusively to financial problems. There are a variety of other reasons. Record keeping problems and medical crises seem to be the leading causes of non-financially motivated failure to file.

Record Keeping Problems. Deb is a lady from Tennessee whose husband runs a small construction company. He travels a lot. For eight years during the 1980s, Deb raised children while her husband operated the business. Deb's husband was not an organized person when it came to record keeping. Like many citizens uneducated in the ways of accounting and record keeping, he operated his business out of his pocket. If he did obtain a receipt, it eventually found its way into a box or bag where it lay, dirty and crumpled, for years.

The standard by which he judged the success of his business was simple. "If I had money, I was doing okay. If I didn't, I wasn't." Who needs an accountant to figure that out?

Deb and her husband were not criminals and they were not tax cheats. They were, however, confused by a complicated system and fell victim to their own reservations and ignorance. In 1984, Deb and her husband did not file their 1983 tax return. That began a pattern continuing until 1991. This is when the IRS finally knocked on the door and put the fear of God into Deb.

Then there is Doug, not entirely unlike Deb and her husband. He too operated his business by the seat of his pants and out of a briefcase. During early 1989, Doug's car was deposited at a local service garage for repair. Before leaving it, Doug removed the items of value but left two boxes containing his 1988 financial records.

While the vehicle was in the care of the service garage, it was broken into and, you guessed it, various worthless items were stolen, including his records. This happened in February, 1989, just two months prior to the 1988 filing deadline. Doug had no idea what to do, so like many who somehow lost records, he did nothing. He filed no return and submitted no extension of time to file. After all, why ask for an extension of time when he did not have any records from which to prepare the return anyway?

Doug's single problem quickly became many. Perceiving that he could not file his 1989 return because of the missing 1988 return, he suddenly had two unfiled returns. Then two became three.

Record keeping problems may be occasioned for reasons other than confusion or ignorance. You may have lost records due to fire, flood, civil disorder or some other casualty. In one case, I dealt with a woman who moved several times within just a few years. Her records ended up with the National Geographics, deep within some recycling bin. This started her on a pattern of non-filing that extended four years.

I know some IRS employees will read this book. After passing this portion they no doubt surely scoff and say, "Those reasons are no excuse for not filing subsequent returns." They might concede that cause existed for not filing the initial return, but they assert there is no justification for allowing the pattern to continue. The hardness of their hearts leads them to exclaim, "It's their own fault and they deserve what they get!"

The following remarks are directed squarely at the IRS. I believe the agency itself is chiefly responsible for a great deal of the non-compliance that exists today. The IRS, no one else, goes to great lengths to terrify the public. It leads the nation to believe that if you run afoul of the agency, you will be destroyed. Why would anybody wish to bring that kind of wrath upon himself by stepping forward after making a mistake?

The IRS, no one else, has lied to the public about the ability to obtain an extension of time to pay taxes. Those lies continue to this day. If the public had any idea of this right, the millions of tax returns which go unfiled because of financial shortcomings would likely be filed on time.

The IRS, no one else, lobbies Congress annually for increased penalty and interest assessment tools with which to club the public when they make mistakes. Using these tools unashamedly, the IRS routinely doubles, triples--or more--a tax bill attributable to failure to file. Then to add insult to injury, IRS lies to the public about the right to cancel those penalties. IRS employees regularly claim that nothing can be done about penalty assessments and that is simply not true.

When a citizen finally does step forward or is found out, it is the IRS, no one else, that imposes enforced collection, often sending the citizen right back into hiding. After all, how can anyone be expected to pay taxes at the expense of feeding his family? I do not care what you may think, the reality is that when faced with a choice between feeding the family and paying the tax, the family will be fed--period.

What I want to know is, when are you people going to realize that compassion for the unintentional, the ignorant, the confused or misled nets the agency more revenue and good will then does the Darth Vader approach? After all, these are *fellow Americans* you grind into a powder! And for what? Is not the right of an individual *to exist* and raise a family *at least* as important as the prevailing financial whims of Congress?

Medical Problems. A Phoenix man I will call Bill was faced with a real crisis. His wife was diagnosed with cancer and the outlook was not good. Bill immediately began to do everything in his power to keep his wife alive. He went from specialist to specialist and from treatment program to program.

The disease progressed but slowly at first. Bill's search for hope and a cure went on. Diverting all his resources to the battle, he used every available dollar to pay for doctors, hospitals and clinics. As financial demands grew, Bill met them by funneling tax money to the war. When faced with the prospect of paying the tax or potentially keeping his wife alive, Bill's choice was simple and he made it without hesitation.

When the time came to file his tax return, he was struck with a harsh reality. His wife's illness and care consumed both his resources and his time. Even if Bill had the money to pay the tax, there was no way to prepare a correct return because he spent no time attending to his financial affairs. Bill's decision, like that of keeping his wife alive, was made quickly. He simply failed to file.

Eventually, Bill and his wife lost their physical battle, but not before piling up several years of non-filing. Having emerged from one critical war a loser, Bill now faced another. And his prospects for winning seemed no better than the first time. In the second fight, however, Bill had nowhere to turn. So in his retreat, the problem only grew worse.

Rod also had a medical problem. He was an alcoholic. It began slowly at first but by the early 1980s, his problem was out of control, so mush so, that he could not hold a job and lost his wife. During that period, Rod went four years without filing. His affairs were in such disarray, he could not begin to construct a return even if he were sober long enough to recognize the requirement.

Eventually, Rod got help with his drinking problem and dried out. While surveying the damage from his new position of sobriety, he realized, among other things, he failed to file several tax returns. He anonymously phoned the IRS seeking advice.

What he learned was not promising. He would have to file the returns, he was told. No surprise there. He was also told that interest and penalties would be added to the bill. While that was not good news, it too came as no surprise. He then asked what terms could be worked out because he could not pay in full. He was told the IRS was not a bank. He was told it does not give loans and if he could not pay, he could expect wage levies and tax liens.

Rod went several years without filing returns and heard nothing. When he voluntarily stepped forward seeking help, he was threatened. His concern turned to fear, then to bewilderment. "Why," he asked, "would they do nothing when I was not filing, then threaten to crush me the minute I stepped forward to fix the problem?"

Good question. There are legal and procedural reasons (which we address later) why this occurs but I have never heard a reasonable explanation as to why the agency's attitude allows it to continue.

Rod could not pay the tax and he could not survive wage levies. The agency gave him no hope. Therefore, he continued in the pattern of not filing. Eight years went by before he came to grips with the trouble.

Rod's story evidences a phenomenon which bears discussion. Citizens can go for ycars without filing tax rcturns. In thc proccss, it is very common that they hear absolutely nothing from the IRS. That is one of the reasons we see the non-filing pattern continue.

When one fails to file the first time, he expects the IRS to be at the door within just a few months. The agency not only does not arrive at the door, it sends no letters and places no phone calls. After the shock and dismay wear off, it becomes slightly easier to skip the second year, then the third. All the while the citizen expects somehow to raise the money, but never is contacted by the agency.

After filing the tax returns, it seems the roof caves in. Almost overnight, IRS records tax liens, sends penalty notices and makes contacts by revenue officers who demand payment *now,* or else!

None of what is written here should be construed as encouraging the failure to file tax returns. Similarly, this should not be construed as encouraging the pattern of non-filing.

What I am attempting to point out, as much for the IRS as any one else, is the *psycho-dynamics* of the non-filer. I know because I speak with hundreds of them every year. I help them solve the problem and break the pattern. If the IRS were doing what I have been doing, I believe there would not be seven to ten million non-filers. Whether the agency wishes to accept it or not, the cold reality is that many non-filers are created by the IRS itself. Those who are not created by the agency are often encouraged by it.

Filing a Return Without the Money

Another common way of becoming indebted is by filing a return that *reports* tax due but without *paying* the tax. Any number of financial, medical or other factors can affect one's ability to pay. However, the prevailing school of thought, encouraged and propagated by false IRS doctrine, is to file the return *without* taking protective measures.

After filing a return, the tax becomes "assessed." The assessment affords the IRS the right to collect the tax. Collection begins with a series of notices and demands. If the tax is not paid after receiving notice, the agency may enforce collection.

This explains why one can go years without filing a return and never hear from the agency only to have the roof cave in just months after filing. The assessment, created at the time of filing, releases the dogs and unless you meet and neutralize the attack, you are fresh meat.

More than anything else, the IRS is responsible for exacerbating this problem. As I mentioned, the IRS deliberately lies to the public about the availability of the extension of time to pay taxes, claiming no such right exists.

To add insult to injury, most tax professionals do not know any better so the media proliferates the IRS' position. For example, the March, 1992, issue of *Money Magazine* contained a story entitled, *What to do If you Can't Pay the IRS this April.* The self-styled experts at *Money* took a crack at helping its readers avoid the problem. Here is the best the know-it-alls could come up with:

> If you find yourself in this predicament, take a deep breath [as if that's going to help]. Applying for an extension won't help: you will still be penalized unless you pay your 1991 liability in full by the April deadline. [That's a real revelation; *the IRS* told me that much!] Make sure you haven't overlooked any salable assets, such as saving bonds or stocks, [There's an idea! I never thought of actually selling something to raise the money!] or any possible sources of loans, such as a cash-value life insurance policy, 401(k) plan or a home-equity line of credit. [Boy, what would we do without the *Money* plan of attack?]

Drawing on a former IRS Revenue Officer for "help," *Money* goes on to explain that if you "can't come up with the full amount, send in as much as you can and file your 1040 on time anyway."

There. Now that is what I call a battle plan! Is it any wonder why so many people find themselves swamped with trouble when they follow this advice?

The article did not say one word about avoiding the entire ugly affair by just properly preparing and filing Form 1127. Nor did it breathe a word about canceling the stiff penalty for not paying the tax, which the article rubs into the nose of the reader.

On April 15, 1992, a *Money* senior editor appeared on a national television broadcast to answer tax questions. He was asked by the host what to do if one could not pay his taxes on time. I will never forget the "expert's" response. The man sat there with a blank stare on his face, then just shrugged his shoulders.

Debt Created by the Tax Audit

The stated purpose of the tax audit is nothing more or less than the process of determining the correctness of a tax return. In the civil tax environment, the citizen bears the burden of proof with regard to all issues claimed on the return. That does not mean you go to jail if the IRS accuses you of a crime and you cannot prove your innocence. It means if the IRS challenges a claim in your return, you must prove the correctness of the claim. If you cannot, it is disallowed. If disallowed, IRS recalculates your tax bill and charges you the difference, including interest and penalties. If you incur tax debt as a result of an audit, you may lay claim to at least one form of forgiveness. Most importantly, you can prevent that debt from driving you underground.

General Tax Audits

The IRS pretends the tax audit is merely a tool to check the accuracy of tax returns. In reality, the audit process leads to big bucks for the agency. Each year, the process leads to additional tax assessments of approximately $4,000 per audit. According to the IRS, 88 percent of all returns are incorrect. When audited, the alleged errors lead to wholesale assessments of interest and penalties.

The premise of my book, *IRS, Taxes and the Beast*, is that many of the techniques employed by tax auditors are carefully contrived bluffs designed to obtain improper tax assessments. This claim is proven each time I speak with another discouraged citizen seeking an explanation for the incredible claims made by the IRS in *his* audit.

As I claim time and again, *no* decision of an auditor is final. When you appeal your audit, your chances of winning increase substantially. For example, the IRS' own statistics show that audit results are wrong between 60 to 90 percent of the time! Statistics also show that the IRS *collects* substantially less from those who appeal audit decisions versus those who do not.

The reality, however, is that most people do not understand that you can say "no" to an auditor and make it stick. Most people cringe at the thought of challenging an IRS official. And the IRS knows this. Consequently, it continues the practice of extracting money from citizens under the guise of correcting return errors.

Because tax auditors have nothing whatsoever to do with collecting the final assessment, they could not care less whether you can actually *pay the bill*. Their job is simply to determine the "correct liability." It is the job of the revenue officer to collect the assessment. Once the case is handed to an RO, his only concern is to collect the tax. He could not care less whether you *actually owe* it.

Each year, hundreds of thousands of citizens are caught in this trap. The result is a tax bill they generally cannot explain and a tax collector who does not care even if they could.

Tax Shelter Audits

Do you know anybody who has much sympathy for tax shelter investors plagued with back taxes? I surely do not. As with other areas of tax debt, however, this situation was at least exacerbated by the IRS.

In the late 1970s and early 1980s, an entire industry grew up around the goal of reducing one's tax bite. This is nothing new. Whenever Congress creates a tax, expert attorneys, accountants and tax planners figure a way to reduce or eliminate it. It is a game that has been played for centuries.

The depreciation and investment credit rules which once existed allowed a person to make, for example, a $10,000 investment in a business. In turn, he could claim as much as $40,000 to $50,000 in tax breaks and deductions. In this manner, a high income citizen faced with a $50,000 tax hit could virtually eliminate it by investing a fraction of the tax bill into a business. The fee paid to the investment advisors nowhere near approached what he would otherwise pay in taxes.

Business ventures formed through limited partnerships sprung up everywhere. The partnerships operated every conceivable business. There were motion picture ventures, oil and gas operations, race horse and race dog consortiums and an endless list of other enterprises.

Recognizing the loss of revenue generated by these programs, the IRS regrouped and influenced Congress to change the laws. With the passage of the Tax Equity and Fiscal Responsibility Act of 1982, the IRS was handed a new toolbox of enforcement statutes. It also won new guidelines by which such investments must operate.

That might seem fair enough, standing alone. But Congress did not merely change the law. It allowed the new rules to apply *retroactively*. That meant the IRS could attack investments made under the old laws, well before any restrictions applied.

And attack it did. Within just a few years, more than 400,000 tax shelter cases found their way into the courts. In litigation, the tax shelters dropped like flies. In my own experience, I have not seen a single victory on the merits of the investment. True, many investors were able to avoid penalties and some were given credit for their out-of-pocket expenses but otherwise, the fight was hopeless.

By the late 1980s, the 400,000 tax shelter *litigation* cases became 400,000 *collection* cases. The horrible thing about tax shelter cases is the length of time it took the litigation to run its course. It was not uncommon for a citizen to make an investment in 1980 which saved him, say, $30,000 in taxes. By 1990, after exhausting the litigation process, that same citizen was asked to pay $100,000 or more, considering interest and penalties.

Another fact I notice with tax shelter investors is that while they certainly were high income citizens, most were by no means rich.

These facts considered, it presents more than just a small problem when such a person is presented with a tax bill of $100,000-plus.

IRS Error

In 1988, the General Accounting Office of the United States Government (GAO) released a study which I made common knowledge. The study was done in response to my claim that the IRS deliberately sends notices to the public which it knows are false. The study revealed that *48 percent* of all IRS computer notices were either wrong or incomprehensible. Still, most citizens just pay because they are largely ignorant of their right to challenge them.

In 1990, the GAO did a follow up to the 1988 report. In it, it asked the question, "What has the IRS done to correct the problem revealed in our first report?" The answer was spelled out very simply and quickly in a two-page document. The IRS did not lift a finger to correct a problem that costs the public billions each year.

Computer Notices

The IRS conducts computerized audits of every tax return filed. Those audits lead to a flurry of notices as well as about one million face-to-face examinations annually. The number of notices is into the tens of millions each year.

When conducting these audits, IRS views at least four items. First, it determines the mathematical correctness of each entry in the return. Second, it ascertains mechanical correctness. By that I mean it verifies whether all necessary supporting schedules are attached and whether all required entries are present and in the proper line, etc. Third, it compares all information returns, such as Forms W-2 and 1099 bearing your social security number, with the income entries on your return. This is to ensure that you accurately report all income. Fourth, it conducts a discriminate function (DIF) analysis of your return.

The DIF program is a sophisticated program that compares every entry on your return with averages for a person in your same income category and profession. If any line of your return does not match the averages, the difference is "scored." This is referred to as a DIF score. The higher the score, the more likely it is for your return to undergo face-to-face audit.

Any of these first three functions regularly lead to demand notices. The notices explain that an error was made in the return and was corrected by the IRS. The notices may explain the nature of the error or they may not. They do, however, point out that interest and penalties were added and demand payment.

In my book, *41 Ways to Lick the IRS with a Postage Stamp,* I dissect these notices and show step-by-step procedures to deal with them. Most people do not deal with them properly. As a result, they find themselves in debt for taxes not legally owed.

Information Returns

Errant computer notices are not always the fault of IRS. Each year, the IRS processes over one *billion* information returns. The mountain of paperwork is prepared by industry and submitted to the IRS in two forms. One is the actual paper documents, prepared by computer or typewriter. The other is computerized forms submitted on machine readable magnetic media. These days, nearly as many machine readable media are submitted as paper returns.

The common thread running through both the paper returns and the magnetic media substitutes is that they are prepared and processed by humans--and humans make mistakes.

According to the IRS, the private sector error rate found in information returns is about five percent. While that may seem like a small number, it means *50 million* errant information statements find their way into the system each year.

With Congress passing new information reporting laws each session, I expect to see the number of information returns to grow steadily. Soon, we all will be required to report the number of times per month we mow the lawn.

When IRS computers detect income from an information return not reported on your tax return, it issues a notice. It demands payment of taxes, interest and penalties. And, they are issued with an error rate of about *48 percent.* For the same reasons expressed in the previous section, most citizens are not successful in correcting errant notices. The result is the IRS demands payment of a tax liability based on income the citizen never received.

Divorce and Spousal Abandonment

The subjects of spousal abandonment, divorce and separation might seem inappropriate for a book treating tax amnesty. Unfortunately, the sad reality is that the consequences of a broken marriage go far beyond the impact it has on the children. Broken marriages carry serious financial implications often reaching well into the sphere of income tax matters.

Virtually without exception, married couples file *joint* federal tax returns--and for good reason. Joint income tax rates are much less expensive than the married filing separately rates.

For example, the tax on $40,000 (using 1997 rate tables) computed at the *married filing jointly* rates, is $6,004. However, if just one spouse earns $40,000 and elects to be taxed at the *married filing separately* rates, the tax is $8,529. Thus, the sole breadwinner pays a penalty of $2,525 to elect separate return rates.

Many people believe the IRS gives the break to married citizens because they generally have children to raise and that is a greater financial burden. However, this is simply not the case. A growing number of single people have children to raise and they do not receive the same break. The same $40,000 of income taxed at the *head of household* rates creates a tax liability of $6,911. That is $907 *more than* the tax on the same income at the *married filing jointly* rates.

As you see, the cheaper rates for married citizens have nothing to do with children. It is designed solely to *induce* the filing of joint returns. When filing a joint tax return, both parties are *jointly responsible* for the debt regardless of who *actually* earned the income. Consequently, a husband could be responsible for earning all the income, file a joint tax return, then desert his wife without paying the tax. Because of the joint return, the wife can be forced to pay the tax even though she earned none of the money.

Why would the IRS do this? The answer is very simple. Virtually all married couples hold their assets jointly. As such, each possesses a legal interest in the property. A problem for the IRS arises when separate returns are filed but the tax is not paid. The IRS *cannot* seize joint property to satisfy the liability of a single spouse without compensating the non-debtor spouse. More on this in chapter six. This makes it difficult for the IRS to collect from joint assets. The problem is eliminated by simply bribing the married couple to file a joint return. That way, both are equally liable for the tax and assets can more easily be seized to pay a potentially unsatisfied bill.

I speak with many women who, after receiving a divorce, believe they are protected from unpaid tax bills by their divorce decree. Typical language holds that the husband is responsible to pay any unsatisfied tax. However, when the IRS cannot find the husband, it ultimately attacks the wife. Unfortunately, the divorce decree is not binding on the IRS. The divorce decree does not pretend to, nor could it vitiate the legal liability established by the federal tax laws. Therefore, when the wife complains that the divorce court held the husband liable, the IRS is unimpressed. Despite the fact that she was left with little or nothing but the children to support, the IRS chases her for the unpaid bill.

Business Debt

During the decade of the 1980s, we saw more business and bank failures than at any time since the Great Depression. In the south, northeast and southwestern United States, property values dropped substantially. With business and farm failures at record levels, you can well imagine that billions in tax revenue went uncollected.

Before embarking on the road to success, many entrepreneurs incorporate their businesses. The general belief is that the corporate structure provides a jacket of insulation from potential creditors which might grow out of the venture. However true this may be of *other* creditors, it *does not* hold water with the IRS.

The theme with businesses gone south is very much the same regardless of the nature of the operation. Bad economic conditions, poor management or a thief in their midst lead to seriously reduced cash flow. At that point, an elaborate juggling act begins, designed to float creditors as long as possible with the hope that sufficient funds materialize to stand the business back on its feet.

Businesses with employees are required to withhold federal income and social security taxes. The withheld funds are referred to as *trust fund* taxes. This is because the law establishes a trust relationship between the IRS and the employer. The employer withholds the money and is required to send it and an accurate report (Form 941) to the IRS. The funds are therefore held in trust by the employer on behalf of the employee and the IRS. The trust relationship is satisfied by paying the tax on time.

In addition, employers are required to make matching payments of social security and unemployment taxes. These funds are referred to as *non-trust taxes*. They are non-trust because the funds do not originate with the employee. Rather, they come from company profits. Non-trust taxes are reported partially on Form 941 (matching social security taxes) and on Form 940 (unemployment contributions).

At the heart of the juggling act is the IRS. When a business finds itself in trouble, it quickly falls behind in the payment of employment taxes (trust fund and non-trust fund alike).

It happens for two reasons. The first is the practical reason. When cash flow is tight, businesses often operate on what is referred to as *net payroll*. They do so because they generally have no other choice. To illustrate net payroll, suppose you have one employee who grosses $1,000 per month. Suppose further that your trust tax withholding obligation is about 25 percent, or $250. Also suppose your non-trust liability is another 15 percent, or $150.

In order to meet the total burden of the $1,000 per month payroll, you must have $1,150 on hand. Because of sour cash flow, you do not. However, due to wage withholding considerations, you actually pay the employee just $750 ($1,000 gross pay minus $250 trust fund withholding). By paying the employee $750 and not paying the taxes, you operate on net payroll. This process reduces your immediate cash requirement by $400. When you extrapolate this over five, or ten, or fifty employees, you easily see how a company gets behind very quickly.

The second reason employment tax debts occur is grounded in emotional factors. Company heads faced with serious financial constraints often fool themselves. They convince themselves that the slow down is only temporary. They sell themselves on the idea that business will turn in two or three months and when it does, they can pay all the taxes at once. They point to this big deal or that pending sale as proof of their contentions.

Too often, the reality is the business does not turn around because this big deal or that pending sale never materializes. The result is things go from bad to worse. Very few companies ever recover from employment tax burdens. The primary reason is because the IRS is unforgiving of the net payroll problem. It considers employers in that position to have "stolen" the money and used it to run their business. When these cases fall into the hands of ROs, the result is always aggressive enforced collection.

After seizing company assets, the IRS turns its attention to corporate officers and business heads. Under the law, the IRS has the power to hold corporate officers and other company officials *personally* responsible for unpaid trust taxes. One can be held personally liable if he was responsible to withhold, truthfully account for and pay trust taxes but deliberately failed to at a time when he knew they were owed. Code section 6672.

When the IRS decides to hold an individual accountable for unpaid trust taxes, it assesses him personally with an amount equal to the delinquent trust taxes. The assessment is known as the Trust Fund Recovery Penalty.

After the assessment, the IRS pursues *personal* income and assets to satisfy the tax. The corporate veil is never an absolute protection from trust taxes. However, amnesty is available to those facing these assessments.

Tax Protesters

Tax Protesters are nothing new. They have been around as long as taxes themselves. Tax laws spawn tax protesters for three reasons. First, some believe the laws are illegal, immoral, oppressive or unreasonable. Second, some do not agree with the way the money is spent. Third, some are simply greedy and do not wish to pay. The United States has its share of tax protesters motivated by all three reasons.

The history of the modern tax protest movement dates to the middle 1960s. It began with individuals who believed our tax laws violate the Constitution in a number of ways. Most notably, the theory was that by signing a Form 1040, you waive your Fifth Amendment right against self-incrimination. Since the Constitution provides that no person may be compelled to give testimony against himself, protesters argued that no one could lawfully be required to sign the form.

This theory and many variations were tested by the courts and IRS over a period of two decades. Since the middle 1960s, the IRS developed a substantial tax protester training manual and instituted detailed policies and procedures for dealing with them. The manual purports to train IRS field personnel in the various protester arguments and how to counter them.

Like any movement, the tax protest movement has its leaders. They travel the country, sometimes appearing on radio call-in shows broadcasting their claims. Some of the more prominent protesters publish how-to books instructing people on the ways to "eliminate" paying income taxes.

Tax protester seminars were very popular during the 1970s and 1980s. Tax protesters met to discuss the latest issues of concern to them. The seminars featured leading protest leaders discussing their most recent research and findings. A common thread was defiant opposition to the tax laws on legal, moral or religious grounds. Another was that each encouraged the audience to take action based upon his particular theory. All had books and literature to sell purporting to support his position.

The speakers at these seminars were particularly adept at selling their position. They would cleverly present select provisions of the tax code or carefully excised portions of court decisions to support their claims. Given the fact that, with the exception of the undercover IRS agents, the audience was made up entirely of tax neophytes, many of whom were easily persuaded by the presentations. The IRS points out in numerous internal memoranda that an ignorant citizen could easily be swayed by some of the tax protester presentations. I also can testify that without a good working knowledge of the tax code, an ignorant person could be made to believe just about anything by selective presentation of code sections.

During the 1970s, 1980s and continuing to this day, thousands of citizens were duped into believing the IRS could do nothing because their particular position was entirely legal. The leaders promised their techniques would work and often guaranteed to stand by and help in the unlikely event some renegade IRS employee did not quite get the picture.

One vocal tax protester was so sure of his theory he offered a $100,000 reward to any person who could prove him wrong! He used the claim as an advertising ploy for his book. Seeing the ad, I wrote a lengthy letter to the man pointing out, with sections of the tax code and supporting case law, how his theory would not work. At the conclusion of the letter, having proved with chapter and verse that his theory was bogus, *I claimed the $100,000 reward!* Sadly, he never paid me. Eventually, the man went to jail--not once, not twice, but *three times*-- making it impossible for both *the IRS and myself* to collect a dime.

Another man made the claim that his theory was so strong, the IRS was forced to dismiss its criminal case against him. He appeared as the feature speaker at tax protester meetings far and wide because of his "victory." Not long after the "win," he released a book showing how *you too* could beat the IRS.

I was flooded with calls during the period of his celebration. "What's this all about?," I was asked. Rather than rely on his word as to what happened, I contacted the California federal courts directly. I obtained copies of relevant court documents and carefully reviewed them. What I found was not surprising, at least not to me.

I found that while it was true that criminal charges were dismissed, the reason was entirely different from what the man claimed. He was arguing that his secret defense (which he offered for sale in his book) won the case and made it impossible for the IRS to do anything to him. I found quite the contrary. The dismissal was instigated by the prosecuting attorney for a critical error the grand jury made in bringing the charges. The reality was, nothing prevented the IRS from recharging. Furthermore, because of the peculiar nature of the case, the decision could not be relied on by anyone else.

After studying the hard evidence, I phoned the man and confronted him. I pointed out the true reason for the dismissal and asked whether he understood why the government closed his case. He said he did. I then asked whether he understood that he could in fact be recharged for related offenses. He agreed he could.

I then accused the man of deliberately misleading the public. I explained that he could not go on with the claim that others could follow in his footsteps when clearly, they would be asking for trouble. Within just a short period of time, that particular claim died on the vine but another soon sprouted in its place, hustled by the same tax protester.

The specific claims of the various leaders are as varied as you can imagine. At one time or another, protesters claimed:

•the tax laws are unconstitutional because they create a condition of slavery, prohibited by the Thirteenth Amendment;

• the tax laws do not apply to wage earners because the law taxes only *income* and wages are not *income;*

• the tax laws are voluntary, that is why the IRS regularly uses the phrase "voluntary compliance" in describing them. Because they are voluntary, one has the option to pay or not pay;

• the tax laws apply only to resident and non-resident aliens, not persons born in the United States.

A more recent scheme involves the claim that one can be "untaxed." The salesmen behind this program sell their magic documents for fees of $2,000 and higher. The process involves sending "untax" documents to every government agency you can name. After mailing the requisite notices containing the secret commands, you no longer have to pay income taxes!

As it turns out, the IRS *raided* the "untax" offices of the leading proponent. They seized his records, including his "untax" documents and the names and addresses of those to whom he sold his program. Later, he was given the opportunity to test his "untax" theory in a federal courtroom, where it failed. Even worse, however, is the fact that the IRS also contacted all his disciples after getting their names and addresses from the records they seized.

Regardless of the nature of the claim or the means by which it is put into effect, all have one thing in common: in the final analysis, they simply do not work. The courts at every level reject them repeatedly and it does not matter what the argument is. They all fail--period.

The irony is the vast majority of citizens involved in the tax protester movement are honest citizens who believe they were doing the right thing. With few exceptions, no one would have taken such steps if they had any idea what the IRS' true reaction would be. Most took the steps because they were convinced by apparently knowledgeable authorities that, a) the stance was perfectly legal, and b) there is nothing the IRS could or would do about it.

The fact is the IRS has a potpourri of weapons available to force compliance. Not the least potent of these is the ability to determine a tax liability for those who do not file a return. After doing so, the citizen bears the burden to disprove its accuracy. If he fails or refuses, the tax is assessed and enforced collection follows. The most potent is criminal prosecution for either failure to file a tax return or tax evasion. Code sections 7203 and 7201. Failure to file is misdemeanor and evasion is a felony. More on this in chapter three.

Nothing can convince a tax protest follower of the error of his ways faster than the one-two punch of tax liens and levies. By the time the matter progresses to that point, most protest followers are absolutely disillusioned with their leaders and bitter about being misled. Further, they are *desperate* to solve the problem and put a major mistake behind them. They are anxious to settle with the IRS and are sure they will never do anything like that again.

The difficulty is that the IRS can be extremely vindictive, especially with tax protesters. It seems IRS leaders are as guilty as tax protester leaders about misleading their followers. IRS leaders have their followers convinced that all tax protesters are dirty cheaters who must be taught a lesson once and for all and in the process, get that pound of flesh! With its foot on the neck of the downed protester, its desire is to press harder rather than let him up.

This unreasonable behavior prevents many protesters from squaring with the IRS. Observing this behavior manifested on their friends who do step forward, those remaining simply dig themselves deeper underground, determined that anything is better than what the IRS has in store for them.

The IRS' behavior in these cases serves only to galvanize the protesters' feelings that the agency is universally unjust and there is no hope of reconciling. Most of these people, people who were misled to begin with, feel lost and trapped. Some feel they can never live a normal life again. We shall see.

Conclusion

Against this backdrop of factual and financial circumstances, I will prove my claim that there truly is *no such thing as a hopeless tax case.* I have proven, and the countless letters in my files verify, that *there is a way out* of the wilderness. I would like Jack to describe for you how his problem was solved. Jack's letter was written to the friend who steered him to me for help.

Dear JoAnn:

About 18 months ago the IRS obtained a levy against my pension. They allowed $325 per month total income for my wife and myself to live on, and IRS took the rest. $325 per month isn't enough for housing, let alone health insurance, food, utilities or any other necessities of life. Any other income we earned would have been immediately confiscated by the government. A depressing future, at best.

I looked for help from Congressman, Senators, IRS ombudsman, Problems Resolution Office, private attorneys and the ACLU. Nobody would help me and didn't want to get involved.

About a year ago, in depression, I called the above agencies for help and was fortunate enough to talk to you, JoAnn, in Senator Boschwitz' office. You informed me that your office couldn't help, but that you had read newspaper articles about Dan Pilla and he had helped people out in like circumstances.

With my hope and confidence levels at their absolute lowest, I contacted Dan Pilla and he said he thought he could help me. Dan showed me how to file documents, initiate proceedings and make arrangements to pay some of the greatly exaggerated tax demands and also avoid the penalty and interest buildup, enabling me to still have about 80 percent of my pension to live on. Dan helped me with all the paperwork, showing me shortcuts, helped me avoid pitfalls, find an attorney and the toughest part, encouraged and supported me when things looked hopeless.

Without Dan Pilla's help, my wife and I could have spent our retirement years in poverty, paying overstated taxes, penalties and interest (being continually compounded), with no final payment ever in sight.

Thanks to you and Dan, the issue is now completely resolved.

JoAnn, I could never repay you for having steered me to Dan Pilla. You and he have given us "the rest of our lives." Thank you so much.

Signed: Jack - Arizona

Indeed, there is no such thing as a hopeless tax case.

"Say therefore to the people of Israel, 'I am the Lord and I will bring you out from under the burdens of the Egyptians, and I will deliver you from their bondage, and I will redeem you with an outstretched arm and with great acts of judgment'"

Exodus 6:6

CHAPTER THREE
Am I Going to Jail?

In chapter two I spoke about my friend Deb, whom I came to know in 1991. Deb was as distraught as any person I have ever met. She and her husband did not file tax returns for a number of years. A revenue officer (RO) from the Collection Division paid an unannounced visit to Deb at home and caught her at a most inopportune time.

Deb just stepped out of the shower and was unclothed. After leaving the bathroom, she found the IRS employee *standing* in her kitchen. Without invitation, the officer saw fit to just walk in the door! The only thing that prevented total humiliation and shock was the fact that the RO was a woman. The officer quickly left after giving strict instructions for Deb to call her.

Deb called and a meeting was arranged. Deb was instructed to bring all books and records for the years 1983 through 1990. She was told that because the returns were not filed, the IRS would "help" prepare them. She was warned to attend the meeting and be prepared to cooperate.

The meeting took place a very short time after the phone conversation. Following an initial laugh about the collision in the kitchen, the RO quickly became *all business.* She demanded all the records and wanted them "now." Deb explained that she did not have time to gather and organize the records. In the few days that passed since the phone conversation, she was "locating, sorting, separating, compiling and posting" the documents covering eight years. There just simply was not enough time to have them fully prepared for the meeting. Deb asked for more time and assured the RO that she recognized her duty to "cooperate fully."

At that, the officer put the fear of God into Deb. The RO explained that because Deb "refused to comply," she could expect "the US

Marshall to arrest me at anytime. No ifs, ands or buts." Deb asked three different ways whether this were the only solution to the problem and why no additional time could be had. Deb was "repeatedly told to expect--without warning--to be picked up by a Marshall" and jailed.

Despite all I said in chapter two about what goes on in the mind of a non-filer, you may still have doubts as to why a person would not simply step forward and say, "Hey, I haven't filed. I need to get that fixed." Stories of what happens to people like Deb get around and they get around fast. And the IRS wants it that way. It wants people terrified so the public dances to all its tunes.

However, the terror campaign has a deepening negative impact. A growing number of citizens simply run further into the woods, more determined to stay out of sight. Hence, the most non-compliant--non-filers and tax payment delinquencies--*are taught* that stepping forward is the last thing any sensible person should do.

The real tragedy in Deb's story is not only did a revenue officer threaten and coerce a citizen honestly attempting to resolve a problem, but she did so by *lying through her teeth!* Under the circumstances of Deb's case, which is very illustrative of the typical non-filer or delinquent citizen, there was virtually *no chance* of going to jail. Even if there were any risk of jail, the RO had nothing whatsoever to say about it. She was simply using her power and position unjustly to further terrify an already extremely fearful citizen.

Because this kind of thing goes on regularly, I define clearly what does and does not constitute a true criminal risk.

The Chances of Going to Jail

The chart in Exhibit 3-1, reproduced on the next page, is taken from the 1992 Edition of *Internal Revenue Service 1992 Annual Report.* The chart indicates criminal investigation activity in 1992, breaking the cases out into the type of crime involved. The numbers are illustrative of any given tax year. (The data for later years are not broken down as clearly as those in the *1992 Annual Report.*)

The chart shows that of the total criminal investigations begun (6,473), about 41 percent (2,669) involved narcotics, organized crime and public corruption. The single largest area of investigations (2,588) centered around white collar crimes that might have some tax law implications but more likely involved non-tax crimes such as bankruptcy and health care fraud, money laundering and other currency violations. In fact, in a 1997 General Accounting Office

Exhibit 3-1

Table 20 — Criminal Investigation Program

	Initiated	Discontinued	Referred For Pros	Info. Indictments	Convictions	Total Sentenced	To Prison	% To Prison
Program: Abusive Compliance								
North Atlantic	159	29	96	75	57	37	33	89.19%
Mid-Atlantic	174	16	88	69	69	73	42	57.53%
Southeast	253	65	140	109	97	83	50	60.24%
Central	135	23	92	57	61	47	37	78.72%
Midwest	105	28	47	41	36	42	30	71.43%
Southwest	206	33	131	109	79	87	60	68.97%
Western	184	51	109	89	87	80	64	80.00%
AC International	0	1	0	0	0	0	0	0.00%
U.S Total	**1216**	**246**	**703**	**549**	**486**	**449**	**316**	**70.38%**
Program: Narcotics Crimes								
North Atlantic	168	68	104	104	101	76	48	63.16%
Mid-Atlantic	190	32	139	104	76	74	65	87.84%
Southeast	366	54	283	287	193	192	153	79.69%
Central	227	43	178	168	137	145	125	86.21%
Midwest	193	42	178	167	147	140	121	86.43%
Southwest	526	96	469	441	214	205	169	82.44%
Western	357	21	219	207	152	123	97	78.86%
AC International	12	2	4	4	5	1	1	100.00%
U.S Total	**2039**	**358**	**1574**	**1482**	**1025**	**956**	**779**	**81.49%**
Program: Organized Crime								
North Atlantic	59	22	46	45	44	26	14	53.85%
Mid-Atlantic	46	11	26	35	22	12	5	41.67%
Southeast	107	24	101	92	65	42	24	57.14%
Central	62	17	63	40	35	44	27	61.36%
Midwest	44	18	41	36	43	33	18	54.55%
Southwest	36	11	40	27	24	29	20	68.97%
Western	57	13	33	28	24	30	18	60.00%
AC International	0	0	0	0	0	0	0	0.00%
U.S Total	**411**	**116**	**350**	**303**	**257**	**216**	**126**	**58.33%**
Program: Public Corruption Tax Crimes								
North Atlantic	44	10	34	32	28	19	9	47.37%
Mid-Atlantic	19	12	20	23	25	19	9	47.37%
Southeast	41	7	37	29	21	20	14	70.00%
Central	16	4	8	9	7	7	6	85.71%
Midwest	29	10	15	7	8	12	7	58.33%
Southwest	49	14	25	21	11	14	9	64.29%
Western	21	1	19	17	20	10	9	90.00%
AC International	0	0	0	0	0	0	0	0.00%
U.S Total	**219**	**58**	**158**	**138**	**120**	**101**	**63**	**62.38%**
Program: White Collar Tax Crimes								
North Atlantic	395	206	197	148	144	115	43	37.39%
Mid-Atlantic	386	105	183	127	123	152	112	73.68%
Southeast	468	194	192	177	170	142	95	66.90%
Central	318	138	149	109	107	92	66	71.74%
Midwest	242	104	139	110	98	82	58	70.73%
Southwest	389	139	210	185	120	109	59	54.13%
Western	381	127	185	148	128	133	97	72.93%
AC International	9	9	5	1	0	0	0	0.00%
U.S Total	**2588**	**1022**	**1260**	**1005**	**890**	**825**	**530**	**64.24%**
Program: All Programs								
North Atlantic	825	335	477	404	374	273	147	53.85%
Mid-Atlantic	815	176	456	358	315	330	233	70.61%
Southeast	1235	344	753	694	546	479	336	70.15%
Central	758	225	490	383	347	335	261	77.91%
Midwest	613	202	420	361	332	309	234	75.73%
Southwest	1206	293	875	783	448	444	317	71.40%
Western	1000	213	565	489	411	376	285	75.80%
AC International	21	12	9	5	5	1	1	100.00%
U.S Total	**6473**	**1800**	**4045**	**3477**	**2778**	**2547**	**1814**	**71.22%**

report, the GAO observed that IRS is spending less time on tax related criminal matters and more time on the growing number of non-tax offenses it is asked to investigate.

Only about 18 percent (1,216) of the criminal investigations involved abusive compliance or what you might consider typical tax crimes. Such offenses include failure to file tax returns, tax evasion and filing false documents. Among these, cases involving tax protester leaders are prominent.

Right out of the chute, you see that your chances of being implicated in a tax crime are reduced by more than 80 percent unless you are a drug dealer, crime boss, politician or white collar corporate heavy.

Keep in mind that in 1992, about 115 million individual income tax returns were filed. When that figure is compared to the 6,473 criminal investigations, you quickly realize you have a greater chance of being struck by lightning than of being implicated in a criminal tax investigation.

Please also note that while 6,473 investigations were undertaken in 1992, just 3,477 ran their full course and actually resulted in a criminal charge. Less than 54 percent of the cases beginning as criminal investigations ever mutated into full scale, liberty threatening criminal prosecutions. Even at that, just 1,814 citizens were sentenced to prison. And the highest majority of those--38 percent--were involved in narcotics crimes.

Just 316 citizens were sentenced to jail time in 1992 as a result of abusive compliance. When you divide that number by 115 million, the number of individual returns filed, you find the true statistical probability that any one citizen will ever do jail time as a result of a tax crime. When considered in this light, I would have to say the answer is, no, *you are not going to jail!*

The Signposts of a Criminal Investigation
There is no need to lay awake at night wondering whether you will go to jail if you *step forward* or whether you will go to jail if you *do not step forward*. There is no need to panic if told by an IRS employee, as Deb was, that you are *in fact* going to jail. You can often answer for yourself, quickly and accurately, whether there is any realistic chance that your case has or may take the shape of a criminal prosecution. Reading the clear signposts along the route of compliance enforcement tells the tale.

The first and most important fact to remember is that the IRS is a decentralized agency. It divides the duties of the agency into distinct divisions, each with a clear responsibility. The three main divisions that citizens encounter are,

•*The Examination Division* - Responsible to audit tax returns and determine tax, interest and penalty liabilities;

• *The Collection Division* - Responsible to collect tax assessments, conduct employment tax examinations and secure tax returns from non-filers;

• *The Criminal Investigation Division* - Responsible to conduct investigations of possible violations of the criminal tax and related federal laws and to assist the Department of Justice in the prosecution of citizens ultimately charged with criminal offenses.

The Criminal Investigation Division (CID) is staffed with special agents highly trained to investigate whether a tax or other financial offense occurred and to gather the needed evidence to prove the crime in court.

Therefore, the first signpost indicating a potential criminal case is, when the case is immediately referred to CID for investigation. The IRS manual requires the referral be made "at the earliest opportunity" upon the discovery of "firm indications of fraud."

Upon receiving a criminal referral, internal evaluations are performed on evidence already in the IRS' possession. If the evidence indicates possible fraud, a "freeze" is placed on the citizen's tax account.

At that point, all audit and collection aspects of the case are immediately suspended. Thereafter, the IRS makes *no effort* to assess or collect taxes. Nor does it attempt to secure unfiled returns. (I explain why later in this chapter.) The freeze is indicated in the citizen's Individual Master File (IMF). The master file is a blueprint of all audit, collection and enforcement activity that occurs in a case. It is available by making a request under the Freedom of Information Act (FOIA) to the service center where you file. A criminal freeze is indicated with the transaction code (TC) 914.

In chapter three of my book, *Taxpayers' Ultimate Defense Manual*, I provide the details for submitting a request under the FOIA and show you how to read an IMF printout and interpret the entries.

At the point the case is frozen, a special agent is assigned and a full scale investigation begins. The second signpost occurs when the special agent begins his investigation. His first task is to contact the citizen and ask pointed questions.

When a citizen is contacted by a special agent, IRS procedures require that he be read his "Miranda" rights. The Miranda warning explains that the special agent's purpose is to conduct a criminal investigation and that statements or documents provided could be used against you in court.

The third signpost occurs either apart from or in connection with the direct contact by a special agent. Because the IRS bears the burden of proof in criminal cases, the agency must gather evidence sufficient to persuade a jury of your guilt. It gathers this evidence by issuing summonses to third parties, such as your banks, employer, credit union, mortgage lender, etc. The summons, Form 2039, requires the named party to release to the *special agent* the requested records. Summonses are also used to obtain testimony from third parties.

It is true that when a criminal investigation begins, special agents are often assisted by revenue agents. They handle the tax liability aspects of the investigation. It is not true, however, that revenue agents or revenue officers act independently of special agents. In a criminal investigation, the special agent is in charge of and directs the case.

Therefore, the fourth and a very important signpost of a criminal investigation is *the absence* of a revenue agent (civil tax auditor or examiner) or revenue officer (civil collection officer). If an auditor is present but is acting in conjunction with the special agent, that is a direct indication of a criminal case.

You may be asking why it is so that civil tax examiners fade from view when the case assumes criminal implications. The answer is found in a thirty-year history of litigation involving criminal investigations and the propriety of the conduct of IRS personnel.

The rules established through litigation indicate that when the IRS obtains evidence from a citizen through deceit, trickery or fraud, that evidence may not be used in a prosecution. Trickery and deceit exist when revenue agents or special agents seek and obtain evidence directly from the citizen without explaining the true nature of the investigation. If an investigation is truly criminal in nature, the special agent must explain its purpose before obtaining evidence. Evidence obtained by misleading the citizen is considered to have been obtained in violation of law. That is the reason only highly trained special agents conduct criminal investigations.

The ultimate indication of a criminal investigation is a recommendation for prosecution by the special agent. When the case is complete, a recommendation is made by the special agent if the evidence establishes that a crime was committed. The recommendation is made to the Office of District Counsel. District Counsel are the IRS' "in house" attorneys. Their function is to review the evidence and possible legal defenses and other potential problems with the case. They determine whether the matter should in fact be pursued.

Assuming District Counsel agrees with the recommendation, the case is sent to Washington. The act of transferring the case to Washington constitutes the formal recommendation for criminal prosecution. Justice Department attorneys in Washington make the final determination whether and to what extent any criminal charges are filed. I know of no exceptions to this rule.

These facts evidence plainly that the claims made to Deb by the revenue officer were false and terribly misleading. The revenue officer acted as though she had the authority to commence a criminal case on her own. As you now know, not only does she not have the authority to instigate a criminal *prosecution*, she does not even have the authority to instigate a criminal *investigation!*

She certainly could have made a referral to CID, but had she done so, all aspects of the civil case would have immediately stopped. She would, at that point, have been required to close her civil tax examination and terminate her contacts with Deb. The fact that she continued her contacts and discussions, continued making demands and eventually received and processed tax returns, proves that no criminal case was ever pending or intended. That RO simply enjoyed the fact that she could terrorize a citizen.

If you are threatened with criminal action by a revenue agent or RO and are unsure of the true posture of your case, you should ask pointedly whether you are, in fact, under a criminal investigation or whether the agent intends to make a referral to CID. While agents have been known to lie, there are consequences for their actions. I already explained that evidence obtained using trickery, deception or fraud is subject to suppression later.

You should also know that the Internal Revenue Manual, at section 4565, expressly provides that no "threat of criminal prosecution shall be made in any case in an attempt to obtain settlement of the civil liability." Not only did the revenue officer lie to Deb, she was in direct violation of the IRS' manual.

Tax Crimes and the Statute of Limitations

There is one very sure way to know whether any substantial risk of criminal prosecution exists for non-filing or non-payment of taxes. That is to determine whether the statute of limitations governing the ability to charge and prosecute a crime has expired.

The Internal Revenue Code contains approximately seventeen provisions defining and setting penalties for criminal conduct. Among these are the more famous crimes of tax evasion, failure to file returns and submitting false documents. Among the less famous are the crimes of failure to collect taxes and making fraudulent statements.

Code section 6531 establishes the limitation period within which a person may be charged with a criminal offense. The statute reads in part,

> No person shall be prosecuted, tried or punished for any of the various offenses arising under the internal revenue laws unless the indictment is found or the information instituted within three years next after the commission of the offense.

As you see, generally speaking, there is a three-year limitation on the power of the IRS to prosecute a criminal offense. The three-year rule applies to approximately one-half of the criminal provisions of the code. There are eight exceptions to the three-year rule built into code section 6531. Let us examine them now. In any one of those eight circumstances, the citizen may be charged with a criminal offense within *six years* after the commission of the offense. These are the exceptions:

1. *Fraud.* Offenses involving fraud or an attempt to defraud the United States in any manner, 18 USC (US Criminal Code) section 1001;

2. *Evasion.* Offenses involving an attempt in any manner to evade or defeat any tax or payment of any tax, code section 7201;

3. *Aiding and Assisting.* Offenses related to aiding and assisting in, or counseling, or advising in the preparation or presentation to the IRS of a false or fraudulent return, statement or other document, code section 7206(2);

4. *Failure to file or pay.* Offenses involving the failure to file returns or failure to pay a tax at the time required by law, code section 7203;

5. *False Return.* Offenses involving the preparation and presentation to the IRS of a false or fraudulent return, statement or other document, code sections 7206(1) and 7207;

6. *Intimidation.* Offenses relating to making threats against or intimidating IRS agents while in the act of performing their duties, code section 7212(a);

7. *Unlawful acts of agents.* Any unlawful act committed by an IRS agent, officer or employee in connection with the performance of his duties, such as extortion, accepting bribes, etc., code section 7214; and

8. *Conspiracy.* Offenses involving a conspiracy, the object of which is to attempt in any manner to evade or defeat the payment of any tax or to defraud the United States by impeding and impairing the lawful functions of the Internal Revenue Service, 18 USC section 371.

Deb was threatened with jail by the revenue officer. Deb did not file tax returns for the years 1983 through 1990. She was sweating bullets by the time the officer finished with her. Deb was convinced she was going to jail. However, in the case of failure to file, the IRS has just six years from the *due date* of the return to commence the prosecution. Deb's return for 1983 was due on or before April 15, 1984. The six-year period of limitation expired on April 15, 1990. By the time the IRS demanded the return, it was October, 1991. Consequently, it was legally barred from charging Deb with any crime for both 1983 and 1984.

Jail threats quickly lose their sting when measured against the yard stick of the statute of limitations. I believe it is important to know and use this information when dealing with oppressive agents. Just by informing them that you understand the limitations placed upon their authority by the plain language of the law, you make great strides toward eliminating potential abuse. That leaves you to deal with the case on its merits, without having to contend with bureaucratic nonsense.

This is not to say that all non-filers have nothing to fear when it comes to criminal prosecution. In fact, when Mrs. Peterson testified to the House Government Operations Committee in June, 1992, regarding the IRS' new attitude, she specifically addressed the non-filer issue. She realizes that most non-filers are not criminals. As we explore in chapter eight, she instituted a non-filer program designed to bring them in from the cold.

At the same time, however, she made it clear that the IRS will use a stick in addition to the carrot to bring non-filers into compliance. In her testimony she stated, "but for those taxpayers who do not accept our encouragement, we will use a more direct approach." That approach is to use "criminal sanctions in appropriate cases." She went on to say that the IRS expects the number of criminal cases against non-filers to increase "as we identify more taxpayers who persist in willfully failing to comply with the law."

What Determines Who Will and Will not be Prosecuted?

Why is it that not every one who fails to file a tax return or fails to pay taxes is prosecuted? One answer is the IRS certainly does not have the manpower to chase every possible case. That is not the only answer. It is, in my judgment, not even the most *significant* reason most tax violations are never prosecuted.

The most significant reason the vast majority of delinquent citizens are never prosecuted is because legally, criminal cases are vastly unlike civil cases. In civil tax examination and collection cases, the *citizen* bears the burden of proof on virtually all matters. If the IRS claims you owe taxes, you must prove you do not. Otherwise, the tax is assessed.

Not so with criminal cases. In every criminal prosecution, including tax prosecutions, the accused enters the case with the protection of the three most important legal concepts ever devised. Every citizen should know and understand these concepts because they form the very heart of our legal system. Let us examine them.

Presumption of Innocence

In any criminal case, the accused enters the prosecution cloaked with the presumption of innocence. This means simply that the defense never has to prove anything. This constitutional safeguard, gradually eroding in our nation, acts as a guarantee that innocent citizens are not punished merely because they are unable to prove a negative.

Burden of Proof

In all criminal prosecutions, including tax cases, *the government* bears the sole burden of proof. The burden of proof refers to the government's affirmative duty to bring forth legally acceptable evidence to prove the accused is guilty as charged. The accused has no burden of proof in a criminal tax case.

Reasonable Doubt

The burden of proof is an extremely strict burden. It rises above the burden often used in civil cases and surpasses the burden applied even in civil tax fraud cases. The burden that must be met in a criminal case is proof beyond a *reasonable doubt*. Reasonable doubt is the kind of doubt that would cause a person to hesitate in making the most important decision of his personal life. When such doubt is shown, the defendant must be considered not guilty.

It is not a simple matter to flippantly accuse a person of tax fraud, evasion or criminal failure to file a tax return. The stringent criminal law environment does not permit the kind of willy-nilly decisions often made by tax auditors. Consequently, before making the decision to prosecute a citizen for a tax crime, IRS conducts a thorough investigation. Thereafter, referrals and reviews take place at the highest levels of both the IRS and Justice Department. The IRS must be sure that before anyone is prosecuted, the government has sufficient evidence to sustain a conviction.

The Element of Willfulness

Most critical of all evidence needed to sustain a tax conviction is proof of the element of *"willfulness."* In reviewing the language of the criminal statutes cited above, you find that the term willfulness appears in each one of them. For example, in the statute addressing failure to file a tax return, the law provides that anyone required to "make a return...who willfully fails to...file such return...shall be guilty of a misdemeanor..." Code section 7203.

Thus, in a failure to file case, the government bears the burden to prove not only that a citizen was required to file a return and did not, but that his failure was due to "willfulness."

The term willfulness is defined as a voluntary, intentional violation of a known legal duty. The requirement to prove willfulness is designed to prevent the conviction of a person who makes an honest mistake or due to negligence or some other non-criminal reason, does not do what the law requires. In order to be convicted of a tax offense, one must know what the law requires and he must deliberately and intentionally *set out* to break the law.

We have all heard the axiom that holds "ignorance of the law is no excuse." That principle applies only to offenses which are characterized as *malum in se* in nature. *Malum in se* is a Latin phrase defined as a wrong in itself; an act involving illegality from the very nature of the transaction, based upon principles of natural, moral and public law. See Black's Law Dictionary, second edition. Examples of such an offense are murder, rape and theft.

Tax laws *do not* fall into this category. Rather, they are classified as *malum prohibitum* offenses. That Latin phrase means an act prohibited; a thing which is wrong only because prohibited; an act which is not inherently immoral, but becomes so because its commission is expressly forbidden by law. See Black's Law Dictionary, second edition. The concept of *malum prohibitum* is the opposite of *malum in se.*

Tax laws are classified as *malum prohibitum* because it is not inherently immoral to fail to pay taxes, as it is to rob or murder someone. Because of the character of the crime, the government must prove the accused had the *specific intent* to break the law. Such intent is a state of mind referred to as *mens rea.* That term is defined as a guilty or wrongful purpose. Without proof of a guilty or wrongful purpose, a criminal conviction is improper.

One judge described it this way, "Even a dog distinguishes between being stumbled over and being kicked." The Supreme Court speaking in *Morissette v. United States*, 342 US 246 (1952). Many a person may stumble over the seventeen thousand pages of law and regulation we call the tax code. Many a person may stumble over the two to three thousand tax forms and the tens of thousands of pages of instructions. Many a person may stumble over the court opinions and IRS rulings so voluminous as to fill a gymnasium. Very few people, however, ever make up their mind in advance to break the law by lying, cheating or deceiving the IRS.

These legal principles dictate that no person should ever be convicted of violating the tax laws where his actions were merely negligent, mistaken, inadvertent or grew out of a good faith misunderstanding of the requirements of the law. The criminal statutes apply only to the willful or intentional violator, not the mistaken, misled or negligent person.

How to Prevent a Criminal Case

Statistics indicating the extremely low probability of something terrible happening are meaningless when *you* are one of the statistics.

When it comes to a criminal prosecution, I rather suspect you would just as soon it not be you. I agree.

What you must understand going into this discussion is that in addition to the legal considerations examined above, the IRS and its attorneys carefully consider the facts and circumstances of each case before undertaking a prosecution. In weighing these factors, attorneys speak in terms of "jury appeal." By that, they are referring to the likely way in which a given factor may influence a jury. If a factor has *positive jury appeal*, it means that from the standpoint of the *IRS*, the factor may tend to influence the jury to *convict* the accused. If a factor has *negative jury appeal*, such factor may weigh more in favor of the accused, influencing the jury to *acquit*.

To prevent a criminal case, one must point up, highlight and underscore the facts and circumstances which balance in favor of the citizen. There are certain ways this can be done effectively and we address them here.

First, I must give this caution. *Please read this carefully.* If, after reading to this point, you still believe you are truly at risk of a criminal prosecution, if you believe the facts and circumstances of your case indicate the government may pursue a criminal case, you should *immediately* consult *experienced* tax counsel. If you have already been confronted by a special agent or recognize one or more of the other signposts of a criminal investigation, you should *immediately* consult *experienced* tax counsel. If you are unsure, make an FOIA request for your IMF to learn whether a freeze is in effect.

A true criminal investigation and potential prosecution is *very serious* and should be handled only by an attorney experienced in dealing with CID, District Counsel and the Justice Department. *Under no circumstances* should you consult a lawyer off the street to handle such a problem.

The Voluntary Disclosure

At one time the IRS administered a formal policy which held that a citizen's voluntary disclosure of a crime *prior* to detection by the IRS *would not* lead to prosecution. The formal policy was criticized and eventually abandoned. The spirit of the policy lives on, however, and the IRS continues to adhere to a softer form of the predecessor.

The policy is expressed in Policy Statement P-9-2. It states that although IRS policy does not necessarily preclude prosecution, the IRS will "carefully consider and weigh the voluntary disclosure, along with all other facts and circumstances, in deciding whether or not to recommend prosecution."

Merely disclosing the possible violation is no guarantee that one will not be prosecuted. Still, a true voluntary disclosure weighs heavily in favor of the citizen. The reason was expressed by a former IRS Commissioner in a speech before the American Bar Association's tax section. There, Commissioner Latham said, "The Department of Justice has learned by what may be termed the 'hard way' that evidence of a truly penitent spirit weighs heavily with a jury."

This policy is expressed in substance in a brochure developed and distributed by the Phoenix district office describing the IRS' Non-filer Program. The brochure is entitled, "Come on In" and it strongly encourages non-filers to step forward. It states, "If you voluntarily come in now, we will help you file your returns and make arrangements for you to pay what you owe."

However the brochure warns, "If you choose not to take advantage of our current efforts to assist Non-filers, you could face criminal charges for failure to file, in addition to severe penalties."

Notice that the treat of criminal prosecution is to those who *do not* step forward. For those who do so voluntarily, there is the offer of help. In fact, the brochure concludes by saying, "Coming forward voluntarily is the best way to avoid criminal prosecution."

In order for a voluntary disclosure to be of any effect, it must be truly "voluntary." That is, it must not have been influenced by the IRS or external events making it likely the IRS would discover the malfeasance. Disclosure is voluntary when,

1. It is made prior to the commencement of any audit or investigation. Certainly it is voluntary when done after a specific solicitation by the IRS such as by the brochure mentioned above;

2. It is made prior to the citizen's knowledge of the IRS' obtaining information from third party sources which may lead to the discovery of the wrongdoing;

3. If an investigation is pending, the disclosure is voluntary if made prior to the citizen having any knowledge of it; and

4. The disclosure is truthful and complete as to all material matters.

In the case of failure to file, the concept of voluntary disclosure may be a moot point if, at the time the return is filed, the statute of limitations has lapsed. One cannot be prosecuted for failure to file after six years from the due date of the return.

However, upon filing a past due return, the IRS *must* be expected to carefully scrutinize it. If it is found to be false, the door is opened to possible prosecution for submission of a false document. The statute of limitations covering a false return expires six years from the date the return is *presented* to the IRS.

Upon making a true voluntary disclosure and all of the facts of the case so justify (particularly the effect of the voluntary disclosure on jury appeal) CID at that moment considers whether to drop the criminal investigation. If the investigation is dropped, the matter is transferred to the Examination Division which studies the civil tax aspects. Any tax owed is assessed, including interest and penalties. The case is then handed to the Collection Division whose job is to secure payment.

Cooperating with the Investigation

If one finds himself the target of a full blown criminal investigation, he is quickly faced with a very difficult decision. The decision *must never* be made in a vacuum and should be reached only after thoughtful consultation with *experienced* counsel.

The decision is whether to cooperate with the investigators or remain silent per your constitutional rights. Experienced attorneys are divided on which is the best approach. Some tell you to keep your mouth shut and hope for the best. Others advise you to disgorge and hope they do not thump you.

It is the classic Fifth Amendment dilemma. If you do not cooperate, they may construe that fact in a negative light. But if you do, *you may* well provide all the information or evidence eventually used against you in court. Often, it is impossible to know which is the best approach. Generally, it is a judgment call made on the basis of the facts of each case.

I personally believe the innocent citizen, the one caught in a tangle of tax regulations or financial suffering or who was misled by purported experts, is better served by cooperating. This involves filing all required returns and providing proof of their accuracy. If possible, make full payment of all taxes. In chapter eight, I discuss at length how to "step forward" *before* the IRS commences a criminal or civil inquiry. The most important thing to remember is that special agents *will interview* you if you choose to cooperate. You should have counsel present during the interview and should discuss your statement *before* making it.

Bearing in mind the government must prove you acted willfully before a prosecution proceeds, take every opportunity to provide tangible evidence that your actions or lack thereof were based on good faith and not out of criminal intent. This is the single most important aspect of the case. It is important because regardless of what you did or did not do, you *cannot* legally be convicted of a crime unless, at the onset, you *deliberately* intended to break the law.

Without saying so, special agents hunt for evidence of this critical element. As a practical matter, you alone can provide it because no one can pry into your head to examine your thoughts from years past. Be prepared to offer detailed explanations of what you were thinking at the time you acted or failed to act. The evidence must support the claim that you did not intend to break the law.

Experienced counsel is able to evaluate the potential impact, or jury appeal, of your statements. Counsel is able to assist in bringing forth and underscoring the factors pointing to good faith and the lack of criminal intent.

Even if the special agent is not persuaded of your good faith, you have an opportunity to meet with District Counsel and later, the Justice Department. Counsel should take these opportunities to press the issue of good faith. After making the decision to cooperate and disgorge, do not turn back. Press to the end in an effort to prevent a criminal prosecution.

If you choose not to cooperate, the investigation runs its course naturally. Special agents pursue third party sources for information, such as banks, brokerage houses, etc., and interview all possible witnesses looking for evidence to prove their case.

The one significant advantage to not cooperating is that the IRS obtains nothing from you which could, in turn, be used against you. In my experience with criminal prosecutions, particularly with tax protester cases, the only evidence of willfulness the government ever has is what it obtains from the citizen's own lips. Many would be much better off if, in protesting their taxes, they just kept their mouths shut!

The major disadvantage of not cooperating, however, is the special agent likely *never* hears an innocent explanation of your deeds. He considers the evidence in a negative light and unless you cast positive favor upon it, none ever attaches.

As you can see, it is a tough call. Almost always, the factors to consider go well beyond those addressed here. All we know for sure is each case is different and special agents are highly trained investigators who *must never* be underestimated. That is why it is important to seek counsel who knows how to match wits with them.

Conclusion

Terror is immobilizing. Overwhelming fear leads an otherwise perfectly rational person to irrational acts. You can never set your tax problems straight until you cast off the chains that bind you to the fear. That begins with understanding what we taught in this chapter. In a letter to me, Roy tells of his problems, how he fell behind in his return filings and how he corrected them.

> This letter is to express my thanks for your book, *How Anyone Can Negotiate with the IRS and Win!*
>
> Because of immense spiritual, emotional and family problems extending from 1986 to mid-1990, I did little but work, try to start a career and sleep. One of the things I did not do was to file federal income tax returns for 1986-1989 in a timely manner. Needless to say, they came after me, desiring a sum total of about $9,100.
>
> The positive attitude which permeates your book, plus the information on forms, dealing with notices etc., became a bastion of moral, emotional, mental and ultimately, financial encouragement to me. Thanks to principles which I have studied in your book and in IRS publications which you recommended, my liability is roughly $1,600 - a far cry from $9,100.
>
> Signed: Roy - New Jersey

"So do not fear, for I am with you; do not be dismayed, for I am your God. I will strengthen you and help you; I will uphold you with my righteous right hand."

Isaiah 41:10

CHAPTER FOUR
The Tax Man Cometh

The one-sidedness with which Congress and the courts view the IRS never ceases to amaze me. Very early I learned that virtually no attack on the constitutionality of the tax laws would be successful. While the sole function of the federal courts is to prevent Congress from overstepping the bounds clearly set by the Constitution, they instead allow virtual unfettered reign in the area of taxation. As a result, the IRS is able to commit acts the courts would never allow any other police force to get away with.

The courts are fond of declaring that "taxes are the life blood of government." Given the fact that federal judges are paid from this revenue stream, it is not difficult to understand why they are reluctant to limit the IRS' reach. Decades before I entered the battle for taxpayers' rights, the question of the constitutionality of the tax laws was settled. Early court decisions established two dangerous precedents.

The first is one entirely unsupported by an honest reading of the Constitution. Used by courts for decades, the principle is now the touchstone of most court opinions directed at the IRS. It holds that the government's overriding need to quickly assess and collect taxes outweighs a citizen's individual rights under the Constitution." To state it another way, because the government needs the money, it can do anything necessary to collect it--and the courts must support that effort. This is true regardless of the impact those actions have on the rights of the individual.

The second principle is based directly upon the first. It dictates that because of government's "overriding need" for revenue, a citizen is required to *first pay* the tax he allegedly owes *before* the courts determine whether indeed he *owes* it. Though there are limited exceptions, this is the axiom responsible for the notion that you "owe the tax unless you can prove otherwise." It is also responsible for the IRS' traditional hard-line attitude when it comes to collection. Because the agency knows courts largely stand in the way of one's efforts to block collection, such action often crosses the bounds of both law and logic, leading to a myriad of cases of IRS abuse.

For more information on these principles, their exceptions and how to handle IRS violations of law and your rights, please refer again to my book, *Taxpayers' Ultimate Defense Manual.*

The IRS' Collection Powers

The practical result of the above is the IRS has more tools to enforce collection than any other creditor or government agency. In fact, that is why Congress continually hands the IRS the task of collecting debts for other agencies, such as delinquent student loans and child support. Here we examine those tools in very general terms. I outline what to expect from the IRS if you owe money. In chapters five, six and seven, I show you how to neutralize collection and put yourself in a position to win tax amnesty.

The IRS' collection arsenal consists of four primary weapons. They are the "summons," the "tax lien," the "tax levy" and the "seizure." Let us address them in turn.

The Summons

The summons is an investigative tool. It is used by all enforcement divisions to gather information. Special agents use the summons to gather evidence for use in a possible criminal prosecution. Revenue officers use the summons to gather information concerning income and assets which is translated into collection action.

The summons used by the Collection Division varies slightly but importantly from that used by CID. Its underlying purpose is to gather information from which to collect taxes. For that reason, the summons is referred to as a *Collection Summons.*

There are two versions of the collection summons in common use. The first is directed at those who filed tax returns but have not paid the tax. That is IRS Form 6637, reproduced as Exhibit 4-1 on the next page. Note that Form 6637 is subtitled, Collection Information Statement.

A Collection Information Statement, IRS Form 433-A or 433-B, is always procured by revenue officers in delinquent accounts. It is a detailed financial statement showing your income and expenses, assets

Exhibit 4-1

Department of the Treasury
Internal Revenue Service

Collection Summons
Collection Information Statement
Form 8537 (Rev. 10-84)

In the matter of the tax liability of

Internal Revenue District of Jacksonville, FL
Periods U.S. INDIVIDUAL INCOME TAX RETURNS (FORMS 1040) FOR THE YEARS ENDING DECEMBER 31, 1983 AND DECEMBER 31, 1984

The Commissioner of Internal Revenue to

at Orlando, FL

You are hereby summoned and required to appear before: L.M. Croskey or her designee

an officer of the Internal Revenue Service, to give testimony and to bring with you and produce for examination the following books, records, papers, and other data relating to the tax liability or the collection of the tax liability or for the purpose of inquiring into any offense connected with the administration or enforcement of the internal revenue laws concerning the person identified above for the periods shown.

All documents and records you possess or control regarding assets, liabilities or accounts that are held in the name of the taxpayer(s) or for the benefit of the taxpayer(s) named above which the taxpayer(s) owns wholly or partially; or in which the taxpayer(s) has a security interest. These include but are not limited to: all bank statements, checkbooks, canceled checks, savings account passbooks, records or certificates of deposit for the periods

all current vehicle registration certificates, deeds or contracts regarding real property, stocks and bonds, accounts, notes and judgments receivable, and life or health insurance policies currently in force. This will enable us to prepare a Collection Information Statement. A blank statement is attached to guide you in producing the necessary documents and records.

from July 1, 1989

to date summons is complied with

Business address and telephone number of Internal Revenue Service employee named above: 3319 Maguire Blvd., #101 Orlando, FL 32803 PH: (407) 648-6550

Place and time for appearance: at 3319 Maguire Blvd., #101 Orlando, FL 32803

on the 3Lt day of May, 19 90 at 1:00 o'clock p. M.

Issued under authority of the Internal Revenue Code this 2Lt day of May, 19 9?

Signature of Issuing Officer
Title Revenue Officer

Signature of Approving Officer (if applicable)
Title

Part 2 to be given to person summoned

and liabilities. It is used as a guide to pursue available assets and to determine whether an installment agreement is appropriate and the amount of the monthly payment. We discuss the Collection Information Statement in detail in chapter five.

The second version of the summons used by revenue officers is directed at those who *have not* filed tax returns. That summons is IRS Form 6638. An example is provided below as Exhibit 4-2.

Exhibit 4-2

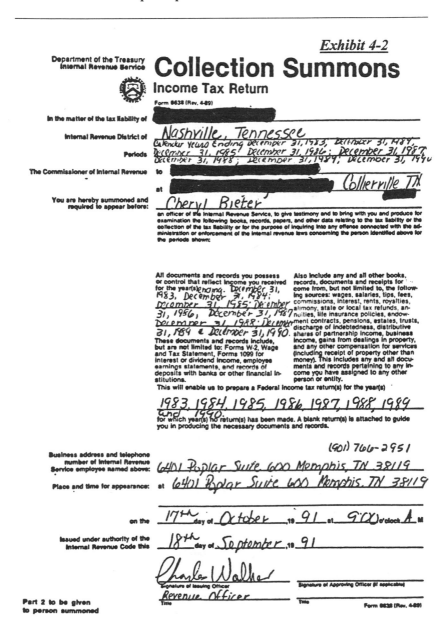

Please observe that Exhibit 4-2 is subtitled, Income Tax Return. Form 6638 is substantively the same as Form 6637. The latter, however, declares that the information to be produced is to be used "to enable us to prepare a federal income tax return." We discuss this form and its uses in more detail in chapter five.

The Tax Lien

The tax lien is the tool the IRS uses to make public record the fact that one owes outstanding debts. IRS Form 668 is the Notice of Filing Federal Tax Lien. It is reproduced below as Exhibit 4-3.

Exhibit 4-3

Form 668 (Y) 487	Department of the Treasury - Internal Revenue Service	
(Rev. January 1991)	**Notice of Federal Tax Lien Under Internal Revenue Laws**	

District	Serial Number	For Optional Use by Recording Office
Detroit, MI		*This Notice of Federal Tax Lien has been filed as a matter of public record.

As provided by sections 6321, 6322, and 6323 of the Internal Revenue Code, notice is given that taxes (including interest and penalties) have been assessed against the following-named taxpayer. Demand for payment of this liability has been made, but it remains unpaid. Therefore, there is a lien in favor of the United States on all property and rights to property belonging to this taxpayer for the amount of these taxes, and additional penalties, interest, and costs that may accrue.

*Penalty and interest accrue until the liability is paid.

*For the amount required to have the lien released, contact the District Office, Collection Division.

Name of Taxpayer

Residence

*See reverse for an explanation of your *Administrative Appeal rights.

IMPORTANT RELEASE INFORMATION: With respect to each assessment listed below, unless such lien is refiled by the date given in column (e), this notice shall, on the day following such date, operate as a certificate of release as defined in IRC 6325(a).

Kind of Tax (a)	Tax Period Ended (b)	Identifying Number (c)	Date of Assessment (d)	Last Day for Refiling (e)	Unpaid Balance of Assessment (f)
1040	12/31/90		05/27/91	06/26/01	26421.12

Place of Filing		Total $	26421.12
REGISTER OF DEEDS OAKLAND COUNTY PONTIAC, MI 48053			

This notice was prepared and signed at Detroit, MI _____, on this
the 06th day of September, 19 91 _____.

Signature for ANTHONY CIPPALONE	Title	REVENUE OFFICER 38-01-1727

(NOTE: Certificate of officer authorized by law to take acknowledgments is not essential to the validity of Notice of Federal Tax lien Rev. Rul. 71-466, 1971 - 2 C.B. 409)

1 - Taxpayer's Copy

Form 668 (Y) (Rev. 1-91)

The purpose of IRS Form 668 is to secure the tax debt to a citizen's property. This prevents him from disposing of property without paying the tax. A tax lien arises at the time the tax debt is established. It becomes perfected when notice is filed with the county recorder's office. It then attaches to "all property and rights to property" owned by the citizen at the time of its filing. The lien also attaches to "after-acquired property," or property acquired after its filing. The fact of the lien appears on your credit report.

The tax lien not only encumbers assets, it destroys your credit. Banks and other lenders refuse to lend money when a credit report reveals a tax lien. Consequently, those seeking to borrow funds to pay the tax are turned away because of the outstanding lien. Ironically, when asked to release the lien to enable a loan (so the tax can be paid), the IRS often refuses. This is a problem we address and solve in chapter six, *Coping with Liens, Levies and Seizures.*

Wage and Bank Levies

Wage and bank levies are perhaps the most crushing blows the IRS can deal in the collection environment. Directed to your employer, bank account or other revenue source, the levy instructs a third party to pay the IRS all funds owed to you. Levies are used to reach not only banks and employers, but pension funds, business accounts receivable, securities dealers or any other third party in possession of funds belonging to the delinquent citizen.

IRS uses several forms to accomplish the levy. The most common are, (1) Form 668-A, Notice of Levy, used on banks and other third parties; and (2) Form 668-W, Notice of Levy on Wages, Salary and Other Income, used on employers to levy wages. See Exhibit 4-4 on the next page.

One troublesome aspect of the wage levy is that it is considered "continuing." That is, it is effective beginning with the date of service until the tax is fully paid or the levy is otherwise released. For example, the IRS need issue only one notice of levy on an employer to seize wages over an extended period of time.

Property Seizures

In addition to the levy, the IRS may collect by seizing and selling assets held by the citizen himself. Examples of this are seizures of homestead property, other real estate holdings, personal property such as boats, automobiles and business equipment, supplies and accounts

Exhibit 4-4

Form **668-W** (Rev. July 1989)	Department of the Treasury – Internal Revenue Service **Notice of Levy on Wages, Salary, and Other Income**

Date: May 17, 1990   **District:** Jacksonville, FL   Telephone number of
IRS Office (407) 648–6558

Name and Address of Taxpayer

TO: ▮▮▮▮▮▮▮▮▮▮   ▮▮▮▮▮▮▮▮▮▮
    ▮▮▮▮▮▮▮▮▮▮   ▮▮▮▮▮▮▮▮▮▮

REPLY: Internal Revenue Service
3319 Maguire Blvd., #101
Orlando, FL 32803   Identifying Number(s)
                                     ▮▮▮▮▮▮▮

Kind of Tax	Tax Period Ended	Unpaid Balance of Assessment	Statutory Additions	Total
1040	12/31/83	34,505.69	18,649.24	53,154.93
1040	12/31/84	25,096.93	17,706.35	42,803.28
			Total amount due ➧	95,958.21

Interest and late payment penalty have been figured to __June 30, 1990__ .

As required by the Internal Revenue Code, notice and demand for the above amount were made on the taxpayer, who neglected or refused to pay. The amount is unpaid and still due. Chapter 64 of the Internal Revenue Code provides a lien for the tax and statutory additions. Items levied on to pay this are: (1) all wages and salary for personal services of this taxpayer that you now possess or for which you become obligated, from the date you receive this notice of levy until a release of levy is issued, and (2) other income belonging to this taxpayer that you now possess or for which you are obligated. These wages, salary, and other income are levied on only to the extent that they are not exempt from levy under Code section 6334 as shown in the instructions. Demand is made on you to pay the total amount due. Do not offset funds the taxpayer owes you without contacting the IRS office shown above by phone for instructions.

Please see the back of this page for instructions.

Signature of Service Representative *L.M. Croskey*   Title Revenue Officer

Part 1—For Employer or Other Addressee   Form **668-W** (Rev. 7-89)

receivable. This includes office furniture, inventory and business fixtures.

After seizing property, the IRS must issue a notice to the owner indicating specifically what was seized. The notice is provided on Form 2433, Notice of Seizure, reproduced below as Exhibit 4-5.

Exhibit 4-5

Department of the Treasury
Internal Revenue Service
Form 2433 (Rev. March, 1988)

Notice of Seizure

Name and Address

Under the authority in section 6331 of the Internal Revenue Code, and by virtue of a levy from the District Director of Internal Revenue of the district shown below, I have seized the property below for nonpayment of past due internal revenue taxes.

Due from	Amount	Internal Revenue District (City and State)
	$ 675,000	Manhattan

Description of property

Beginning at a point on the westerly side of Main Street, distant 260 feet from the northerly corner formed by the intersection of the westerly side of Main Street, with the westerly side of Park Place, measured along the westerly side of Main Street, running westerly on a line which is the extension of the radius of a circle of which the westerly side of Main Street is the circumference, 100 feet; thence northerly 65 feet to a point which is 115 feet weste... from the westerly side of Main Street measured on a line which is the radius of said circle and passes through the westerly side of Main Street, which is the circumference of said circle at a point 55 feet northerly from the point of beginning.

Said premises being known as One Main Street.

Signature of Revenue Officer making seizure	Address	Date
Signature of accompanying employee	Address	Date

Part 1 — Taxpayer Copy   Form **2433** (Rev. 3-88)

Once seized, the property must be sold as soon as possible. It must be sold "not less than 10 days or more than 40 days" from the date of seizure. Notice of the sale must be given to the citizen using Form 2434, Public Auction Sale, reproduced below as Exhibit 4-6. It explains when the sale is to occur, what is to be sold and the terms.

Exhibit 4-6

Department of the Treasury / Internal Revenue Service

Notice of # Public Auction Sale

Under the authority in Internal Revenue Code section 6331, the property described below has been seized for nonpayment of internal revenue taxes due from

_____ .

The property will be sold at public auction as provided by Internal Revenue Code section 6335 and related regulations.

Date of Sale: _____ 19_____

Time of Sale: _____ (am) pm

Place of Sale:

Title Offered: Only the right, title, and interest of _____
in and to the property will be offered for sale. If requested, the Internal Revenue Service will furnish information about possible encumbrances, which may be useful in determining the value of the interest being sold (See the back of this form for further details.)

Description of Property:

Property may be inspected at: _____

Payment Terms:
☐ Full payment required on acceptance of highest bid
☒ Deferred payment as follows:

Form of Payment: All payments must be by cash, certified check, cashier's or treasurer's check or by a United States postal, bank, express, or telegraph money order. Make check or money order payable to the Internal Revenue Service.

Signature	Name and Title *(Typed)*	Date
Address for information About the Sale		Phone

Form **2434** (Rev. 3-84)

Property Exempt From Levy and Seizure

A levy can potentially reach all property owned by the citizen. There is no specific class of property *exempt* from levy or seizure. However, the law does specify some *limitations*. The limitations are pointed at certain types of property or property rights and are set forth in code section 6334. Thirteen categories are specified as beyond the reach of the IRS. They are:

1. Wearing apparel and school books necessary for the citizen and his family.

2. Personal household goods, furnishings, food and fuel, the value of which do not exceed $2,500.

3. Tools and equipment necessary for the citizen to carry on his trade or business, the value of which do not exceed $1,250.

4. Unemployment benefits in any amount.

5. All undelivered mail.

6. Railroad Retirement Act pension benefits and special pension benefits payable to a person listed on the Medal of Honor roll of any military branch.

7. Workman's compensation benefits in any amount.

8. So much of the salary or wages as are necessary to comply with court ordered child support.

9. A minimum amount of wages or salary determined by reference to one's filing status and personal dependent exemptions. More on this important item in chapter seven.

10. Service-connected disability payments in any amount.

11. State, local and Federal government public assistance or aid payments.

12. Payments to a participant under the Job Training Partnership Act in any amount.

13. The principal residence of a citizen unless written approval is given by the district director or assistant district director or unless the collection of tax is in jeopardy.

Chapter seven puts into perspective these various limitations. There I illustrate the manner to best insure they are observed by the Collection Division.

What to Expect From Enforced Tax Collection

Let us now address how the IRS is most likely to utilize the four collection tools.

As you read chapter two you noticed that collection cases fall into two general categories. The first is where you *file* a tax return but do not pay the tax (including liabilities determined after you file, such as through an audit, etc.). The second is where you *fail to file* the return. These two categories apply whether the debt is for personal or business taxes. What follows is an explanation of the procedures pursued by the IRS in both situations.

When you File But Do Not Pay

Filing a tax return triggers a series of events within the IRS' service center designed to place the agency in position to legally collect the tax. When a return hits the service center, it is processed in the manner discussed in chapter two, under the heading, *IRS Error.*

What we did not address there is a very important legal principle governing the collection of taxes. The principle is that unless there exists a legitimate tax *assessment* obtained in accordance with all administrative procedures, no tax is owed. An assessment is born when an assessment officer signs an assessment certificate, generally IRS Form 23C. The certificate must show the amount and type of tax, the year in question and the name and social security number of the citizen. When the certificate is signed, the assessment is recorded in that citizen's Individual Master File for the year involved.

This procedure is followed in cases where a return is filed without full payment or when assessments are made *after* filing the return. The latter assessments occur following tax audits, Tax Court decisions or other similar situations.

The assessment, now an official tax debt, is then offset by withholding credits or payments submitted with the return. If there is an outstanding liability, the matter is then handed to the service center's Collection Branch for action. The Collection Branch operates a function known as Automated Collection. Automated Collection was installed in 1984. It features numerous Automated Collection Sites (ACS) located throughout the nation. ACS is responsible to collect, to the fullest extent possible, all outstanding amounts.

Collection begins with a friendly reminder from the service center, generated by ACS. The first notice follows the filing of your tax return by about sixty to ninety days. It states that an outstanding balance is due and requests immediate payment. It explains that interest and penalties continue to accumulate until you submit full payment. See Exhibit 4-7, reproduced on the next page.

Exhibit 4-7

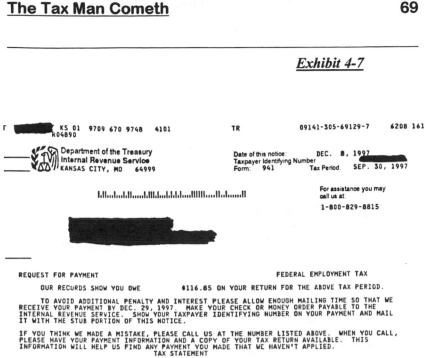

If full payment is not made, the IRS may issue as many as three further notices. The notices arrive at intervals of approximately three to four weeks. The last notice is a Final Notice, Notice of Intention to Levy. The final notice explains that unless the IRS receives full payment within thirty days, it may commence enforced collection action, including the use of liens, levies and property seizures. Exhibit 4-8, reproduced on the next page, is an example of a final notice.

Exhibit 4-8

P 901 290 712

Department of the Treasury
Internal Revenue Service
KANSAS CITY, MO 64999

011721   9709
Notice Number: CP 504
Notice Date: 01-12-98
SSN/EIN:
Caller ID:

003945 1 AT   0.254

411764177221

Final Notice !!

We intend to levy. Please respond NOW.

(To avoid additional penalty and interest, pay your overdue tax in full today.)

Our records indicate you have not paid your overdue tax. The law requires that you pay your tax at the time you file your return. This is formal notice of our intent to <u>levy</u> (take) your paycheck, bank account, auto or other property if we do not receive your payment in full. We can also file a Notice of Federal Tax Lien, if we have not already done so.

PAY YOUR TAX TODAY
Account Summary

Form: 941	Tax Period: 09-30-97
Prior Balance:	$116.85
Last Payment:	$0.00
Penalty to date:	$0.00
Interest to date:	$1.01
New Balance:	$117.86

See enclosed Publication 594 that explains
your rights and responsibilities as a taxpayer.

Questions? Call us at   1-800-829-8815

Please mail this part with your payment, payable to Internal Revenue Service

Notice Number: CP 504
Notice Date: 01-12-98

write on your check:

| 941 | 09-30-97 | |

Amount Due: .
. $117.86

411764177 KS TAXF 01 2 9709 670 0000001178b

Internal Revenue Service
KANSAS CITY, MO   64999

010296

During the period between the first and final notice, you may receive a phone call from an ACS employee. You may also receive a letter from ACS entitled, "Request for Telephone Contact." The letter asks you to call ACS to discuss the outstanding balance. The purpose is to gather information to carry out collection. You are asked to provide financial data over the phone, including the location and balances of your bank accounts. Often, if the matter is approached properly, you may reach an installment agreement in that conversation. In chapter five I discuss several rules for dealing with ACS. Read them carefully before discussing any aspect of your case over the phone.

When you cannot make satisfactory payment, ACS may begin enforcement action. It generates tax liens as well as wage and bank levies if it has knowledge of your employer and location of your bank accounts. If ACS lacks sufficient information to carry out automated collection or other reasons justify, the case is transferred to the district office. At that level, the IRS operates the local Collection Division. There, revenue officers work collection cases handed off by the service center.

When a case is handled locally, the revenue officer makes contact with the delinquent citizen, usually in person. The contact is designed to obtain payment of the outstanding balance. If you cannot make payment in full, the RO demands that you complete a financial statement. He uses the information either to enforce collection or to establish an installment agreement.

As with ACS, revenue officers wield the power to lien, levy and seize assets. Expect this treatment if you do not cooperate with the collection process. In addition, expect the RO to issue a collection summons to secure financial data if it is not provided upon request. See Exhibit 4-1, page 60. In addition or as an alternative to the summons, the RO may immediately begin enforced collection action.

Revenue officers also possess the power to accomplish something ACS is reluctant to do. They may *stay collection* under terms we discuss later. Further, they are the first line of defense when it comes to implementing the amnesty programs discussed in this book.

Revenue officers can be extremely intimidating and are often very demanding, as we saw in Deb's case. However, when handled properly, the face-to-face meeting with the RO may be the first step toward a final and satisfactory resolution to your delinquency problem. Chapters five and six provide the secrets to successfully dealing with both ACS and a revenue officer, placing you well on the road to tax amnesty.

When You Did Not File

If you did not file a tax return, tax collection enforcement must naturally take a different course. The fundamental difference between filing and non-filing is, after filing a return, the IRS possesses a legal assessment which it may collect immediately. When no return is filed, it must *first* obtain a legal assessment *before* commencing collection action.

This legal axiom explains the phenomenon discussed in chapter two where we examined the case of a citizen who went years without filing a return but was never contacted. When he finally filed the returns, the IRS came down on him with both feet. "Why," he asked, "did they do nothing all those years I was in hiding only to clobber me when I finally attempted to resolve my non-filing?" The answer is, all those years he did nothing, the IRS had no assessment to collect. Once he filed the returns, the IRS quickly obtained an assessment and the matter was handed to ACS. ACS is nothing more than a huge computer designed to chase delinquent citizens. Unless you have some understanding of how to handle it, it can swallow you quickly.

Because of the assessment requirement, the IRS' first contact with delinquent filers is designed to secure that assessment. The approach can be either benign or malignant, but both eventually lead to an assessment. Once an assessment exists, the IRS pursues collection in precisely the manner outlined above. Because of the similarities in actual collection action, I limit the following conversation to the manner in which the agency obtains an assessment.

The benign approach. IRS computers are designed to compare information returns, such as W-2s and 1099s, with income tax returns. The computers search for both non-filers and underreporters. When an underreporter is unearthed, the computer corrects the return and issues a notice and demand for payment.

After detecting a non-filer, the agency establishes a Tax Delinquency Investigation (TDI). The TDI begins with a notice to the citizen explaining that no return was filed, though IRS records indicate one was due. The notice is referred to as a tax delinquency inquiry. It demands the return be filed or an explanation as to why one is not due. See Exhibit 4-9 on the next page for an example of such a letter.

Upon filing the return, an assessment follows and in turn, collection. If a return or adequate explanation is not submitted, expect the TDI to take another course. That would be the malignant approach.

The malignant approach. I refer to this as the "malignant approach" because it is occasioned by demands, threats and the

001122

```
                                        ** IF YOU HAVE ANY QUESTIONS, **
                                        ** REFER TO THIS INFORMATION: **
                                     NUMBER OF THIS NOTICE:   CP-518 M
Department of the Treasury           DATE OF THIS NOTICE:     04-28-97
Internal Revenue Service             TAXPAYER IDENT. NUM:
CINCINNATI, OH   45999               TAX FORM:  1040                    9722
                                     TAX PERIOD:  12-31-93
```

```
                             * 3 8 6 6 4 1 4 5 3 1 0 2 *
```

```
        YOUR TAX RETURN IS OVERDUE  -  CONTACT US IMMEDIATELY

     Our records show that you still haven't filed the following
tax return.

        Form number:  1040        Tax period ENDING:   12-31-93
        Title:  US INDIVIDUAL INCOME TAX RETURN

     Please contact us immediately, or we may have to take the
following actions:

     1.  Summon you to bring us your books and records.
     2.  Begin criminal proceedings which may include a fine,
         imprisonment, or both if you willfully fail to file a tax
         return.

     To prevent these actions, file your tax return today, and attach
your payment for any tax due.  Even if you can't pay the entire
amount, it is important that you file your return.  Pay as large an
amount as you can, and tell us when you can pay the rest.  We may be
able to arrange for you to pay in installments.

     If you aren't required to file or have previously filed, please
contact us at 237-0800 LOCAL DETROIT
              1-800-829-1040 OTHER MI
```

potential for punishment. The malignant approach grows out of a tax delinquency inquiry which is ignored. It can also spawn on its own without prior notice of any kind. As you recall from our discussion in chapter three, Deb's initial contact was a personal visit from a revenue officer. Deb's case is the quintessential example of the malignant approach. The malignant approach is undertaken by either the Collection or the Examination Division.

The Examination Division is solely responsible to conduct audits and determine tax liability. Consequently, it is natural for the Examination Division to secure unfiled tax returns. When Exam becomes involved in a delinquency case, it immediately assigns a revenue agent. The agent then issues a notice to the citizen explaining his tax affairs are under examination. He sets a meeting at which he requests you present all records of income and expenses. Alternatively, the agent may demand that you file the returns together with all necessary supporting documentation.

Generally speaking, revenue agents are much easier to deal with than revenue officers. The simple reason is revenue agents have no power. Unlike revenue officers, they cannot lien, levy or seize assets. Furthermore, they cannot render unilateral determinations of your income tax liability. Their every decision is subject to appeal.

The questions of how to handle audits and revenue agents are beyond the scope of this work. However, my book, *IRS, Taxes and the Beast* provides details and step-by-step procedures for handling every aspect of the audit and appeals process.

A revenue agent is less likely to issue a summons for records than a revenue officer. That is because revenue agents have the authority to make *recommendations* concerning your tax liability in the absence of records. The recommendations may be based on (1) prior years' tax returns, (2) Bureau of Labor Statistics, or (3) a good solid (or not-so-solid) *guess*. In computing the tax in one of these ways, the agent affords the benefit of only a standard deduction and one dependent exemption. Of course, his recommendation may be appealed. Please see *IRS, Taxes and the Beast* for more information.

The revenue officer's approach is slightly different. Rather than holding out for records, he is likely to merely demand that returns be filed. Revenue officers are not tax auditors. They are not trained in the practices of determining a tax liability. They are tax collectors--period. Therefore, they are likely to demand returns and threaten a terrible future if they do not receive them.

Let us look back at Deb's case for a moment. She was contacted by a revenue officer in the first instance. There was no tax delinquency inquiry. The RO explained the nature of the contact, set a meeting and demanded Deb appear with completed returns or records with which to prepare them. Because of the magnitude of the work and minimal time allotted, Deb was unable to do either. When she appeared at the meeting, the threats and intimidation began in earnest.

Next, the revenue officer served a summons on Deb. See Exhibit 4-2, page 61. It demanded production of all documents needed to prepare the unfiled returns. Again, despite working diligently, Deb was unable to comply. As a result, the revenue officer went ballistic. She made it clear that Deb would be "hauled off to jail" some night, without warning and in the presence of her children.

This grossly unprofessional conduct coupled with outright lies reduced Deb to a puddle of tears. She was terrified at the thought of being hauled away to jail while her children slept in their beds, at a time when her husband was thousands of miles away attempting to earn a living. Through various maneuvers I explain later in this book, we were able to completely neutralize the revenue officer. We were able to communicate the fact that we knew she was lying and could not in fact, carry out any of her threats. Though the revenue officer clearly did not like learning this lesson, she was in no position to do anything about it.

It is equally clear, however, that if Deb did not have the benefit of this information going into her confrontation, there is no telling how much damage could have resulted. As it turned out, Deb ended up in total control of a situation which began entirely out of control.

Collecting Employment Taxes

For reasons explained in chapter two, under the heading, *Business Debt*, the IRS pursues unpaid employment taxes with great tenacity. Whether returns are filed timely or not, the course of action does not vary widely. Naturally, the agency uses all the collection tools at its disposal in much the same fashion as outlined above. For example, when dealing with unfiled returns, expect the malignant approach.

In the case of an operating corporation, the IRS demands current financial statements covering both the business and the corporate officers. It seeks financial data from the corporate officers for the purpose of determining whether to immediately pursue assessment of the Trust Fund Recovery Penalty (sometimes referred to as the 100 percent penalty). If the corporation has liquidated all its assets (or had none to begin with), IRS assesses the Trust Fund Recovery Penalty and collection is pursued from the personal assets of the corporate officers.

To avoid immediate assessment of the penalty, make every effort to pay the *trust fund* portion of the tax as quickly as possible. More on this in chapter five, under the heading, *Employment Taxes and the Installment Agreement*. Do not expect the IRS to forestall enforced collection, either personally or otherwise, for any length of time unless you immediately agree to an *aggressive* installment payment. Often, however, because of the agency's attitude toward squandered trust fund taxes, the amount of the payment chokes the life out of the business. It becomes impossible to pay suppliers or purchase other necessary services.

Do not be surprised if the RO exhibits a less than sympathetic attitude. When trust fund amounts are concerned, they often feel they are doing you a favor by closing the business. At least that way, you do not sink further into debt.

Another risk is the reality that the IRS may pursue accounts receivable for collection. This often negatively impacts the business by discouraging otherwise faithful customers from continuing their relationship, not to mention the effect of lost revenue. Nobody wants to be mixed up in an IRS problem if they can help it.

Despite the fact that employment tax collection cases are very sensitive, it is possible to avoid utter destruction. Furthermore, even in the worst case, amnesty is available to prevent the mistakes of the past from following you into the future.

Conclusion

Fear of the unknown and misinformation about what the IRS can do are the biggest reasons delinquent citizens do not step forward. For many, however, IRS makes the choice for them. As happened with Deb, the IRS simply "finds you." You must then take steps to resolve your tax delinquency in a manner which satisfies the IRS and at the same time, does not destroy you. This can be done, but if you are unaware of the IRS' usual approach to these cases, you will likely melt into a puddle.

In Deb's case, her faith and a little help pulled her through in a fashion she never thought possible. These are her own words:

> Expectations, disappointments, chaos, rebellion, destruction, bankruptcy, despair, selfishness, pride...I have enough excuses to make a glass eye cry. The truth is that God will call it sin and so will I. My personal, spiritual and financial life were in ruin when God called me to the Truth and I gave my life to Jesus Christ. God loved me and saved me, but He did not part the Mississippi and swallow up the IRS.
>
> However, He did lead me to Precept Bible Study and Christian Radio. It was on *Point of View Radio* that I first

heard of Daniel Pilla. He believed people could actually negotiate with the IRS. I was persuaded that he loved the Lord and would be Godly counsel . . . so I ordered all his books and began to seek solutions to my problems. Somehow, bookkeeping was an ovary-related job in this family, therefore it was relegated to me. I did not want to do it, I had not done it, and neither had anyone else. (Rebellion, perhaps?)

My Day of Accountability came in September, 1991. Two IRS employees delivered a summons for nine years of returns to be filed and paid within thirty days. Thirty days?!?!?! There was a mountain of boxes filled with records that no human could organize and accurately file in thirty days! "Could we have more time, please?" NOOOOOOO. They left, I cried and then I determined in my heart to be obedient and committed everything to reconciling with the IRS.

Next, I called Daniel Pilla. What a comfort to receive, in person, clear and helpful advice. I wrote a letter to my revenue officer requesting more time. It was denied. Mr. Pilla persuaded me to keep my appointment for compliance and take another letter explaining what I had been doing for the past thirty days and again, asking for more time. It was denied.

However, I was asked to fill out papers and answer questions that I was not prepared to do. So, I exercised the rights that I read about and I left. I was turned over to District Counsel for "non-compliance" and ordered to meet with my revenue officer. I did not want to go. Nothing was completed. Mr. Pilla persuaded me to attend. I arrived with a copy of a letter I had sent to District Counsel the night before. My revenue officer was enraged. Our meeting was short. She was to the point. I could expect federal marshals to arrive and snatch me from my home--before the eyes of my children, and oh, by the way, "they usually come at night." GREAT! And with the next breath, she issued a threat she thought was even more frightening--"the IRS would make out the returns themselves and we would pay what they decided we owed." Who was she kidding? I had read my books. I knew I could appeal that decision.

I sat and listened and then I did it--I asked for more time, please. The officer went livid and asked me to leave because I was wasting her time. I drove home on Romans 8:38-39. I called Mr. Pilla and all I could do was cry about putting up

Christmas decorations and writing checks at the grocery store and I wept for my children and the horror they might face . . and he was so very kind to me.

Mr. Pilla assured me that I would not be thrown into prison. We made a plan of action and a proposal for compliance to the summons. I wrote another letter to district counsel and threw myself on their mercy. Then I put up Christmas decorations with my children. One week before Christmas, the letter came from District Counsel accepting our proposal and setting up a defined schedule for filing. I also received assurance from that office that I would not be arrested by federal marshals and no further steps would be taken as long as I met the given schedule.

Thank you, Merciful, Father God.

So began months of ledgering and filing. Many, many days I would sit before another box of records and pray, "Father, please rapture us today. I cannot do this another month, I cannot do this another day." But I always remembered what I had learned in Hebrews 12:6-14 and I endured.

When the payment of penalties and interest became a factor, I consulted Mr. Pilla and wrote another letter to District Counsel to ask for a temporary stay of interest and penalty collection. This was denied. With another call, Mr. Pilla and I agreed that the next solution was to seek a second mortgage on the house.

Doors were opened that allowed us to refinance the first mortgage at a much lower rate and payment. We also were given a second mortgage. This was far more than I ever hoped for. God's economy has also provided abundant income and job contracts for my husband, who works very hard to meet our financial responsibilities and pay off this tax debt. There is not enough room to detail how completely God has provided and cared for us.

I could never have completed this year without God's Word and Godly Counsel. Only one week before my Day of Accountability, I had begun Precept Bible Study in the Book of Daniel. This was God's perfect timing. I learned to take courage and stand alone, to have peace and joy in the fire of trial and I also learned to trust my God who still, today, humbles the heart of the proud and rebellious, who still shuts the mouths of lions and who still raises up Godly men, like Daniel, to lead others by their examples.

Thank you, Daniel Pilla, for your example and your kindness. May God bless you and keep you and yours.

Signed: Deb - Tennessee

"Then he said to me, 'Fear not, Daniel, for from the first day that you set your mind to understand and humbled yourself before your God, your words have been heard, and I have come because of your words'."

Daniel 10:12

CHAPTER FIVE
Damage Control--
How to Stabilize Collection

Who does not believe an ounce of prevention is worth a pound of cure? If you believe it applies to life's everyday events, then most certainly it applies to the IRS. Unfortunately, my experience proves unequivocally that too many people do not stay on top of the matters of greatest importance to them. When the topic is the IRS, folks would just as soon believe the agency will go away as face the problem head on.

As I pointed out in chapter four, it does not transpire that enforced collection nightmares evolve without warning. Before collection action develops, the warning signs abound. This is particularly true when the tax debt grows out of a return filed without full payment, from an audit or some other examination program. In these cases, the many notices make it clear that unpleasant action is ahead if the matter is not resolved. Yet, in the vain hope that it will just disappear, many take the "ostrich" approach. The head goes deep into the sand, exposing the posterior in an extremely vulnerable position. Do not for a moment believe the IRS will not tee off on one so ideally situated.

If you are to prevent such a thing, you must understand, a) that enforced collection can be at least minimized and in many cases, avoided, and b) to stabilize the collection environment, you must go on the offensive quickly in a very carefully prescribed manner. Pay close attention as we examine how to *stabilize* the volatile collection environment. The primary goal is to establish either an installment agreement or in some cases, "uncollectible status."

An installment agreement based on your ability to pay enables you to pursue one or more of the amnesty programs. In a few cases, the installment agreement by itself can solve the problem. In the majority of cases, however, it is but a stepping stone to other relief programs.

In cases where there is a financial hardship and one is unable to make a monthly payment, the IRS institutes a collection "freeze." This is what is referred to as uncollectible status. Upon declaring uncollectible status, the IRS effectively pushes the "hold" button on its collection machine. It *does not* eliminate the tax, however. The debt remains viable but collection is not pursued due to the financial shortcomings of the citizen. We discuss uncollectible status in detail in chapter eleven.

Now let us turn our attention to stabilizing the collection function. First we address the case of filers unable to pay, then we examine non-filers with the same problem. Lastly, we address business tax debts.

Avoiding Automated Collection

Treat ACS demands very seriously and respond to them immediately. Without a prompt response, the IRS pursues enforced collection with all available tools. There are two schools of thought when dealing with ACS. The first suggests you should make every attempt to have your case transferred from ACS to the local Collection office. That enables you to deal face-to-face with a revenue officer and may place you in a better position to negotiate reasonable payment terms.

The second school of thought suggests that by dealing directly with ACS, your case may be handled more expeditiously and in assembly-line fashion. That may prevent drawing the IRS' full collection attention and hence, its wrath. That theory, however, has some inherent flaws, as we examine later.

Nevertheless, it is a simple matter to *attempt* to win an installment agreement or uncollectible status from ACS and you should make that attempt in the first instance. Let us examine the procedures.

Negotiating with ACS

The first order of business in obtaining an installment agreement or uncollectible status is to utilize IRS Form 9465, Installment Agreement Request. Please see the Forms Kit. Form 9465 is a simple form stating, "I cannot pay in full. I need an installment agreement." Next, the form says, "I can afford to pay $_____ per month." You fill in the blank, sign the form and mail it to the IRS using certified mail, return receipt requested. If you cannot make a payment, enter the number "0" and declare that you need "uncollectible status" due to your current "financial hardship."

Use Form 9465 upon receipt of the *initial* collection notice. See chapter four under the heading, *What to Expect from Enforced Tax Collection.* This sets the wheels in motion to establish an installment payment or uncollectible status quickly and potentially without the need of involving a local RO. If you cannot pay at the time of first filing your return, attach Form 9465 directly to the return.

In addition to Form 9465, include a letter explaining the following points: (1) you do not have sufficient money or assets to pay the tax in full, (2) you have no creditors who can be put off, thus allowing you to pay in a short time, and (3) monthly bills needed to meet necessary living expenses make it impossible to pay more than you suggest. Include a simple worksheet of your income and expenses to show that the payment is reasonable. When seeking uncollectible status, be sure to show that monthly expenses meet or exceed income. See chapter eleven for details.

If you are unable to reach a satisfactory agreement with ACS, push for transfer of the case to an RO.

Why Attempt to Transfer Your Case?

My comment suggesting you may receive expedited, assembly-line treatment from ACS is not intended to suggest its ultimate goal of collecting money is somehow overlooked. On the contrary, while it sometimes happens that ACS more readily accepts payment terms, the risks inherent in dealing with ACS are not often outweighed by the potential benefit.

The overriding disadvantage of dealing directly with ACS is revealed in its name, "*Automated Collection.*" ACS cases are on the collection fast track. At particular risk are W-2 employees whose paychecks and bank accounts are within easy reach. Unless you take clear and definitive steps quickly, expect ACS to accomplish two goals. First, it issues a tax lien which devastates your credit and ironically, often stands in the way of your obtaining a loan to pay the tax.

Second, but just as quickly, ACS reaches out for the source of revenue most easily plucked--your paycheck and bank account. All that is necessary to seize your paycheck or bank account and separate you from your financial lifeline is for you to do *nothing.* ACS is impersonal and need not be dissatisfied with the progress of a collection case to issue wage or bank levies. Given the fact that ACS is

programmed to move quickly, it is a miracle when it *does not* commit
those acts.

In my mind, these factors almost always weigh in favor of pursuing
a transfer to the local Collection Division. As you learn in our later
discussions concerning your relationship with a revenue officer, your
options are generally greater when the case is managed at the local
level. Furthermore, it is my opinion that success with the amnesty
programs is more likely when the case is managed by the human
element. Policy changes allowing the spirit of amnesty cannot be
recognized or acted upon by a machine.

How to Transfer your Case from ACS

Transfer from ACS to the local Collection office is not routine and
the request must come from the citizen. At section 5548.2(2)(a)1, the
Internal Revenue Manual (IRM) specifies that a case will be
transferred when the "taxpayer requests a transfer . . ." The manual
goes on to state that such requests must be supported by the facts of
the case and meet the requirements of IRM part 5521(15). That section
explains that the IRS does not honor requests for transfer "based
merely on taxpayer preference for personal contact where the facts do
not justify the transfer."

The manual is silent as to what exactly constitutes "facts justifying
the transfer." However, it does suggest that transfer is appropriate
when "taxpayers are currently working with a field employee on
another case or where the case seems unusually complex." Further
guidance comes from IRM part 5534.5, entitled *Cases Requiring
Special Handling*. There are six points listed which, if raised by the
citizen, require special handling. They are:

- taxpayer claims liability is paid;
- taxpayer claims tax is not owed;
- taxpayer requests explanation of balance due;
- taxpayer in bankruptcy;
- levy on state income tax refund paid tax;
- taxpayer out of business.

*Request the transfer at the first sign that ACS is not seriously
considering your Installment Agreement Request.* Do not wait for the
final notice and do not wait for enforced collection. Make the request
in writing and be specific. Mail it to the address appearing on the top

of your notice. Always communicate in writing and by certified mail, with return receipt requested. Allege that the complexity of your case necessitates a transfer. Where appropriate, raise one or more of the issues set out above and provide facts and argument to support your request.

Your letter must also make every effort to persuade ACS that enforced collection action is not warranted. In this respect, point out that you cannot make full and immediate payment. Also point out that enforced collection action is sure to cause economic hardship by making it impossible to pay your monthly living expenses.

In order for ACS to act on your letter, clearly establish these several points:

1. You do not have sufficient funds available to pay in a lump sum;

2. You do not have sufficient assets which can be liquidated in order to pay in full;

3. You have no creditors to whom payments can be stalled thus enabling you to pay in full within a very short period of time; and

4. Monthly expenses necessary to meet your personal "health and welfare needs," such as food, clothing and shelter and the support of dependents make large monthly installment payments (or *any* monthly payment) impossible.

List three final requests in the conclusion of your letter. First, request the case be transferred to a local collection officer with whom payment arrangements can be negotiated. Second, request that enforced collection be postponed in the meantime. And third, request the IRS accept temporary installment payments (or grant uncollectible status) in the amount you suggest. Include the first suggested payment in the letter.

If successful, you avert enforced collection action and an RO is assigned to your case. Soon thereafter, expect to meet with the RO to discuss payment terms and of course, entertain the prospect of employing one or more tax amnesty programs.

If the Case is not Transferred

If ACS *does not* transfer the case, it is likely to respond to your letter in one of two ways. It may mail the needed installment agreement forms, principally a financial statement (discussed later), by return mail with a cover letter explaining what to do with them. In other cases, an ACS representative simply phones the citizen to secure the financial statement. Phone calling is not uncommon in cases involving small amounts of tax.

Whenever you engage in a phone conversation with anybody from the IRS, keep careful notes of your discussion, including the date, name of the person you spoke with and his return phone number and mailing address. Follow up your conversation with a letter reiterating all you discussed, including any agreements reached. This is the only way of making a written record of the conversation.

If you received any forms by return mail, promptly and accurately complete and return them as requested. Later in this discussion, I address the particulars of completing the financial statement and other needed documents and give cautions on which ones to avoid, if possible. Send all documents, including your initial letter and payment via certified mail, return receipt requested. Keep a copy of each document for your records, including the payment devices.

When you win an installment agreement in this fashion, you effectively stabilize the collection process. This eliminates all enforced collection activity. You may then turn your attention to one or more of the amnesty programs discussed later.

Negotiating with a Revenue Officer.

After the case is transferred to the local Collection Division, the next step is a visit from a revenue officer. The initial visit from the RO is often a shocking experience. An RO does not generally phone or otherwise announce his visit. Further, IRS policy always has been to attempt to collect all the tax in the first visit. Therefore, expect the RO to demand immediate, full payment of the entire tax.

You must take the initiative here if you are to achieve a realistic installment agreement. If your response is simply that you cannot pay, the RO generally asks when you can. Unless you take some affirmative action to direct the course of the conversation, expect the RO to merely make demands, issue potential levy threats and push paperwork under your nose.

To begin installment negotiations, explain that you cannot pay in full. Ask for all paperwork necessary to establish the agreement. At this point, it is critical to communicate your desire to cooperate. State that you recognize your obligation but need assistance in reaching amicable terms.

At no time should you make statements to the effect of, "I don't owe the money. I'm not paying." The last statement you ever want to make to an RO is that you will not pay the tax. In response, he is likely to resort to the full arsenal of collection weapons at his disposal.

Even if you believe you do not owe the tax, follow the guidelines outlined above *first*. Only after you establish favorable working terms with the RO should you address the merits of the tax. Keep in mind, you generally have the right to challenge an assessment in some fashion and always have the right to make a claim for refund of taxes improperly paid or collected. See chapter five, *Taxpayers' Ultimate Defense Manual* for more on the refund process. Other suggestions for challenging the underlying assessment come later in this work.

My policy is that you should never sign documents on the *first* visit from an RO. It is not uncommon for ROs to make demands for financial statements or to sign Form 900 on the spot. The Form 900 is a Tax Collection Waiver and acts to extend the statute of limitations for collection of the tax. It is reproduced below as Exhibit 5-1.

Exhibit 5-1

Form **900** (Rev. January 1968)	Department of the Treasury — Internal Revenue Service **Tax Collection Waiver**			
Name(s) and address of taxpayer(s)				Statutory period extended to
Tax form number	Tax period ended	Assessment date	Taxpayer identification number	Amount Outstanding

The taxpayer(s) and the District Director of Internal Revenue agree that the above amount outstanding (plus interest, penalties, and other additions provided by law) may be collected from the taxpayers by levy or a proceeding in court begun on or before the date to which the statutory period has been extended. Further, they agree that if an offer in compromise is made by the taxpayer(s) on or before the date to which the statutory period has been extended, then the time for making any collection will be further extended beyond that date by the number of days (1) the offer is pending, or (2) any installment remains unpaid, or (3) that provisions of any related collateral agreement are not satisfied, plus 1 year.

Taxpayer's signature	Date	Taxpayer's signature	Date
By (If signed by someone other than the taxpayer)			Date
District Director's name		By Delegated Representative (signature and title)	Date

Part 1 — IRS Copy   Form **900** (Rev. 1-88)

Signing forms under these conditions is generally a serious mistake. With respect to financial statements, if it is later shown to be in error, that nullifies any installment agreement. Furthermore, the financial statement must be signed under penalty of perjury and it is a felony to deliberately and knowingly submit false information. Therefore, provide only absolutely correct and complete information. This *cannot* be done on the spot.

Signing Form 900 can have long-term negative effects. Form 900 extends the statute of limitations governing the IRS' right to collect. In some cases it is necessary to sign the form before executing an installment agreement but never sign it without careful consideration of the implications. Furthermore, never sign a so-called "open-ended waiver." An open-ended waiver is one which does not establish a new date for the expiration of the collection statute. An open-ended waiver allows tax collection to continue *indefinitely*.

A very polite but effective way to "borrow time" in the face of demands for immediate signatures or information is to explain that you wish to consult counsel first. You have the absolute right to counsel *whenever* dealing with the IRS. Further, by explaining you need additional time to ensure that all statements are complete and accurate, it becomes virtually impossible for the RO to offer tangible objections.

Negotiations with a revenue officer can be sensitive and sometimes stressful. However, if you recognize the purpose of the meeting and the goals of both parties, they do not have to be difficult. As mentioned earlier, the job of the RO is to get the money--period. Your success depends upon your understanding this premise and working toward achieving that goal.

It is no secret that satisfying the revenue officer will not be easy. After all, if you were capable of paying the tax, you surely would not be reading this book. Yet, citizens experience the most trouble with an RO when they do not cooperate with the collection process. In my experience, when you step forward and in essence, do the collector's job for him, you fare much better than if you attempt to dodge the collection process. This is true even if you feel you do not owe the tax. The merits of the liability may always be addressed after neutralizing threats of enforced collection.

This is particularly true when you are not capable of full payment. It is under those conditions that tax liens, wage and bank levies and property seizures create the most havoc. To avoid financial disaster, you must do the revenue officer's job for him.

Explain that you understand he must have a financial statement and supporting documents. Explain that you know his job is to collect. Work faithfully to meet all your responsibilities.

That is not to say that you should roll over to every demand regardless of whether it is reasonable or proper. Clearly, you should not. The line to walk is that which divides the area between good faith cooperation and mindless capitulation. You may be surprised to learn that when you stand up to unreasonable or improper demands, the RO often gains a measure of respect for you. That makes the job of handling his reasonable and legitimate requests that much simpler. It also tells him that you are not an easy mark and cannot be run over.

What follows is a specific discussion of how to win an installment agreement in negotiations with a revenue officer. Bear in mind, however, that the rules and techniques relevant to the RO apply equally to ACS. Use this procedure even if you are not successful in winning a transfer from ACS.

First, I address all those cases in which an assessment is pending because of filing a return without paying the tax in full. This includes any situation where the IRS assessed additional tax liabilities such as through an audit.

Later, under the heading, *The Tax Delinquency Investigation,* I address the non-filer. There, we examine all aspects of handling the RO in the face of demands for delinquent returns.

Lastly, we explore the pressing problem of employment taxes. Given the nature of employment taxes, the IRS takes a different, generally more aggressive stance when addressing those debts. Consequently, the citizen burdened with such debt must also be more aggressive in resolving the situation.

How to Win an Installment Agreement

Prior to passage of the Taxpayers' Bill of Rights Act (TBRA) in 1988, there was no legal authority permitting the IRS to enter into installment agreements. It was purely discretionary with the RO and his immediate supervisor. Often, the agreement was looked upon as doing the citizen a "favor." It does not require much experience to know the IRS is not in the business of granting favors to delinquent citizens. Therefore, installment agreements were difficult to come by and involved intensive negotiation. Once instituted, the IRS was notorious for arbitrarily increasing the payment or disregarding the agreement altogether.

As a result of the TBRA, the authority for the installment agreement grows from code section 6159(a). In relevant part, it provides,

> The Secretary is authorized to enter into written agreements with any taxpayer under which such taxpayer is allowed to satisfy the liability for payment of any tax in installment payments if the Secretary determines that such agreement will facilitate collection of such liability.

The law does not grant an "absolute right" to an installment agreement but the agreement is available when it will "facilitate collection." Thus, before the agreement is considered, you must show that it is the IRS' only hope of collecting a reasonable amount of money in a reasonable period of time. If you have significant assets that can be liquidated to pay the bill or have substantial borrowing power, the RO expects you to tap those resources first.

Moreover, there is no specific statutory or regulatory provision stating a time limitation on installment agreements. As a result, citizens hear many statements concerning the "required" or "maximum" term of the agreement. Some say all taxes must be paid in ninety days. Others say the agreement cannot go beyond one year, etc.

The regulation makes it clear, however, that there is no specific time limit. Revenue Regulation section 301.6159-1(a), states,

> A district director, a director of a service center, or a director of a compliance center (the director) is authorized to enter into a written agreement with a taxpayer that allows the taxpayer to satisfy a tax liability by making scheduled periodic payments *until the liability is fully paid* if the director determines that such an installment agreement will facilitate the collection of the tax liability. (Emphasis added)

As we plainly see, the installment agreement continues "until the tax is paid." That may be ninety days in some cases or several years in others.

As a result of the open-ended nature of installment agreements, the chief question is not how long the agreement runs, but rather, how much you can afford to pay. The more you pay, the less time it takes to liquidate the debt and vice-versa. Of course, the IRS always looks for the largest possible payment with an eye toward satisfying the liability in the shortest time. Too often, the agency demands payments which simply are not reasonable or feasible under the circumstances. Let us therefore turn our attention to the process by which one establishes the amount of the installment agreement.

How to Establish the Installment Payment Amount

The heart and soul of any collection case is the financial statement. The RO's first job is to obtain a financial statement if the citizen expresses inability to pay the tax in full. The IRS does not entertain alternative payment methods unless you provide a financial statement signed under penalty of perjury. Submit the financial statement on Form 433-A (individuals) or 433-B (businesses). See the Forms Kit.

The purpose of the statement is two-fold and you must understand *both*. First, the IRS determines from the financial statement whether, in fact, you are unable to pay the tax in full. The RO considers all income and assets as well as expenses and liabilities. If the statement reveals sufficient income and assets from which to pay, negotiating a long-term installment agreement is very difficult.

However, short-term arrangements are possible. A short term agreement enables you to selectively liquidate certain assets or otherwise make arrangements to raise funds. Of course, along with revealing your income and assets--and their locations--you provide the RO with possible sources of levy action. And that is the second purpose of the financial statement--to ascertain the whereabouts of your assets. However, this is an unavoidable risk since you cannot win an installment agreement without a financial statement and any financial statement must be true and accurate to avoid the risk of prosecution for submitting a false document.

Next, the RO analyzes your monthly income and expenses to determine the payment you can afford. You are not at liberty to declare, "I will pay you $100 per month" and expect the RO to accept it without question.

On the other hand, his demand is not supposed to be arbitrary either. It is supposed to be based upon your net take-home pay and personal living expenses. The difference between take home pay and personal living expenses is defined by the Internal Revenue Manual (IRM) as "disposable income." IRM 5323.12(5). "Disposable income is the amount available to apply to the tax liability." Ibid.

Establish your take-home pay. The first step, then, is to establish your take-home pay. Pay particular attention to the portion of the financial statement seeking information concerning your present income. See Form 433-A, Section V (see the Forms Kit). This information should be complete and entirely accurate. For example, do not list income which is not certain and recurring money *each month.*

Be sure to consider all amounts "deducted from gross income, including deductions required by law to be withheld, or any child support or alimony payments that are made under a court order or legally enforceable written agreement." IRM 5323.12(5). Such items include but are not limited to federal and state income taxes, FICA and Medicare taxes and wage garnishment payments. Other deductions might include union dues, life insurance (if not to the level of investment) and other payments required by your employer.

The IRM stipulates the amount of the monthly payment "will be at least the difference between net income and allowable expenses." IRM 5323(4)(e); see Form 433-A, Section V. The difference between gross pay and withholdings is considered "net income." From net income, subtract your allowable monthly living expenses to arrive at the installment payment amount; see Form 433-A, line 53.

Figuring allowable expenses. Determining what constitutes "allowable expenses" is another matter. It involves a wide range of discretion on the part of the RO. The RO has the power to disallow certain of your expenditures. The result is, he demands that funds committed to those items be used to increase your payment to the IRS. This demand is made without regard to the effect on other creditors or your overall lifestyle.

The second step in the process, therefore, is to provide proof of your monthly expenses. Before the expenses are allowed against income, they must meet certain criteria. First, the expenses must be classified as either "necessary" or "conditional." Second, they must be "reasonable in amount." IRM 5323.12(1)(a).

A "necessary" expense is one which provides for the "health and welfare" of the citizen and his family. Another type of "necessary" expense is one which is incurred for the "production of income." Ibid.

Health and welfare expenses include housing, food, medical care, personal care items, clothing, utilities, transportation, child care, insurance, payments for legally secured or perfected debts, etc. These expenses establish the "minimum" a citizen and his family need to live. Ibid.

Some often overlooked necessary living expenses are,

• Legal and accounting fees necessary to deal with the IRS or that are otherwise necessary to produce income;

- Charitable contributions necessary as a condition of employment or somehow provide for the health and welfare of the family;
- Child care expenses including baby-sitting, day care, preschool, etc., when they are reasonable and necessary for the production of income, i.e., parents need day care in order to work;
- Court ordered payments such as alimony, child support, or other court-enforced payments;
- Dependent care for persons other than children, such as elderly, handicapped or invalid family members;
- Education expenses when required for a physically or mentally handicapped child or when required as a condition of employment;
- State and local tax payments;
- Health care, medical services, prescription drugs, supplies, doctors, travel, eye glasses, contact lenses, etc.;
- Involuntary deductions from pay, such as union dues;
- Life insurance if the payment is for a term policy;
- Unsecured debts for such things as credit cards and personal loans, but only minimum payments when it is shown that the payments are necessary for the health and welfare of the family or are necessary to produce income.

Expenses necessary to earn income include necessary travel, transportation, telephone, supplies, office expenses, etc. They can also include educational expenses when required by law or by your employer and child care expenses.

"Conditional" expenses are all those which are not "necessary" to maintain minimum living standards. However, they are allowable only if the tax, including accumulating interest and penalties, can be paid within three years. IRM 5323.12(1)(b).

In figuring the amount of disposable income available for an installment payment, the IRS *must allow* all necessary expenses which are reasonable in amount. It allows conditional expenses when the tax can be paid within three years. However, excessive necessary expenses and conditional expenses *are not* allowed if the tax and accruals cannot be paid within three years.

Excessive necessary expenses are those which are not reasonable in amount. When an expense is disallowed, the IRS expects the citizen to increase his installment payment by the amount of the disallowed expense. The citizen is, according to the IRS, expected to adjust his lifestyle in any way necessary to pay the amount demanded.

National and local expense standards. Effective September 1, 1995, the IRS introduced what it calls "standards" for determining one's allowable expenses. On line 42 of Form 433-A, the IRS asks for the "National Standard Expenses." The National Standard (NS) expenses include the following six items: food, utilities, housekeeping supplies, clothing and clothing services, personal care products and services and miscellaneous items. The first five items are established by Bureau of Labor Statistics, the sixth is established by the IRS.

NS expenses vary depending upon income and family size. As income and family size increase, the allowable expense increases. The specific amounts are changed from time to time. The chart, reproduced below as Exhibit 5-2 shows the NS expenses as of January, 1997.

Exhibit 5-2

NATIONAL STANDARD EXPENSES
(Item 42)

Expenses Include: Housekeeping supplies, Clothing and clothing services, Personal care products and services, Food, Miscellaneous

Total Monthly Income	Number of Persons in Household				
	One	Two	Three	Four	Over Four
Less than $830	315	509	553	714	+120
$830 to $1,249	383	517	624	723	+130
$1,250 to $1,669	448	569	670	803	+140
$1,670 to $2,499	511	651	731	839	+150
$2,500 to $3,329	551	707	809	905	+160
$3,330 to $4,169	590	840	948	1,053	+170
$4,170 to $5,829	665	913	1,019	1,177	+180
$5,830 and over	923	1,179	1,329	1,397	+190

ALLOWABLE TRANSPORTATION EXPENSES

Ownership Costs		
	One Car	Two Cars
National	$350	$550

Line 43 of Form 433-A calls for housing and utility expenses and line 44 calls for transportation expenses, including normal car maintenance, parking, tolls, etc. These items have been codified into what the IRS calls its Local Standards (LS). LS amounts are determined on the basis of living expenses within a given county or IRS district. They are based upon Bureau of Labor Statistics. Since September 1, 1995, the IRS has imposed these standards throughout the nation.

Prior to establishing NS and LS expenses, a citizen was called upon to substantiate every expense claimed on Form 433-A. The IRS would, in some cases, verify the expense before allowing it. Under present procedures, however, NS and LS amounts need not be substantiated or verified. The amounts are allowed automatically in computing disposable income.

It would seem these procedures make it easier to negotiate a reasonable installment agreement. However, that has not been the case. The IRS uses the NS and LS expenses more as a sword with which to extract higher installment agreements.

For example, citizens whose reasonable necessary living expenses exceed the NS amounts are told simply to stop paying such bills and pay the difference to the IRS. In the case of LS expenses for housing and transportation costs, citizens whose fixed house payment exceeds the standard amount are told, in essence, "tough." They are expected to pay the IRS the difference. In fact, the manual describing these standards states in numerous places, "taxpayers are responsible for deciding how to adjust or eliminate expenses." IRM 5323.5(6)(b)2.

Unfortunately, but not surprisingly, this amounts to something of a return to the draconian attitude that prevailed in the Collection Division before former Commissioner Peterson instituted the tax amnesty programs. That attitude can be summarized very simply: "get the money"--period--regardless of the facts and circumstances--regardless of the hardships and limitations of the individual. Just get the money.

That is what I call the Darth Vader approach to tax collection. This is where the IRS grabs the citizen by the throat and simply squeezes him to within an inch of his financial life. In many cases, NS and LS expenses force the citizen to make a choice between paying his taxes and feeding his family. IRS does not wish to accept the citizen's notion that feeding his family should come first. After all, *why* do you need to eat? Instead, force the citizen to reduce his standard of living to the lowest possible level so he can pay IRS every remaining dime. The NS and LS standards are clearly at odds with the spirit of resolution expressed in the "new attitude."

Facing down NS and LS expenses. The RO's position often is that NS and LS expenses are carved in stone regardless of your actual expenses. However, this is simply *not* supported by the manual. IRM section 5323.421 describes the operation of NS amounts. At subsection (2)(c), the manual states,

> That a taxpayer spends more than the total amount allowed by the National Standards does not automatically constitute a justification for the Service to consider the expense to be necessary. A taxpayer who claims more than the total allowed by the (NS) must substantiate and justify as necessary each separate expense of the total.

From this plain language we learn two things. First and foremost, expenses exceeding NS amounts can be allowed, despite the fixed standards. Second, *before* allowing them, the citizen must justify each and every expense and show it is necessary to provide for the health and welfare of the family or to produce income. He must also demonstrate the amount is reasonable under the circumstances. Frankly, this is precisely the position we were in prior to adoption of the standards.

At IRM section 5323.422, the IRS discusses the LS amounts. At subsection (1) we find this statement:

> These standards (LS amounts) should be used to ensure that taxpayers who spend more than locally-established standards justify their expenses.

Both in the case of NS and LS expenses, amounts in excess of the standards are allowable under appropriate circumstances. On January 10, 1997, I received a letter from A.C. Zack, Chief, IRS Collection Division, St. Paul, Minnesota. Zack responded to my inquiry regarding NS and LS expenses. Zack states, "The maximum stated allowance under each expense is a *guide* and *may be adjusted* based on the circumstances of each individual case" (emphasis added).

In the manual, the IRS gives an example with regard to food expenses exceeding NS amounts. The excess is allowed where a citizen has "special prescribed or required dietary needs." IRM 5323.421(2)(c).

In another such example, the citizen's housing expenses exceed the standards. But *before* requiring him to pay the excessive amount, the RO is instructed to consider,

- the increased cost of transportation to work and school which might result from moving to lower cost housing;
- the tax consequences resulting from selling a home, including capital gains taxes and the lost interest and real estate tax deductions; and
- the actual cost of moving to lower cost housing. IRM 5323.422(3)(a)1a-c.

The IRS has even provided a set of questions and answers to its ROs for the purposes of further explaining NS and LS expenses. IRM Exhibit 5300-47. In one question, the IRS discusses the issue of what to do when a citizen's actual expenses exceed the NS amount. Consider the language of Question 7:

> 7. Q. A taxpayer claims that she needs more than the amount provided by the National Standards because she has five teenage children. Can she get an increased amount?
> A. Yes, if she can fully pay the tax liability within three years. Otherwise [that is, she cannot paid within three years], she has to substantiate and justify all the expenses included within the National Standards. The fact that she spends more than the National Standards allow for one category of expense, such as clothing, does not in itself, constitute a justification.

The unfortunate reality is that too many IRS employees simply do not read their own manual. This is one reason why so many citizens have run into a brick wall when trying to support expenses exceeding these standards. Be prepared to cite chapter and verse of the manual to support the position that expenses in excess of the standards are allowed when they can be justified and shown to be reasonable in amount.

It is important to note that the NS and LS standards *do not apply* to expenses necessary to produce income. The standards only apply to *personal living* expenses. Therefore, before completing Form 433-A, carefully analyze all monthly expenses. Those which can fairly be said to constitute expenses necessary to earn income should be so classified. To be allowed, they must be verified and reasonable in amount.

A W-2-type wage earner may have substantial unreimbursed employee business expenses. They might include business licenses, car expenses including tolls, parking, etc., office supplies, tools or equipment, meals and entertainment and similar expenses.

The self-employed must use IRS Form 433-B (see the Forms Kit) to show business expenses. *Do not* show production of income expenses on Form 433-A. Form 433-B shows gross business receipts and business expenses. The net is transferred to Form 433-A as personal income to the business owner. From there, deduct personal living expenses to arrive at disposable income.

By placing as many expenses as possible on the Form 433-B (or classifying them as production of income expenses by the W-2 wage earner on 433-A), you minimize dispute arising when actual living expenses exceed NS and LS amounts.

When a citizen has expenses considered to be excessive, the IRS disallows them and demands payment of the overage in the form of a higher installment. The citizen is then expected to decide how to "adjust his lifestyle" and standard of living in order to make the extra payment.

The "one-year" rule. If you are paying excessive necessary or conditional expenses, the so-called "one-year" comes into play. It is described in IRM section 5323.12(4) as follows,

> It provides a taxpayer up to one year to modify or eliminate excessive necessary or not-allowable conditional expenses if the tax liability, including projected accruals, cannot be fully paid within three years.

Under this rule, you may be asked to sell a residence or a vehicle if the expense is considered excessive. In the worst case, use the one-year rule to buy time to adjust living expenses. This way, you can hold off enforced collection action, thus preventing levies and seizures of bank accounts and property.

Other factors bearing on the payment amount. There are two further categories of expenses we should address because they constitute generally "allowable items" in determining the installment payment amount. Minimum payments on secured, legally perfected debts are generally allowed. However, if the payment is for a luxury item such as a boat, expect the RO to ask you to sell the asset then commit the additional revenue--and profit--to the IRS. If you do not, expect the RO to seize it if there is any likelihood of realizing net proceeds from its sale.

The IRS generally attempts to disallow payments on unsecured debts such as credit cards. Look for the RO to ask you to discontinue such payments if by doing so, IRS will be paid in full within ninety days. If that does not pay the debt within ninety days, however, you must argue that minimum payments to unsecured creditors must be allowed. If not, those creditors could commence legal action against you thereby impairing your ability to pay the tax. In these discussions, expect the IRS to impose the "one-year" rule described above.

In some cases, a fixed, level monthly payment cannot be determined. The reason is many self-employed people and those working on strict commission do not always realize the same cash-flow or profits from one month to the next or from season to season. In this case, make that point clear at the outset of negotiations. I find it helpful to prepare a detailed cash-flow projection showing your expected income and expenses for the ensuing twelve or twenty-four month period.

By doing this, the RO (who probably has no understanding whatsoever of how real-world businesses operate) is taken by the hand and shown how your business and hence, income, fluctuate. You can then structure an elastic payment plan which expands and contracts with your income.

It is within this broad framework that you negotiate to determine the amount of your monthly payment. After reaching an agreement, the details are reduced to writing in IRS Form 433-D, Installment Agreement, reproduced on the next page as Exhibit 5-3.

Recognize the RO's job. In these negotiations, never lose sight of the fact that the RO's job is to *get the money!* Everything he says and does revolves around that general goal. As a practical matter, he attempts to reach that goal by doing the following:

1. Obtaining information on possible sources of levy, including the location and value of assets, bank accounts, etc. The financial statement serves this purpose.

2. Obtaining a Signed Form 900, Tax Collection Waiver, if the financial statement indicates that immediate or short-term collection is not possible.

3. Filing a Notice of Federal Income Tax Lien in the county in which you live. This protects the IRS' interest in your assets and may legally "secure" its claim.

Exhibit 5-3

Form **433-D**
(Rev. February 1995)

Installment Agreement

check box if
installment agreement
fee was paid ☐

Name and address of taxpayer(s)

Waukesha,

Social security or employer identification number	
(primary)	(secondary)

Telephone number (home)	(business)

Kinds of taxes (form numbers) 1040	Tax periods 90, 91, 92, 94
Amount owed as of 8/95	Earliest CSED 6/15/2002
$ 80,452.00	

For assistance:
Call 1-800-829-1040 or write:

_____ Service Ctr.

Employer (name and address)

Financial institutions (names and addresses)

Waukesha,

City, State and Zip Code

I/We agree that the federal taxes shown above, PLUS ALL PENALTIES AND INTEREST PROVIDED BY LAW, will be paid as follows:

$ 3715.00 will be paid on 9/15/95 and $ 3715.00 will be paid

no later than the 15th of each month thereafter until the total liability is paid in full. I/We also agree that the above

check box if pre-assessed modules included ☐

installment payment will be increased or decreased as follows:

Date of increase (or decrease)	2/15/96	3/15/96
Amount of increase (or decrease)	$ (350.00)	650.00
New installment amount	$ 3365.00	4015.00

AGREEMENT LOCATOR NUMBER: __ __ __ __
(circle)
0   No future action is required
5   Financial review date: 02/96
        m   y   y
6   SCCB — Monitor ES compliance:
        Amount per quarter $ _____
        (If amount(s)/quarters will vary, provide details.)

Conditions of this agreement:
* We must receive each payment by the date shown above; if you have a problem, contact us immediately.
* This agreement is based on your current financial condition. We may change or cancel it if our information shows that your ability to pay has changed significantly.
* We may cancel this agreement if you don't give us updated financial information we ask for it.
* While this agreement is in effect, you must file all federal tax returns and pay any taxes you owe on time.
* We will apply your federal or state tax refunds (if any) to the amount you owe until it is fully paid. (This includes the Alaska Permanent Fund dividend for Alaska residents.)
* You must pay a $43 installment agreement fee.
* If agreement defaults, you must pay a $24 reinstatement fee if agreement is reinstated.

Additional Conditions: (To be completed by IRS)

* If you don't meet the conditions of this agreement, we will cancel it, and may collect the entire amount you owe by levy on your income, bank accounts or other assets, or by seizing your property.
* We will cancel this agreement at any time if we find that collection of the tax is in jeopardy.
* We will apply all payments on this agreement in the best interest of the United States.
* This agreement may require managerial approval. If it is not approved, you will be notified.
* **A NOTICE OF FEDERAL TAX LIEN** (check one)
    ☒ HAS ALREADY BEEN FILED
    ☐ WILL BE FILED IMMEDIATELY
    ☐ WILL BE FILED WHEN TAX IS ASSESSED
    ☐ MAY BE FILED IF THIS AGREEMENT DEFAULTS

Your signature X	Title (if corporate officer or partner)	Date	Originator's name, title and IDRS assignment number (or district):
Spouse's signature (if a joint liability) X		Date	K. Cederholm
Agreement examined or approved by (signature, title, function)		Date	Originator Code:

YOU MAY HAVE YOUR INSTALLMENT AGREEMENT PAYMENT DEDUCTED FROM YOUR CHECKING ACCOUNT EACH MONTH (DIRECT DEBIT); IF YOU CHOOSE THIS OPTION, FOLLOW THE DIRECTIONS ON THE BACK OF YOUR COPY OF THIS FORM.

If you agree to Direct Debit, initial here: _____

and attach a blank voided check.

* I (we) authorize the IRS and the depository (bank) identified on the attached voided check to deduct payments (debit) from my (our) checking account or correct errors on the account. This authorization remains in effect until I (or either of us) notify IRS in writing to stop or until the liability covered by this agreement is satisfied.
* I (we) understand that if the depository is unable to honor IRS's request for payment due to insufficient funds in my (our) account on the payment due date I (we) will be charged a penalty of $15 or two percent of the payment request, whichever is greater. If the payment request is for less than $15, the penalty is the amount of the request.

4. After analyzing the financial statement, expect the RO to seek liquidation of assets in which there is an equity interest sufficient to generate positive revenue. If, for example, you own a lake home and would realize substantial revenue by selling it, the RO wants it sold. He may threaten to levy the asset if you do not sell willingly.

The RO also wants you to explore the possibility of obtaining a loan by re-mortgaging property. Be careful, however, not to use credit cards as a means to raise cash for *partial* payments. That merely increases your monthly expenses without eliminating the IRS collection problem.

Before finalizing any agreement, the RO submits it to his immediate supervisor for approval. You *may* be forced back to the table. On the other hand, you have the right to appeal to that supervisor if you cannot agree with the RO.

Life Under the Installment Agreement

Once in place, the installment agreement remains in full force throughout its duration unless, a) the citizen provided incorrect or incomplete financial information prior to finalizing the agreement, b) he fails to carry out all the terms of the agreement (see Form 433-D, Exhibit 5-3) or, c) collection of the tax is in jeopardy. A tax is in jeopardy when the citizen takes steps to dispose of or conceal his assets or is preparing to flee the jurisdiction of the IRS.

Installment agreements can operate automatically, through the cooperation of either your employer or your bank. Expect the RO to push for either of these automated programs. The reason is payment of the tax is taken out of your hands. Under the Payment Deduction Agreement, Form 2159, your employer mails the payment to the IRS at the time of issuing your payroll check. Under the Direct Debit Installment Agreement, Form 433-G, your payment is debited directly from your bank account each month on the agreed upon date.

The fundamental disadvantages of each of these programs is they both require disclosure of your tax problem to either the bank or your employer and each requires an agreement from the affected third-party. For example, in order to operate the Payment Deduction Agreement, your employer must sign Form 2159 and agree to mail the checks to the IRS. Certainly, this may cause some strain between you and your employer. Whether to pursue either of these programs is up to you and depends on the facts and circumstances of your case.

What to Expect While the Agreement is in Effect

Throughout the duration of the agreement, expect the following:

First--installment agreements are generally short-term propositions. The IRS does not fancy itself as a bank and does not routinely enter into long-term agreements. By this I mean an agreement extending beyond thirty-six months. This *does not* mean, however, you must pay substantial debts, say $15,000 or $20,000, in just a few months.

What the IRS does, however, is establish a *series* of short-term agreements. This means that when a citizen is placed on a $100 per month installment agreement, the IRS reviews the agreement in one to two years to determine whether it should be modified. The agency bases modifications upon substantial changes in your ability to pay. Should your income rise substantially or your fixed expenses diminish, expect the payment to increase.

Second--whenever it is apparent that the liability cannot be satisfied within a very few months, the revenue officer often demands that you sign a Form 900 (see Exhibit 5-1, page 86) as a condition of the agreement.

Normally, the collection statute of limitations expires ten years after the date of assessment. With it, the IRS' collection power expires. But Form 900 extends the statute, keeping the agency's collection power alive throughout the period of a prolonged delinquency. Take care when the IRS seeks a signed Form 900. The implications are substantial.

Third--a condition of every installment agreement requires the citizen to be current and remain current with all his other income taxes. The IRS will not enter into an agreement or permit an agreement to operate if the citizen has other outstanding tax liabilities or delinquent returns. For example, you cannot expect the IRS to enter into an agreement to pay 1995 income taxes if your 1996 tax return is unfiled. Further, once finalizing an agreement, it is considered in default if subsequent returns are unfiled or taxes are unpaid by the due date, including any legitimate extensions. See chapter eight for details on how to get and stay current.

Because of the special problems presented to the non-filer in his efforts to negotiate with the revenue officer, they are treated separately in this chapter. See the discussion under the heading, *The Tax Delinquency Investigation.*

Fourth--the agency routinely requests updated financial statements (Forms 433-A and B), usually on twelve to twenty-four month intervals. The update is used to determine whether to alter the terms of the agreement. Such alterations are based upon any changes in financial status. If your income rises or expenses decrease, expect the IRS to increase the payment. On the other hand, the citizen may use the same review process to *reduce* his payment when his income *decreases* or expenses *escalate*.

Fifth--the agreement remains in effect throughout its duration, subject, of course, to the review process discussed above. However, the agreement is considered defaulted if the citizen provided inaccurate or incomplete financial data. Further, the agreement is considered defaulted if the IRS determines that collection of the tax is in "jeopardy" as defined earlier.

Sixth--the very *least* the citizen can expect once the agreement is formalized is to *make the payment!* You cannot expect the IRS to keep the installment agreement in force if you do not meet the terms of the agreement. After formalizing an installment agreement, the IRS monitors your performance. If one misses payments, the appropriate notices are quickly mailed. The citizen thus runs the risk of defaulting and once again igniting enforced collection action.

A caveat--I have always maintained that installment agreements are not and *should not* be looked upon as the *final solution* to a collection problem. Even in the best of cases, we cannot say the problem is solved until the tax is *paid in full*. Short of full payment, the citizen runs the risk that the IRS may exert some type of enforced collection action, installment agreement or not. Therefore, I view the installment agreement as a mere stepping stone, albeit an important and necessary one, to the financial promised land.

I caution any citizen who is either currently under an installment agreement or contemplating such an agreement, to use that tool in conjunction with other techniques which more fully address the problems you face. The installment agreement is not an end in itself. The reason is accumulating interest and penalties almost always negate the monthly payment. The result is the tax continues to build even while making payments.

On the other hand, when the payment is substantial, it is often so at the expense of necessary living expense or current tax payments. And while progress may be made on the delinquent tax debt, the individual actually gets further behind the financial eight-ball because delinquencies arise in other areas.

The installment agreement is an important tool needed to stabilize an otherwise volatile collection situation. Once in place, you may pursue other techniques to ultimately resolve the delinquency. The techniques to which I refer are the tax amnesty programs outlined in subsequent chapters of this work. Only by entirely resolving the delinquency do you finally eradicate the threat of enforced collection.

When the IRS Alters or Rejects Your Agreement

I state clearly throughout this discussion that the installment agreement is subject to review. I also clearly state that if the IRS feels the agreement is based upon incorrect or incomplete information or it feels collection of the tax is in "jeopardy," it can be rejected. Code section 6159(b)(2). The agreement may also be "altered, modified or terminated" at any time a substantial change occurs in your financial condition.

After making such a determination, the IRS must notify you in writing of its decision and must set forth the reasons for its decision. The IRS must provide the notice no later than thirty days *prior* to the date of the action. Code section 6159(b)(5).

The Taxpayers' Bill of Rights Act 2 (TBR2), passed July, 1996, gives you the right to challenge an IRS decision to alter, modify or terminate an installment agreement. Upon receipt of the notice to alter, modify or terminate the agreement, you may demand "an independent administrative review" of the action. Code section 6159(c).

To appeal the decision, file a written protest letter. Submit it within thirty days of the date of the letter communicating the IRS' intended action. IRS Publication 5, Preparation of Protests in Unagreed Cases (see Forms Kit) illustrates how to prepare the protest. It is a simple letter presenting just a few facts and a brief argument to support your position. Chapter eleven of my book, *IRS, Taxes and the Beast* details how to craft a written protest and carry out an appeal.

Under section 6159(b), the IRS has limited reasons why it may alter, modify or terminate an agreement. They are,

1. You provided inaccurate or incomplete information prior to entering into the agreement;
2. The IRS believes collection of the tax is in jeopardy;
3. The IRS believes your financial condition has significantly changed;
4. You fail to pay an installment on time;
5. You fail to pay another tax liability on time; or
6. You fail to provide a financial condition update as requested.

When challenging the IRS' action, be prepared to document the fact that you continue to meet the terms of the agreement as established. You must prove that none of the reasons stated in the IRS' notice (one of the six reasons outlined above) applies in your case.

Re-negotiating Your Agreement

Many citizens suffer under unreasonable installment agreements they never should have agreed to. In addition, financial circumstances sometimes change for the worse after consummating an agreement. In either case, you have the right to re-negotiate your agreement.

To re-open the negotiations, send a written request to the Chief of the Collection Division for your revenue district. Explain that your payment is too high and give the reasons why. Be clear and specific and include a financial statement to support your claims. Explain that the unreasonable payment is causing economic hardship. Specifically ask that the payment be lowered to the amount you believe is reasonable and justified.

While it is unlikely your request will be automatically honored, expect the case to be assigned to an RO for consideration. At that juncture, all of the points we discussed above come into play in re-negotiating the agreement.

If your letter is not successful in getting a review, write to the Taxpayers Advocate. His function is to help citizens solve enforcement problems. I provide the details of the Taxpayer Advocate in chapter seven.

The Tax Lien

A natural outgrowth of an installment agreement is a tax lien. The lien secures the government's interest in your property, preventing sale without payment of the proceeds to the IRS.

The tax lien is the one element of enforced collection over which we have the least control. The lien generally issues from ACS long before other signs of enforced collection manifest themselves. If not issued by the time an RO is assigned to the case, its filing is usually his first order of business, often before making direct contact with you.

The good news is, short of potentially disrupting your personal or business credit, the lien has little impact. However, if you intend to secure a loan, do that *prior* to the issuance of the lien, if possible. I have been successful in several cases in persuading the RO to forestall filing a lien until we pursue all potential loan avenues. This is no great trick since ROs are well aware of the fact that tax liens almost always eliminate the potential of obtaining a loan. If you present facts to establish the prospect of obtaining credit, the RO is likely to delay filing the lien. In chapter six, I discuss several options for dealing with troublesome liens.

The Tax Delinquency Investigation (TDI)

The goal of this discussion is to illustrate exactly how the non-filer is to contend with the demands of an RO. When dealing with a non-filer, the RO is often more intimidating than when dealing with payment delinquencies. Therefore, we afford special attention to that problem.

The Tax Delinquency Investigation begins as outlined in chapter four under the heading, *What to Expect From Enforced Tax Collection*. You avoid a potential TDI if, prior to detection by the IRS, you file the delinquent tax returns. How to step forward to file delinquent returns is the subject of chapter eight.

Upon filing, the IRS processes delinquent returns like any other. If you are able to pay the tax, naturally do so at the time of filing. Then, expect a bill from the service center assessing interest and penalties. Methods for dealing with penalty assessments are discussed in chapter nine.

If you cannot pay the tax due at the time of filing or cannot pay subsequent interest and penalty assessments, be prepared for contact by ACS. Handle ACS as outlined above. Your goal is to win transfer of the case to a local revenue officer and negotiate an installment agreement.

The lessons of Deb's case teach that the best approach may be to file the delinquent returns *before* the IRS instigates a TDI. By doing so, you potentially stand to avoid direct contact with the Examination Division or the Collection Division in the context of a TDI. That is certainly a worthwhile goal.

Upon detection of unfiled returns, the IRS establishes the TDI and hands the case either to Exam or Collection to secure the returns. When the case finds its way to the revenue officer, the Tax Delinquency Investigation becomes a Tax Delinquency Account (TDA). At that point, the RO's job is both to secure returns and collect taxes.

Another lesson learned in Deb's case is that revenue officers are not necessarily *friendly*. They often go to great lengths to intimidate. Rather than offering a feasible way to solve the problem, they routinely present demands which render compliance virtually impossible. It is almost as though their primary objective is not to secure returns and payment of the tax but rather to make life as miserable as possible.

No doubt you were left with a horrible taste in your mouth after our discussion of Deb's bout with her revenue officer. I did explain, however, that certain maneuvers allowed us to diffuse the threats and intimidation. Eventually, Deb won a reasonable amount of time to do her job without further harassment from the RO.

Before we examine those maneuvers, let us understand the two possible approaches used by a revenue officer in filing a delinquency case. As it happened, both approaches were used in Deb's situation. First, the RO demanded she file tax returns for numerous prior years "within thirty days." When Deb made it clear she could not comply with such a request, the RO issued a collection summons demanding records with which to prepare the returns. When Deb could not produce the records with sufficient speed, the RO huffed and puffed, then threatened to blow the house down.

Let us discuss how to handle both demands.

"File the Returns within Thirty Days"

At the first contact by a revenue officer working a TDA, he demands the filing of returns. Expect to be lectured on that fact that your returns are years late and you had all that time to file. Some revenue officers may be willing to extend a reasonable amount of time to do the job. Others, however, like Deb's RO, may be entirely unrealistic.

The key to winning time to file the returns is to show a willingness to cooperate. Make it perfectly clear you *understand* your obligation to file a "true and correct return." Explain that if you are forced to file a return without adequate time to gather, organize and classify all your records, you cannot file a truthful and accurate return. Ask the RO whether he wants your returns to be true, correct and complete in all respects, as indicated on the signature line of Form 1040.

What do you suppose will be his answer? It is highly unusual for an IRS employee to suggest you file anything other than accurate reports. Once securing the admission, explain that accurate returns can be prepared only if you have sufficient time.

At that point, you effectively corner the revenue office with a principle he believes in and accepts. That principle is the one stating we all must file *correct* returns. It is extremely contradictory to recognize, on the one hand, the obligation to file a correct return, then on the other hand, refuse to provide adequate time to do so.

Be prepared to provide a definitive timetable in which to prepare and submit the returns. A generally acceptable timetable is thirty to sixty days *per* return. Suppose you have four unfiled returns. Your filing proposal could suggest one return every sixty days. After submitting the final return, you address, if necessary, any *financial* delinquency.

The number one key to diffusing a revenue officer and winning cooperation is to do the RO's work for him. I mentioned this earlier. In this context, that means affirmatively recognizing the delinquency. It means definitively proposing a means to correct the delinquency. It means setting forth a firm timetable in which to do so.

Contrast this approach with the vast majority of delinquent citizens who generally run and hide. They do not return phone calls. They duck written contacts and the only way the IRS gets their attention is to bash them with liens and levies.

When you make it clear you understand the purpose of his visit and intend to make his job easier, you reap dividends in terms of his cooperation. Naturally, the lip service does little if you do not meet the obligations you claim to recognize. When that happens, expect the RO to force the issue by using the collection tools at this disposal.

You should never forget, however, that an RO cannot legally utilize the tools of lien, levy and seizure unless and until there is a valid assessment. That assessment usually does not exist if no returns are filed. The assessment is not born until you either file the returns, sign a consent to assessment of the tax or after a formal notice of deficiency is issued and ninety days expire from the date thereof. For more information on tax assessment rules, please see the *Taxpayers' Ultimate Defense Manual.*

Therefore, do not be taken in by threats to immediately enforce collection if the returns are not filed TODAY. Please recall Deb's letter. She mentioned her RO made such threats. But she explained she knew her rights and as intimidating as the RO was, Deb exercised her rights.

Provided the revenue office is the least bit reasonable, expect to win sufficient time to prepare and file accurate returns. After filing the returns, the RO's focus changes. He now demands payment of the tax, interest and penalties. To handle this aspect of the TDA, revert to the techniques for negotiating an installment agreement.

The Collection Summons Demanding Records

If the RO is not the least bit reasonable or you did not clearly communicate the points I outlined, expect a collection summons demanding the production of books and records. See Exhibit 4-2, page 61. Obtaining records enables the IRS to prepare the returns for you. This threat was also made against Deb. "If you do not get those records in here," she was told, "we will prepare the returns for you." The threat did not have much impact because Deb realized that the IRS' tax liability determination is appealable. If you disagree, you have the right to challenge it before the assessment becomes final.

Without a doubt, however, Deb was terrified and the RO did her best to maintain the terror. When Deb appeared in response to the summons, she did so without any of the requested records. Instead, she pointed out that she could not organize them in such a short period of time. Thus, she could not possibly prepare truthful returns.

Deb was threatened with jail but I knew she would not go to jail and I told her so. The demands were real, however, and they had to be handled. To understand the significance of what we did, you must appreciate some background on the nature of an IRS summons.

When a citizen does not comply with a summons, the IRS may seek "judicial enforcement" of it. That involves a *civil proceeding*, not a criminal prosecution. Because the summons is not self-enforcing, the courts must back it up. If the IRS believes the facts justify, it seeks judicial enforcement by filing a civil petition with the federal district court where you reside. You have an opportunity to present your side of the story before the court decides.

The decision to commence a summons enforcement proceeding can*not be made* by the RO. It is made by the Office of District Counsel. District Counsel are the attorneys who represent the IRS in court. They alone make the decision based upon all the facts and circumstances of the case. If the record reveals a recalcitrant citizen evading his obligations, expect District Counsel to commence a summons enforcement proceeding.

However, I would never expect District Counsel to take action when a citizen makes every possible effort to comply in face of unreasonable demands and I said exactly that to Deb. When the RO explained she was submitting the case for "court action," I explained to Deb what that meant and we wrote a letter to District Counsel.

The letter explained all Deb had done to comply with the summons. It explained the nature of the RO's demands and the fact that she was unwilling to afford even minimal time to gather and organize records, never mind prepare accurate returns. The letter stressed that at no time did Deb ever refuse to cooperate. We stressed that she never failed to appear at any meetings. We stressed that Deb recognized her obligations and intended to cooperate fully, in fact, *was cooperating*, but simply needed more time. We proposed to file delinquent returns in thirty-day intervals.

The letter was sent via certified mail, return receipt requested, to the Office of District Counsel covering Deb's revenue district. The letter we received in reply arrived just one week before Christmas, just days after the RO promised Deb would be arrested, at home and probably at night and taken away to jail in the presence of her children. (By the way, the details of that threat were also plainly spelled out in our letter.)

District Counsel's response was music to Deb's ears. Not only did the IRS attorney agree to our filing schedule, but he pointedly assured Deb that she would not be arrested and would not be hauled off to jail, at night, in the presence of her children. And he went one step further. He assured Deb that "no further enforcement" steps would be taken provided Deb met the filing schedule.

Deb was never forced to talk with the revenue officer again. Her next meeting was solely for the purpose of delivering the first of the required returns. Thereafter, at thirty-day intervals, Deb presented another return. Each time she did, she displayed only her classic, southern, lady-like politeness.

And the RO *hated it!* She was livid that Deb went over her head. She was incensed that a citizen had the audacity and know-how to short circuit her threats and power. *But what upset her the most was the reality that she could do absolutely nothing about it and Deb knew it!*

Once you get past a belligerent revenue officer and comply with the filing requirement, your attention must focus on paying the overdue taxes. To establish an installment agreement, follow the steps and procedures outlined above. If you do not owe any money after filing the returns, your tax problem is over!

Employment Taxes and the Installment Agreement

Employment tax delinquencies present special problems because the IRS views them in a more serious light. Consequently, it moves to enforced collection faster and with more tenacity. To understand the special problems, let us begin by exploring what constitutes employment tax liabilities.

The total employment tax liability is comprised of two segments. The first is the trust fund portion. Trust fund taxes are those which are withheld from the employee on account of his personal income and social security tax obligations. The trust amounts are withheld by the employer and he bears the burden to truthfully account for and pay them on time. They are referred to as trust taxes because a fiduciary relationship exists between the employer, the employee and the IRS. The employer acts as a trustee over the funds he withholds from the employee.

The second portion is the non-trust portion. Non-trust taxes are comprised of the employer's matching social security (FICA) and unemployment compensation (FUTA) tax payments. Those taxes, generally about 20 percent of the total employment tax burden, do not originate from the employee's pay. They represent excise taxes placed directly on the employer based upon his payroll. Those taxes are therefore paid directly by the employer from company profits. Because they are not withheld from the employee's pay, they create no trust relationship.

Businesses find themselves in trouble with employment taxes for many of the reasons discussed in chapter two, under the heading, *Business Debt.* Whether the business is a corporation, partnership or sole proprietorship, expect the IRS to pursue collection in precisely the same manner. However, an additional factor must be considered when the delinquent taxpayer is a corporation. In that case, when it is not possible to collect from the income or assets of the corporation itself, the IRS assesses the Trust Fund Recovery Penalty against corporate officers and other responsible parties. I discuss the Trust Fund Recovery Penalty in chapter four under the heading, *Collecting Employment Taxes.*

First, Stop the Bleeding

The single most important aspect of stabilizing the employment tax problem has nothing whatsoever to do with the IRS. The patient will not get well until you *stop the bleeding!* In this context, I mean very simply that you must immediately cease the practice of operating on net payroll! If you are filing 940 and 941 tax returns without paying the tax, you must end that practice *immediately.* If you do not file due to lack of funds, you must stop that practice *immediately.*

I emphasized earlier that the key to any successful installment agreement negotiation is to *be and remain current* in your tax return filings and payments. Nowhere is this more important than with employment taxes. The revenue officer will *not for a moment* entertain an installment agreement or, for that matter, anything short of full liquidation, if filing or payment delinquencies continue. As a matter of fact, the RO believes putting you out of business actually *does you a favor!* At least that prevents further delinquencies.

There are only two ways I know of to stop the bleeding. While the answer is simple, I do not pretend that implementing it is. Very simply, you must reduce the number of employees to a level that allows you timely pay the employment taxes on those remaining. If you cannot afford to pay any employment taxes in a timely manner, then all employees must go and they must go now! Naturally, the problem of making timely payments disappears when the employees disappear. If you cannot operate without help, find a way to do it without employees. That might mean working longer hours yourself or using legitimate independent contractors. So be it. You have no choice.

I once consulted with a man who operated a small business with about a dozen employees. He was tens of thousands of dollars behind in his employment taxes. The IRS threatened liquidation and he needed help.

My first suggestion was he cut the employees to a level that would allow him to pay current taxes when due. He said, "I can't do that. I need these people to operate my business."

I said, "Bob, if you don't immediately stop the net payroll game, you will not have any business to operate. They will shut you down." I explained that he would have to find a way to turn out the work with fewer employees *or none at all.*

Next, Bob protested that if he did not have the employees, he could not operate profitably. Knowing the answer, I asked an obvious question. "Are you presently earning a profit?" As I suspected, he said "no." After all, if he were, he would not have employment tax problems, would he?

I then asked, "If you aren't making a profit *with* the employees, how can matters get any worse *without* them?" Bob had no answer.

Finally, I said, "Look Bob, you are the captain of a sinking ship. You must either plug the hole or get the heck out because as it stands, the ship is *going down.* You don't have *any* other choices. The longer you continue in your inability to pay the taxes, you make matters worse--you take on more water."

I know it is very difficult to do, but the small businessman must recognize the point of no return. In all my experience with employment tax disputes, I very seldom see companies work out of the problem. It can be done, but it takes firm managerial resolve and the ability to make hard choices fast and stick with them.

The first hard choice is to cut employees--*now*. If the level of employees remains constant, your problem only grows. The second challenge is to generate cash flow--*now*. Without cash flow, you cannot pay the trust liabilities when due. And the third challenge is you must make your company profitable--*now*. Without profit, the non-trust taxes cannot be paid and the IRS does not permit a company to continue operations without paying *all its current taxes--on time!*

If you cannot do those three things in the ratios needed to stop the bleeding, then you must move to the fourth step. That is to shut down the business--*now*. You have no choice. Do not allow your emotions and wishful thinking to stand in the way of the cold reality that the IRS *will* shut down the business for you, without hesitation or remorse and in a fashion that serves its best interests, *not yours*.

Only after you prove your company can remain current on its employment taxes does the RO entertain the idea of an installment agreement. File prior delinquent employment tax returns as soon as possible, then address the matter of payment. Carefully follow the steps discussed above to secure an installment agreement and pay close attention to the special considerations discussed below.

Special Considerations for Employment Taxes

The most important special consideration is the fact that when collecting employment (or any other) taxes, revenue officers never disclose a significant reality. The reality is when receiving partial payment, they apply those payments in a manner which best suits the agency, not the company or citizen.

More specifically, the RO applies the partial payment first to non-trust taxes. Only after paying the non-trust taxes for all delinquent quarters does he apply payment to the trust amounts. Why do you suppose that is? I promise, they will *never* tell you what you are about to read.

If the taxpayer is a corporation, the non-trust taxes *cannot* be assessed against an individual. Only trust taxes may become personal liabilities through the Trust Fund Recovery Penalty. Therefore, as long as the IRS milks funds from an active corporation, it applies them to the tax which cannot be passed on. It theorizes that if the corporation closes its doors, it will never be able to collect the non-trust amounts. However, the trust amounts may always be collected by pursuing the responsible corporate officers individually through the Trust Fund Recovery Penalty.

If the taxpayer is a non-corporate entity such as a partnership or sole-proprietorship, it is not necessary to assess the Trust Fund Recovery Penalty. The nature of the business structure renders trust tax debts personal liabilities from the beginning. However, as you learn later in this book, non-trust taxes may be discharged in bankruptcy while trust taxes cannot. Consequently, the RO makes every effort to apply as much as possible to the non-trust taxes before his actions force a citizen into bankruptcy.

To avoid the difficulty and potential burdensome liability of unpaid trust taxes, be sure to "designate" your payments at the time of making them. When a citizen makes a voluntary payment to the IRS, he may designate that payment to apply in the manner which best suits the individual, not the IRS. This is an important point because in their haste to apply all payments first to non-trust taxes, I have seen revenue officers lie about this right many times.

The law is expressed in the case of *O'Dell v. United States*, 326 F.2d 451 (10th Cir. 1964). The rule is enforced by all the courts in the land and the IRS knows full well that it exists. See also *Amos v. Commissioner*, 47 T.C. 65 (1966). In fact, in the IRS' own statement of Taxpayers Rights, right number seven declares, "Taxpayers have the right to designate how voluntary (as opposed to enforcement proceeds) payments should be applied to their accounts." Problems Resolution Program Handbook, section 313(7) (5-27-92).

The key to enjoying this right is to make a "voluntary payment." A payment is voluntary when it is not procured by levy or distraint or by a court proceeding in which the government seeks collection. Under this definition, payments made by the citizen to the RO are voluntary payments. When properly designated, they must be applied per the election of the citizen.

To constitute a proper designation, it must,

1. Be made by the citizen. In the case of a corporation, the corporate president or other responsible officer must make it;

2. Be made at or before the time of submitting the payment;

3. Be specific. Funds designated only to a specific quarter but not directed to trust taxes for that quarter may be applied to non-trust taxes for that quarter; and

4. *Be in writing*. I recommend making the designation on both the payment device itself and with an accompanying cover letter. The

statement should read, "Apply to trust fund taxes for _____
quarter (i.e., 2nd quarter, 1995). Apply any excess to trust fund taxes
for _____ quarter." Include your social security number or
employer identification number on both the payment device and the
cover letter. Keep copies of both the letter and the payment device for
your records. Mail the payment using certified mail with return receipt
requested.

To follow the progression of your payments, obtain a statement
from the RO reflecting the outstanding trust and non-trust assessments
at the time the payments commence. Monitor the balances to ensure the
payments are applied in the manner you designate. Do this by
reviewing the Business Master File (BMF) record covering the periods
in question.

Be aware of the fact that if you intend to work the corporation out
of the tax problem, you must eventually pay the non-trust taxes. The
IRS does not look favorably upon an operating corporation with
outstanding employment tax debts, even if they do represent non-trust
amounts.

How to Determine the Employment Tax Installment Payment

Substantive negotiations on the amount of the installment payment
for employment tax liabilities are no different than those used for
personal taxes. The heart and soul of the process is the financial
statement. For businesses, the financial statement is Form 433-B. See
the Forms Kit.

Form 433-B shows business income and expenses. From there, you
ascertain the amount of the monthly payment in negotiation with the
revenue officer. Unlike personal taxes, however, ROs generally do not
allow substantially protracted payment arrangements. This is
particularly true with an operating corporation. To settle the matter
purely in the installment arena, be prepared to make aggressive
payments while at the same time, remaining current with all filing and
payment obligations.

Often, installment negotiations are accompanied by two further
demands. First, the RO asks you to complete and submit Form 4180.
Form 4180 is entitled, Report to Determine Liability for Trust Fund
Recovery Penalty. Its purpose is to ascertain who is to be targeted with
assessment of the Trust Fund Recovery Penalty. See the Forms Kit.

Secondly, the RO may ask you to consent to an assessment of the
Trust Fund Recovery Penalty. I recommend that not be done if
possible. Keep in mind, however, that the RO does not need your

consent to assess the penalty. If you do consent, you are likely to find yourself dealing with two collection problems, not one.

Conclusion

I must end this discourse by repeating an observation made earlier. The installment agreement is not an end unto itself. It is the means to an end, that being the final resolution of the tax dispute. An installment agreement to pay $100 per month against a $20,000 tax liability will *never* resolve the tax dispute. The interest and penalties more than consume the meager monthly payment.

Therefore, pursue other avenues to ultimately resolve the issue. The chapters to follow address those alternatives. Whether they are applicable to you depends on the facts of your case. Rest assured, however, that an installment agreement alone is almost never the only answer. Still, it permits you to address the other aspects of your case free of the threat of wage and bank levies or property seizures. That peace of mind is worth much more than the effort needed to negotiate the agreement.

Listen to Paulette describe exactly what that peace of mind means to her and her family:

> Dear Mr. Pilla:
>
> Words cannot express my gratitude to you. After reading *How Anyone Can Negotiate with the IRS and Win!* and *The Naked Truth,* we were able to secure from the IRS an offer in compromise based upon collectibility. Following your suggestions, such as sending all correspondence certified mail, keeping ourselves very available by phone or visiting, we were able to reduce our liability from $25,000 to $9,000.
>
> A few years ago, we were involved in a college food service business which was great at the beginning but began a sharp spiral downward after a while. Young and inexperienced, we were too proud to close the doors before it was too late. We ended up in deep financial trouble. Throughout 1988 and 1989, we were plagued by calls, field visits and letters-downright harassment. Until one day, my mother heard you on a local radio station in New York. She ordered your books for us immediately. Armed with a new-found determination and positive attitude that we need not be victims of the system, we used your techniques and today our

account has been resolved, as shown on the enclosed letters. We wouldn't have done it without your help.

We now realize how important it is to educate ourselves about taxpayer's rights. If we hadn't read your books, we might have handed over $16,000 more than we had to!

Once again, sincere thanks for all of your help. I am sure your efforts have helped many Americans become aware of their rights as taxpayers.

Signed: Paulette - New York

"Because you have made the Lord your refuge, the Most High your Habitation, no evil shall befall you, no scourge will come near your tent. For he will give his angels charge of you to guard you in all your ways. On their hands they will bear you up, lest you dash your foot upon a stone."

Psalm 91:9-12

CHAPTER SIX
Coping with Liens,
Levies and Seizures

Liens, levies and seizures are the cause of most tax collection trauma. They destroy credit ratings, interrupt paychecks, close businesses and generally mess up a person's life. These weapons are responsible for driving millions of people underground. And while there are useful tools for handling them, the IRS almost never talks about them. Therefore, this chapter presents remedial procedures for handling liens, levies and seizures and we address them in that order.

The Federal Tax Lien

The Taxpayers' Bill of Rights Act (TBRA) and the Bill of Rights 2 (TBR2) have given us new tools for dealing with liens. What follows is detailed discussion of seven strategies.

The Lien Withdrawal

TBR2 added a tool that can effectively to override tax liens. Code section 6323(j) gives the IRS the authority to "withdraw" a lien after it is filed, even if the tax *is not* paid. The statute delineates four possible grounds. They are,

1. The lien was premature or otherwise not in accordance with IRS' administrative procedures;

2. The citizen has entered into an installment agreement, unless the agreement specifically provides for a lien;

3. Withdrawal of the lien will facilitate the collection of the tax; or

4. With the consent of the citizen or the Taxpayer Advocate (see chapter seven), withdrawal of the lien would be in the best interests of the citizen (as determined by the Taxpayer Advocate) and the United States.

Generally speaking, the formal installment agreement, IRS Form 433-D, allows the IRS to file a tax lien. However, that is not always the case and you can get it withdrawn if it is not specifically provided for in the written agreement.

Further, if the lien is not in accordance with IRS' normal administrative procedures, it must be withdrawn. In this regard, the IRS must first follow the deficiency procedures to obtain an assessment (rare exceptions apply). If not, the assessment is invalid and the IRS does not have the legal right to enforce collection. That means the lien is likewise invalid. The deficiency procedures are outlined in detail in chapters eight and nine, *Taxpayers' Defense Manual.*

In addition, before IRS may pursue enforced collection even in the case of a valid assessment, it must first issue the so-called Final Notice, Notice of Intention to Levy as required by code section 6331. It demands payment of the tax in full within thirty days. If full payment is not made within that time, enforced collection action can begin. See chapter four.

Perhaps the two most compelling elements of section 6323(j) are items three and four. Item three gives the IRS the authority to withdraw a lien when it will "facilitate tax collection." This is a broad, undefined phrase I believe operates to the citizen's advantage. As noted in chapter four, a tax lien not only encumbers your property (preventing sale), but it destroys your credit. That makes it impossible get a loan to pay the taxes.

Suppose, for example, you have substantial equity in your home sufficient to pay a tax. However, banks and other lenders usually spook at the idea of lending money when a tax lien is involved. The bank may be perfectly willing to lend money--*if* the lien is removed first. But the IRS does not release its lien unless the tax is paid--first. Of course, you cannot pay the tax unless the lien goes away, since the source of funding is the bank loan. The standoff creates a situation where tax collection is *not* facilitated *because* of the lien. Under the circumstances, withdrawal does indeed "facilitate tax collection."

A similar example is sketched in the case of one wishing to sell his home. Substantial equity in the home makes it possible to pay off the debt but the lien prevents a clear title from passing to the buyer. Therefore, the title company will not close the sale unless the lien is removed. Even if it were to escrow money to pay the tax, the buyer cannot be assured of a clear title unless the lien is removed. That is because the lien attaches to the *property* itself, *not* just the citizen who owes the tax. It therefore *follows* the property from owner to owner when transferring title. Under our example, if the lien is withdrawn, title may pass to the new owner, allowing the title company to close the sale. Under the circumstances, withdrawal does indeed "facilitate tax collection."

Item number four allows the lien to be removed when the Taxpayer Advocate (see chapter seven) agrees that withdrawal is in the "best interests" of the citizen and the IRS. This too is broad, undefined authority which can operate to the advantage of a citizen.

What the IRS is unwilling to do through its field offices, such as Collection, it can sometimes be forced to do through the Taxpayer Advocate (TA). Code section 7811(a), specifying the power of the TA, provides the office with the authority to order the IRS to take any action, or refrain from taking any action against a citizen if he is "suffering or about to suffer a significant hardship." See chapter seven for details on the TA and "significant hardship."

When it is demonstrated to the TA that the presence of the lien does more to prevent collection or otherwise cause financial hardship than it does to protect the IRS' interests, the TA can order its withdrawal.

Make the application for lien withdrawal in writing. Direct it to the Chief, Special Procedures staff in your local district. Special Procedures is an adjunct to the Collection function and handles the legal paperwork. Follow the general format of IRS Publication 784, Application for Subordination of Federal Tax Lien (see Forms Kit), in drafting the application. More on the lien subordination and Pub 784 is provided below, under item four, *The Subordination*.

When the IRS agrees to withdraw, it must be accomplished with as much fanfare as when the original lien was filed. That is, a written notice must be filed in the same government office as the original lien. You must be given a copy of the notice. What is more, when you ask *in writing*, the IRS must "promptly make reasonable efforts to notify credit reporting agencies, and any financial institution or creditor whose name and address is specified in such request, of the withdrawal of such notice." Code section 6323(j)(2).

If the lien was filed in error, the IRS must so state in its certificate of release. Code section 6326(b). This goes a long way toward "repairing" your credit. You have the duty to provide the IRS with the names and addresses of those you want notified. Thereafter, it is the agency's duty to send the notice vindicating you from the damaging lien.

The Bond

Tom owed the IRS $50,000. The debt came as a result of a failed business that eventually led to a tax lien. Tom decided to sell his condominium and use the equity to pay creditors and the IRS. The real estate agency located a buyer who came to terms with Tom. The only hitch was the tax lien. The closing company made it clear that unless the lien was removed, the sale would not close.

Tom took his case to the RO who filed the lien. He logically suggested that if the IRS released the lien and permitted the sale to close, it would receive full payment out of the profits.

But equity or no equity, the RO would not release the lien without full payment. What often happens under these circumstances is after killing the sale, the IRS seizes the property, then sells it for a fraction of what it would have realized had it simply permitted the sale to close in the first place. The result is the owner loses all his equity and ironically, the IRS receives but a fraction of the tax bill in payment.

Given the fact that Tom had significant equity in his home, I recommended he provide the IRS with a bond. If accepted, it leads to release of the lien.

Code section 6325(a)(2) authorizes the IRS to release a tax lien within thirty days after being provided with a bond for the tax, "together with all the interest." We contacted a local bonding company to write the bond. After paying the fee, the company issued a bond meeting IRS requirements. To be valid, the bond must provide for full payment within six months prior to expiration of the collection statute of limitations. Chapter ten explains how to calculate the collection statute expiration date.

At last check, the IRS has no pre-printed form for preparing the bond. Your local Special Procedures staff can provide the information you need. The bond is completed by the citizen or his bonding company and signed by both. For general information, see IRS Publication 1450, Instructions on How to Request Release of Federal Tax Lien.

In creating the bond, the bonding company agrees to be responsible for the tax liability. In exchange for this promise, the company is assured that if it had to pay the liability, you have sufficient assets to cover its loss. In Tom's case, his asset was the equity in his home.

The bonding company generated the paperwork and we picked up the completed documents. We hand-carried the bond to the RO. We had a pre-arranged agreement to exchange it for a certificate of release of the lien. We hand-carried the release to the closing company. After reviewing it, they were satisfied that the lien was removed and the sale could be finalized. At last, we filed the certificate of release with the county recorder.

After the sale was consummated, we made another trip to see the RO. This time we brought money Tom realized from the sale. He paid the tax with interest, well within six months before expiration of the collection statute. Again, we had a pre-arranged agreement with the RO to exchange cash for the bond.

Now that we had the bond in our possession, we marched off to the bonding company and had it canceled. Thus, Tom was assured he would never be called upon to make good on its promise. However, we had to satisfy the bonding company that *it* would not be called upon by the IRS to fulfill its promise. Therefore, we provided a receipt from the RO verifying the tax was paid in full.

The bond enabled Tom to guarantee that the sale of his home would not be killed by the tax lien. At the same time, it took his home out of the grasp of the IRS. The bond gave Tom the time he needed to raise the cash necessary to pay his taxes with the least amount of financial harm.

Property Double the Amount of the Liability

Because of the all-inclusive nature of the tax lien, the IRS regularly ties up property significantly greater in value than the liability. The lien need not identify a particular parcel of property. It is a "general" lien, attaching to "all property and rights to property." This can lead to seizure of most, if not all of your property. Code section 6325(b) can prevent that.

Suppose, for example, you own three homes. The first is your principle residence and the other two are rental properties. Assume your home is paid for and worth $75,000. Each rental property is also worth $75,000 but the bank has a first mortgage on each unit equal to $25,000. Based upon all of this, your net worth (assuming no other assets or liabilities) is $175,000.

Now assume you owe the IRS $25,000. IRS filed a lien and because of it, the bank will not make a loan. As we know, banks will not lend when their security interest is secondary to a tax lien. If the bank were to lend money against the homestead (worth $75,000), the mortgage lien created by that loan is secondary to the IRS' lien since the tax lien was created prior to the mortgage.

The negotiation goal is to induce the IRS to release its lien from the homestead. This allows the bank to make a loan of $25,000 to pay the tax. Full payment releases the remaining parcels from the lien.

Under code section 6325(b)(1), the IRS may discharge a portion of property from a lien when,

> [T]he fair market value of that part of the property remaining subject to the lien is at least double the sum of the amount of the unsatisfied liability secured by the lien and of the amount of all other liens upon the property which have priority over the lien.

Let me explain. Under our example, we have three parcels of property. The combined fair market value (what a willing buyer would pay a willing seller) is $225,000. The prior liens for the bank mortgages equal $50,000 (two mortgages at $25,000 each). Now add the value of the unsatisfied tax liability ($25,000) to the amount of the prior liens ($50,000). The sum is $75,000.

Before the IRS releases the lien on the homestead, you must demonstrate that the fair market value of the remaining properties (the two rental homes) is at least twice the amount of $75,000 (the sum of the liability and the two prior liens). In this case, the combined fair market value of the rental properties is $150,000 ($75,000 each). That is "at least double" the value of all liens in question.

To win partial release of the lien, present the RO with the accounting necessary to demonstrate these calculations. This move allows a person to obtain financing to pay the tax. In turn, it prevents the IRS from selling *all* property at a fraction of its worth. Your presentation should be in writing, fashioned after the "subordination." See Publication 784 discussed in the next section. There is no IRS form covering this procedure.

The Subordination

Another effective method of dealing with liens is a process known as "subordination." Under this technique, the IRS agrees to make its lien subordinate, or secondary, to that of another creditor, such as a bank. Like the other methods, it prevents the IRS from selling your property for pennies on the dollar.

Jim was a brilliant psychiatrist with a successful practice until his business and personal tax returns were audited with a vengeance. Jim ended up owing $53,000.

Jim owned a home on three acres of land. It was worth about $250,000 and the bank held a $100,000 mortgage. The $150,000 equity was more than adequate to pay the bill and Jim made arrangements to borrow the money. The sole proviso was the IRS must agree to lift its lien, allowing the bank's mortgage to be first in line.

Hoping to put the matter behind him, Jim phoned the RO and presented his plan. He would pay the tax in full "within three days" if the IRS would simply lift the lien. The answer was as unreasonable as it was short, "no." Jim was eventually pushed into bankruptcy by a combination of IRS incompetence and unwillingness to find a solution.

The RO failed to explain that under code section 6325(d), the IRS has authority to subordinate its lien when,

1. The IRS is paid an amount equal to its lien or interest in that property; or
2. The IRS will ultimately collect more by subordinating the lien and collection of the tax is facilitated by subordinating.

The very purpose of the subordination procedure is to "facilitate tax collection." That is, to allow the IRS to do its job. Just as with the procedures mentioned earlier, there is no form on which to submit an application for subordination. IRS Publication 784 describes "How to Prepare" the application. Publication 784 is included in the Forms Kit.

Revenue regulation 301.6325-1(d)(1) speaks directly to this matter. It states, in part,

> For example, if a notice of Federal tax lien is filed and a delinquent taxpayer secures a mortgage loan on a part of the property subject to the tax lien and pays over the proceeds of the loan to a district director after an application for a certificate of subordination is approved, the district director will issue a certificate of subordination. This certificate will have the effect of subordinating the tax lien to the mortgage.

Jim "secured the mortgage" and intended to pay the proceeds to the IRS. This would have satisfied his liability. But Jim was unaware of the requirement to make an application and the RO refused to tell him.

According to the above regulation, the application must be "in writing." It must be made in triplicate and must contain,

1. Your name and address;

2. Whether the subordination is made under the first criterion (relating to "payment of the amount subordinated" or the second criterion (relating to "facilitating the collection of tax") of regulation sections 301.6325-1(d)(1) and (2);

3. A detailed description of the property in question, including the street address and legal description;

4. A copy of the Notice of Federal Tax Lien (Form 668) including a statement showing the IRS district originating the lien, the name and address of the citizen shown on the lien and the date and place of its filing;

5. A copy of the proposed documents which create the liability to which the tax lien will be subordinate. An example is a mortgage for a bank loan. You must also submit a description of the transaction, such as "mortgage to pay tax" and the date the transaction is to be completed;

6. If other encumbrances exist upon the property, they must be disclosed, including the name of the holder of the encumbrance, the date it was created, the principle amount due and a description of the encumbrance;

7. An estimate of the fair market value of the property;

8. When seeking the subordination to obtain a mortgage, you must state the amount of money to be paid to the IRS if the subordination is granted;

9. When seeking the subordination in order to "facilitate the collection of taxes," you must state why you believe this is accomplished if the subordination is granted;

10. Any other information you believe has a bearing on the decision to subordinate;

11. Your signature over a statement declaring that, "under penalty or perjury, all facts contained in the application are true and correct" and which specifically requests that the application be granted.

Under the circumstances of Jim's case, there was no justifiable reason for not granting the application. Jim's only downfall was that he did not know what you have just learned. His ignorance cost him his home.

The "quiet title" Action

A quiet title action is a suit in the district court that seeks to settle the question of property ownership. The action is usually brought when one party disputes another's claim of ownership interest in real property. By filing a tax lien against real estate, the IRS effectively claims an ownership interest in it, to the extent of its lien. A quiet title action can sometimes clear the lien.

Doug underwent an audit in which the IRS disallowed several of his deductions. He ended up paying the tax and believed the matter was closed. Over two years later, however, he began receiving collection notices. They stated the tax liability was not paid and Doug owed $2,500.

Knowing the tax was paid and confident that someone had merely overlooked this fact, Doug sent a pleasant letter pointing this out. For convenience, he enclosed copies of the canceled checks. A few months later, he received another letter. Like the first, it stated that he owed taxes and they better be paid. This time, Doug got on the phone.

He was able to persuade someone to recognize that, yes, an error had been made. If he would just send another copy of his canceled checks, the discrepancy could be rectified. Faithfully, Doug re-mailed copies of the canceled checks with a cover letter reciting the details of the conversation. About a month later he received *another* threatening notice and then, much to his bewilderment, IRS filed a lien. It came at just the time he was attempting to sell his house.

Frustrated, Doug turned to the federal courts for help. A little-known federal law contained in the United States code of civil procedure authorizes one to sue the United States if the purpose of the suit is to "quiet title to . . . real estate or personal property on which the United States has or claims a mortgage or other lien." 28 USC section 2410. When circumstances are ripe, the quiet title statute is an effective way to force the IRS to settle the issue of a tax lien.

The specific procedures for filing a quiet title action are set forth in chapter ten, *Taxpayers' Ultimate Defense Manual*. An important point is that before suing the IRS, one must pursue and exhaust all administrative remedies. One key administrative remedy is the right to "appeal" the filing of a tax lien, which we examine later in this chapter.

After filing suit, an attorney was assigned to represent the IRS. The attorney made contact with Doug and discussions began. Doug provided proof that his tax liability was paid. By the time they completed discussions, the attorney agreed to lift the lien if Doug would drop his suit. When the final paperwork changed hands, Doug obtained a certificate of release of federal tax lien which he carried to the courthouse and filed. With the death of the lien, Doug's house sold without further delay.

Expiration of the Lien

Chapter ten presents the law regarding the collection statute of limitations. In general, the IRS has just ten years from the date a tax is assessed in which to collect it. Thereafter, unless the statute is extended by one or more of the methods outlined in chapter ten, the tax is unenforceable. Regulation section 301.6325-1(a) provides that the IRS must release its lien when "the entire tax liability listed in such notice of Federal tax lien has been fully satisfied . . . or has become legally unenforceable."

The above regulation provides that when requesting a release of lien, your written request must,

1. Be sent to the district director for the district in which the lien is filed. Mark the request to the attention of the Chief, Special Procedures staff;

2. State the name and address of the person making the request;

3. Include a copy of the lien in question;

4. State "the grounds upon which the release is sought;" and

5. Contain a declaration made under the penalty of perjury that the facts contained in the application are "true and correct in all respects."

There is no IRS form for this application. However, IRS Publication 783, entitled, "Instructions on How to Apply For" a certificate of discharge provides some guidance. It is included in the Forms Kit.

The ultimate responsibility for obtaining a lien release lies on your shoulders. You must make the application or the IRS is not likely to remove the lien. This is true even if the tax is paid and even if the collection statute has expired. If an application is not made, there is nothing to suggest the IRS will voluntarily release the lien. However, if the IRS fails to release an improper lien, turn to code section 7432. It allows you to sue the United States when the IRS "knowingly, or by reason of negligence, fails to release a lien." The statute allows the citizen to recover the actual, direct damages sustained as a result of the lien, plus the costs of the action. Chapter ten of the *Defense Manual* guides one through this process.

The Lien Appeal

Code section 6326 authorizes an administrative appeal of "the imposition of a lien." The circumstances under which one may execute the appeal are,

1. The tax liability that gave rise to the lien was paid in full prior to its filing;

2. The tax liability was assessed in violation of the deficiency procedures described in code section 6213;

3. The tax liability was assessed in violation of Title 11 of the United States Code (the Bankruptcy Code); or

4. The collection statute of limitations expired prior to filing the lien. Regulation section 301.6326-1(b).

File a written request for appeal with the Chief, Special Procedures staff. The appeal documents must include,

1. The name, current address, and social security number of the person appealing the lien;

2. A copy of the notice of lien in question; and

3. A clear and concise statement of the grounds upon which the lien is appealed. Regulation section 301.6326-1(d)(2).

If the lien is appealed on the ground that the tax liability was satisfied prior to the lien's filing, you must provide proof of payment in the following form:

1. An IRS cashier's receipt showing full payment of the tax prior to the date of filing the lien;

2. A canceled check to the IRS in an amount sufficient to satisfy the tax; or

3. Any other proof acceptable to the district director. Regulation section 301.6326-1(e).

If you argue that filing the lien is in violation of the deficiency procedures (code section 6213), explain how the assessment is erroneous. Detailed guidance on the deficiency procedures is set forth in the *Taxpayers' Defense Manual*, chapters eight and nine.

If you argue that the lien is in violation of the Bankruptcy Code, you must provide,

1. The identity of the court and the district where the bankruptcy petition was filed; and

2. The docket number and the date of filing the bankruptcy petition. Regulation section 301.6326-1(d)(2)(C).

The appeal must be filed within one year after the citizen "becomes aware of the erroneously filed tax lien." Regulation section 301.6326-1(d)(2)(C)(3). Note this language carefully. The one-year rule does not start with the date of *filing* the lien. It begins with the date you become *aware* of it. Exercising the right of lien appeal is a necessary prerequisite to filing suit and obtaining damages under code section 7432. For more details on the lien appeal, a sample lien appeal form and filing suit for failure to release the lien, see the *Defense Manual*, chapter ten.

Releasing Wage and Bank Levies, Generally

Section 6343 of the code provides authority to release a levy or property seizure for any one or more of the following five reasons:

1. The tax liability is satisfied or is unenforceable by reason of the expiration of the collection statute of limitations;
2. Release of the levy will facilitate collection of the tax;
3. The citizen has entered into an installment agreement, unless the agreement specifically allows for the seizure;
4. The IRS has determined that the levy is creating an economic hardship due to the financial condition of the citizen; or
5. The fair market value of the property exceeds the liability and release of the levy on a part of the property could be made without hindering collection.

The IRS routinely engages in wage and bank levies and other property seizures after it has entered into installment agreements. However, such action is not legitimate unless the agreement expressly provides for the levy, which is unlikely. This law gives you the right to have such a levy removed and the seized property returned.

As to item number four, it is not difficult to imagine how wage and bank levies cause "economic hardship." When the IRS enforces collection, it often places one into a position of having to choose between paying his taxes and feeding his family. In fact, it is just this kind of action that drives people underground.

To show economic hardship, send a letter by certified mail, return receipt requested in the manner outlined later in this section. Illustrate in writing exactly how the levy is causing hardship. In the case of a wage levy, show your fixed monthly living expenses and the amount you are left with after the levy. Assuming a negative difference, argue that the levy is making it impossible pay your necessary living expenses. As a result, you risk the loss of your home, auto, health insurance, etc.

Bank levies are similarly damaging. When IRS issues a bank levy, it does not immediately take possession of the funds but it freezes the account. The law requires a twenty-one day holding period before transferring funds to the IRS. This holding period allows you to take action before the losing the money.

Illustrate that the freeze on your account may cause outstanding checks to bounce, in turn ruining your good standing with creditors. In addition, the lack of funds makes it impossible to pay necessary living expenses or business operating expenses. Prove this as outlined in the previous paragraph.

Item number two uses the broad, undefined phrase, "facilitate the collection of the liability." As already stated, this general language invites any reasonable argument to remove the levy when it can be shown that the IRS' action is likely to do more harm than good. IRS regulations give some idea of just how broad this remedy may be. Regulation section 301.6343-1(b)(2) provides,

> A director has the discretion to release the levy in *all situations*, including those where the proceeds from the sale will not fully satisfy the tax liabilities of the taxpayer, under terms and conditions as he or she determines are warranted. (Emphasis added.)

To win a release under this section, show that the IRS' action will make full payment *more* difficult. The following scenario provides an example of how the release can facilitate collection.

Suppose you are an independent contractor doing business with several customers. The IRS issues levy notices to all your customers. Afterward, your customers make it clear they will not continue doing business with you if they must contend with the IRS in the process. You risk losing your primary source of income and hence, your means of paying the tax and supporting your family. By releasing the levies, the IRS ensures that your customers do not abandon you. You are thus able to structure and fund a plan to work out of your debt and stay alive at the same time.

Some companies have written policies stating that wage levies will lead to termination. Certainly the loss of one's job constitutes both economic hardship and destroys your capacity to pay. Collection of the tax is clearly "facilitated" by removing the wage levy.

Under item number five, when the fair market value of the property seized exceeds the tax debt, the IRS must release so much of the property as exceeds the debt. The IRS gives this factual example in regulation section 301.6343-1(b)(5):

> The Internal Revenue Service levies upon ten widgets which belong to the taxpayer to satisfy the taxpayer's outstanding tax liabilities. Subsequent to the levy, the taxpayer establishes that market conditions have increased the aggregate fair market value of widgets so that the value of seven widgets equals the aggregate anticipated expenses of sale and seizure and the tax liabilities for which the levy was made. The director must release three widgets from the levy and return them to the taxpayer.

In your written request for release of levy, provide the facts and information needed to establish the value of the property in question.

Return of Seized Property

TBR2 expanded section 6343 to allow the IRS to return to the citizen any property levied upon, if the IRS determines,

1. The levy on the property was premature or otherwise not in accordance with IRS' administrative procedures;

2. The citizen has entered into an installment agreement to satisfy the tax, unless such agreement provides otherwise;

3. The return of the property will facilitate the collection of the tax; or

4. With the consent of the taxpayer or the Taxpayer Advocate (see chapter seven), the return of the property would be in the best interests of the citizen (as determined by the Taxpayer Advocate) and the United States. Code section 6343(d).

This statute contains the broad and undefined use of the phrases, "facilitate tax collection" and "the best interests" of the citizen and the IRS as determined by the TA. As we discussed earlier, this provides an invitation to use creative, logical arguments to win return of property the IRS has levied upon.

Request for Release of Levy or Return of Property

To make a request for release of levy or return of seized property under section 6343, submit a letter to the district director, marked to the attention of the Chief, Collection Division. The written request must contain,

    1. Your name, address, and social security number or TIN;

    2. A description of the property levied upon;

    3. The type of tax and the period for which the tax is due;

    4. The date of the levy and the originating Internal Revenue district, if known; and

    5. A statement of the grounds upon which the request for release of the levy or return of property is based. Regulation section 301.6343-1(c)(1). There is no form for making this request and it should be submitted as quickly as possible.

If the property levied upon is personal property "essential" to carrying on your business, your request for release of levy should so state. At section 6343(a)(2), the statute declares,

> In the case of any tangible personal property essential in carrying on the trade or business of the taxpayer, the Secretary shall provide for an expedited determination . . . if levy on such tangible personal property would prevent the taxpayer from carrying on such trade or business.

In your request for release, describe the specific property taken, its relationship to the operation of your business and how denial of such property prevents the carrying on of your business. The expedited review and response to the request for release of business property must occur within ten days of making the request. Ordinarily, a decision on the request must be made within thirty days. Regulation section 301.6343-1(d)(1).

Using the Taxpayer Advocate

If your request is not successful, take your complaint to the Taxpayer Advocate (TA). Use the same type of letter, stating your case clearly and using specific examples and statutory references to buttress your claims. Provide a copy of your initial request and explain that the IRS has failed and refused to correct the damaging assault on your financial life. Ask the TA for specific relief in the form of removing the levy and establishing a reasonable installment agreement. See chapter seven for more details on the TA.

Coping with Property Seizures

Property seizures can be the most destructive of all collection techniques. Property seizures include homes, automobiles, businesses, inventory and personal property of every description. A delinquent citizen faces the risk that any property he either owns outright or in which he has an ownership interest may be seized. This means we must understand how to neutralize the impact of seizures. To this end, I offer the following eight strategies for dealing with property levies and seizures.

Your Principal Residence

With the 1988 TBRA, Congress added a mild protection for your principal residence. Code section 6334(a)(13) provides that one's principal residence is generally exempt from levy. Under no circumstances can an RO acting alone or in concert with his immediate supervisor seize your home. However, section 6334(e) allows for its seizure if,

> A district director or assistant district director of the Internal Revenue Service personally approves (in writing) the levy of such property.

Sadly, there are no objective guidelines which allow us to determine the conditions under which a district director may authorize this action. The district director is, however, the highest management official within an IRS district. Basic reason and common sense suggest there must be some egregious behavior on the part of the citizen or the presence of other aggravated conditions to justify the action.

This much is true--when the seizure and sale of a principal residence will cause economic hardship or when some other condition of code section 6343 is met, the levy must be released. Seizure of a principal residence is also subject to the right of collection appeal as discussed in chapter seven. What is more, as I explain in detail in chapter seven, directives from Washington promise to further limit the IRS' attack on one's residence.

The Minimum Bid Worksheet

The minimum bid worksheet is submitted to the citizen after his property is seized but before it is sold. It communicates the figures used to calculate the minimum amount the IRS will accept when selling it. You have five days to object to the minimum bid price.

Don's house was seized by the IRS and was about to be sold. Though the market value of Don's house was about $85,000, the minimum bid worksheet showed the IRS initially planned to sell the property for just over $2,000 (that is not a misprint).

Within the five-day period, we responded by pointing out in specific terms how the minimum bid was both grossly understated, and that raising it would only serve to "facilitate tax collection."

The letter caused the RO to re-compute the minimum bid, raising it substantially. This benefited Don in a number of ways. First, with the substantially higher minimum bid price, the chances of selling the home were greatly diminished. The higher the price of an item, the fewer buyers there are willing to purchase it.

More importantly, the RO was forced to postpone the original sale date. This allowed Don time to maneuver into position to keep the IRS from selling his home altogether. See chapter thirteen.

The Lawsuit for Injunction

What would you do if the IRS mailed you a tax bill for $25,000? What would you say if they told you the tax was on $33,000 you never received? How would you act if they showed up at your doorstep threatening to seize your home if the money was not paid?

Curtis and Rachel faced these very questions. One year, the couple earned combined wages of just over $50,000 and they prepared a tax return reporting that income. Next, they brought the return to a tax preparer to have their figures checked and the return filed. The tax liability came to just about $10,000 which was almost entirely paid through wage withholding. Shortly after filing, they received a letter stating their income had been adjusted--upward--to $83,229.94, over $33,000 *more* than they earned.

Next, IRS mailed a notice of deficiency confirming the adjustment. With interest and penalties, the IRS demanded $25,149.54. Even more bizarre was the reason for the increase. The IRS stated that "the amount reported as gross receipts on Schedule C has been moved to Line 7, form 1040."

The problem was, they filed no Schedule C. They filed a joint return with Forms W-2. There had to be a mistake. Instead of petitioning the Tax Court, Curtis sent a letter demanding that the matter be cleared up without further delay. The letter brought results-- or so it seemed. Just prior to the expiration of the time limit for petitioning the Tax Court, the IRS declared that their account showed a "credit balance of $9,892." Apparently, the problem was fixed.

Believing that, Curtis discarded the notice of deficiency and filed no Tax Court petition. That is when the trouble really started. One month *after* the expiration of the ninety-day grace period, the IRS reversed itself and demanded payment of $25,000. The couple was informed that "enforced collection" would begin if the amount was not paid.

Next, the IRS filed a lien and soon issued a wage levy to Curtis' employer. The liability had now escalated to over $27,500. Curtis was told by his employer that if he did not "obtain a release by five o'clock" the next day, his paycheck would be turned over to the IRS.

The problem seemed insurmountable. The IRS wanted over $27,500. The couple had given up their right to petition the Tax Court by allowing the ninety-day grace period to lapse, *something you should never do!* True enough, the IRS misled them by stating there was a credit on their account but nevertheless, the time to petition the Tax Court passed and they should not have let that happen.

One solution was to sue the IRS. This route posed a new hardship due to a federal law preventing many such suits. Code section 7421 is known as the anti-injunction act and generally deprives federal courts of jurisdiction to stop the IRS. But the couple invoked one little known and even less understood exception to that rule based upon the Supreme Court case of *Commissioner v. Shapiro*, 424 U.S. 614 (1976).

Under *Shapiro*, when an assessment is arbitrary and erroneous and the citizen can demonstrate that, (1) collection of the tax will cause irreparable harm and (2) no adequate remedy exists to prevent the harm, a court can enjoin collection despite section 7421. For greater detail on this process, including forms for carrying it out, see the *Defense Manual*, chapters eight, nine and twelve.

When you show that a tax assessment is both arbitrary and erroneous, it is no longer considered a "tax" subject to section 7421. Rather, it is considered an "exaction in the guise of a tax." *Miller v. Standard Nut Margarine Co.*, 248 U.S. 498 (1932). If the IRS cannot support its assessment with facts sufficient to establish the substantial likelihood that you in fact owe it, a court may decree that the tax is "arbitrary and erroneous." See the *Defense Manual*, for more details.

Curtis filed supporting documents consistent with the *Shapiro* rules. Then, just five days before the levy was to take effect, a federal judge signed a temporary restraining order preventing the levy from going forward. Curtis then went to work with a local RO assigned to figure out what happened. Curtis was able to prove how the IRS made a serious error in computing his income. As a result, the IRS agreed to abate the excessive tax. Throughout all this time, not one penny of Curtis' wages was levied upon and no action was taken to seize the family home.

The Separate Interest

Very often, property is owned jointly by a husband and wife. It is also common for one spouse, say, the husband, to owe taxes but not the wife. Despite the fact that the wife may not owe taxes, the Supreme Court has ruled that the IRS may sell joint property to liquidate the debtor's (the husband's) interest. *United States v. Rogers*, 461 U.S. 677 (1983). (Note, however, that if both spouses sign a joint return for the delinquent year, the IRS can collect from assets owned by either or both parties, even though only one earned the income. The exception to this is where one spouse is considered an "innocent spouse" under code section 6013(e) or 63(c). For more on the innocent spouse, see the discussion below and chapter twelve of the *Defense Manual*.

While the property may be sold, the non-debtor spouse (wife) must be compensated for her interest. This means simply that while the IRS may sell joint property when just one owner owes taxes, it may not retain 100 percent of the proceeds. The non-debtor must be treated as if she holds a lien against the property equal to half its equity.

The IRS inevitably overlooks this minor detail. You learn of its intentions by reviewing the minimum bid worksheet. If the IRS proposes to sell any more than a one-half interest in the property, assume it does not intend to consider the ownership interest of the non-debtor spouse.

A little-known federal statute provides a remedy when one is faced with this problem. The statute is known as the "wrongful levy statute," code section 7426. This statute allows a person to enjoin a levy or sale if the IRS proposes to overlook the ownership interests of a non-debtor.

Margaret filed such a suit in the district court in Chicago. Her husband owed thousands of dollars in taxes and the IRS seized the couple's jointly-owned rental property with the intention of selling it. In her suit, Margaret established her ownership interest by presenting the court with copies of the deed of title. In its order, the court instructed the IRS to restructure its sale in order to protect Margaret's interest.

The law generally requires that one exhaust "administrative remedies" before suing the IRS. In chapter twelve of the *Defense Manual*, I take you through the process of filing an administrative claim for release of wrongfully levied property as well as the process of filing a suit under section 7426.

Another important way to employ the wrongful levy statute is where the IRS intends to sell your homestead residence. In *United States v. Rogers*, the Supreme Court ruled that courts possess the power to *prevent* the sale of one's principle residence under certain circumstances. The court held that code section 7403 (the statute which authorizes the sale of property) does not "require" the property be sold. Rather, when the non-debtor spouse cannot be adequately compensated with money, a court should prevent the sale. The Supreme Court observed that "money is not always adequate compensation for a roof over one's head."

When you can demonstrate that the non-debtor will be irreparably harmed if the home is sold and that "money's worth compensation" is not adequate to rectify the damage, sale of the home can be prevented. By asserting the separate interest claim under the wrongful levy statute, a non-debtor spouse can be spared the misery of such a great loss.

The Premature Assessment

Under code section 6213(a), the IRS generally may not assess a tax unless it has first issued a notice of deficiency. The most common exception to this rule is where the citizen *consents* to the assessment. The notice of deficiency provides ninety days in which to file a petition in the Tax Court for redetermination of the proposed assessment. After mailing the notice, the IRS may not assess until after the ninety-day period expires. If the citizen files a petition in the Tax Court in time, the IRS may not assess until the Tax Court renders a final decision. Even then, the assessment must be in accordance with the court's decision. Code section 6215.

However, the IRS routinely makes premature assessments. Most often, this is done when a citizen fails to file a tax return. Under those conditions, the IRS files for him, using what it calls a "substitute for return" (SFR). Once the SFR is filed and the tax is assessed, collection notices begin. More on the SFR in chapter eight.

Assessments made in violation of the deficiency procedures are invalid. Various code sections we examined throughout this chapter speak to assessments made contrary to the IRS' administrative procedures. In such cases, the IRS must both terminate enforcement action, including releasing liens and levies and it must abate the assessment. If it is convinced that the tax is truly owed, it must follow the deficiency procedures to obtain a valid assessment before undertaking enforcement action.

Levy on an IRA or 401(k)

Perhaps the single largest and most dangerous misunderstanding about the IRS' levy power is the question of whether it can reach an IRA or 401(k). Ordinary creditors cannot reach these assets since in order to qualify for favorable tax treatment, they must meet the requirements of the Employees' Retirement Income Security Act (ERISA). This law requires a so-called "spend-thrift" clause in pension contracts. Simply put, it prevents creditors from attaching retirement funds.

However strong and sound the ERISA safe-guards are vis-à-vis other creditors, *they do not apply to the IRS*. Code section 6334 specifies property exempt from IRS levy. We examine those exemptions in chapter four. Code section 6334(c) states,

> Notwithstanding any other law of the United States (including section 207 of the Social Security Act), no property or rights to property shall be exempt from levy *other than the property specifically made exempt by subsection (a)* (emphasis added).

Subsection (a) of section 6334 *does not* create an exemption for IRAs or 401(k)s. Therefore, the fact that ERISA exempts pensions from the reach of other creditors does not prevent them from being reached by the IRS. They can be *and routinely are* levied by the IRS. And when they are seized, the IRS rubs salt in the wound in a big way. Therefore, preventing seizure of these assets is of paramount importance.

Suppose you owe back taxes of $25,000 and you have $10,000 in an IRA. Now let us suppose the IRS seizes the IRA. When it seizes assets, it has the right to apply the proceeds of the levy in a manner which best suits the IRS. It does not have to take your interests into consideration and you can be sure it does not. Thus, the entire $10,000 is applied to the *back tax* debt.

This does two things. First, it reduces the delinquency by $10,000. However, it also creates a current tax liability equal to about one-half the amount seized. That is because when a premature withdrawal is taken from an IRA, you create a liability for both federal and state income taxes *plus* the 10 percent penalty for early withdrawal. "But wait," you say. "I didn't withdraw the money. The IRS did."

That is true, but the withdrawal operated to your economic benefit because the proceeds reduced *your* delinquency. Therefore, *you are* liable for the current tax and penalty on $10,000 worth of income--the amount of the withdrawal--in the year the IRA is seized. That amounts to a current tax bill of about $5,000, which of course is *unfunded* because the IRS applied 100 percent of the money to the delinquency.

As a result, you lose *150 percent* of the value of your IRA. One hundred percent of the proceeds (the cash value of $10,000) is applied to back taxes and 50 percent more (the current tax obligation) becomes an unfunded debt in the year the money is levied. And, the IRS looks to *you* for payment.

It takes no economist to realize that such an act creates a substantial economic hardship. Any levy attack on an IRA must be quickly attended to with a request for release on two grounds. The first is that it creates an economic hardship. This is manifest in the fact that you will lose all your retirement funds. The second is that it is not in the best interest of either the IRS or the citizen to carry out the levy due to the creation of a current, unfunded tax debt.

If the IRS in fact levied the IRA, make quick application for full release based on the points just articulated. At a minimum, however, *you must insist* that one-half the proceeds be applied to current taxes and be sure to insist that the state income tax be paid in the process. Otherwise, the levy does nothing more than create another set of problems.

Generally speaking, if the IRS makes levy overtures toward your IRA, you are best served by taking the money yourself. By doing so, you can provide for payment of the current taxes and early withdrawal penalty through estimated payments. These must be honored if they are clearly marked in writing as payments designated to the current year. See our discussion of designing payments in chapter five. The balance of the money is then left in your possession. In turn, use it to fund an Offer in Compromise (see chapter twelve) or otherwise resolve the debt.

By following this process, you lose 100 percent of your IRA. However, if you allow the IRS to seize it, you lose 150 percent of your IRA.

The Injured Spouse

One way the IRS collects a delinquent tax is to seize the tax refund owed for the current year. The process is known as "offset." The IRS offsets the refund against the outstanding tax. A problem arises when the citizen files a joint return and his spouse does not owe the debt.

The spouse who does not owe the debt is considered a non-debtor. That spouse is "injured" when her share of the refund is seized to pay a debt (including non-tax debt such as delinquent child support, etc.) she does not owe. As an example, a married couple files a joint tax return and is owed a $1,500 refund. However, the husband has a delinquent tax debt for years prior to their marriage. The IRS seizes the entire refund and applies it to the debt. The wife is "injured" by this action to the extent that a portion of the refund belongs to her but she does not owe the debt.

The law provides special remedies for recovering the non-debtor spouse's share of the refund. The first step of the process is to establish that you are an "injured" spouse. To meet this burden, you must prove:

- You *do not owe* the past-due debt;
- You *earned and reported* income on the joint tax return;
- You *made and reported* tax payments on the joint return; and
- You do not live in a community property state.

The rule of law that applies here is simple. While signing a joint income tax return creates a joint tax liability, it *does not* create a joint interest in the overpayment unless you live in a community property state. In non-community property states, any overpayment must be returned to the person who made it. Only the portion of the overpayment belonging to the debtor can be offset.

The rule is different in community property states. Under community property rules, each spouse has a vested, one-half interest in the property of the other spouse. This includes both wages and other property, including a tax refund. However, state law determines the extent to which community property can be offset for the separate or premarital debts of one spouse.

In Texas, California, Idaho and Louisiana, state law generally allows complete offset. As a result, the IRS does not issue injured spouse refunds in these states. However, the law is different in Arizona, Nevada, New Mexico, Washington and Wisconsin. There, state law provides that community property is not subject to the separate or pre-marital debts of either spouse. As a result, the IRS must issue injured spouse refunds in those states.

If you live in a community property state, please check the status of your law before pursuing an injured spouse claim. The question you must answer is whether community property can be used to satisfy the separate or pre-marital debts of one spouse.

To establish the four points outlined above and make the injured spouse claim for refund, use IRS Form 8379, Injured Spouse Claim and Allocation. It is reproduced in our Forms Kit. File Form 8379 as soon as the IRS notifies you that the refund is to be offset. Send it via certified mail to the service center where you file your return. As a cautionary measure, you can submit Form 8379 with your joint return *at the time of filing.* Do this if you know the IRS intends to offset the refund. Place the form on top of Form 1040 and mail the entire package using certified mail, return receipt requested.

The amount of refund you are entitled to as an injured spouse is based upon your share of the joint income tax liability and the payments you personally made against it. If, for example, your joint income tax return shows only payments made through the husband's wage withholding, there will be no injured spouse refund if the husband owes the debt. You face a similar result if the joint return shows income earned only by the husband.

Therefore, to compute refund, first calculate your income tax liability separately. This process is referred to in Form 8379 as "allocation." Set forth both the income and deductions which are attributable to either spouse. The income you personally earned should be allocated to you.

If you claimed a standard deduction, each spouse is entitled to one-half the deduction. However, itemized deductions can be allocated "in any manner." If the deductions are not allocated on the form, they cannot be allocated later.

Exemptions must be allocated as whole numbers. That is, if you have three exemptions, you cannot allocate one and one-half to each spouse. Each spouse must claim the exemptions they would have been entitled to if separate returns were filed.

After allocating income and deductions, compute your share of the joint tax liability. Figure your share using "married filing separately" rules. That is not to say, however, that you must now be subjected to the married filing separately *rate*. The applicable rate is the *married filing jointly* rate. It is only *your share* that is computed under the married filing separately rules. For a more detailed explanation, see Revenue Ruling 85-70, 1985-1 C.B. 361 and instructions for Form 8379.

Having calculated your share of the joint tax liability, now allocate payments against the tax. Allocate wage withholding payments to the spouse who paid them. Similarly, allocate separate estimated tax deposits to the spouse who made them. However, joint estimated payments, payments made with the return or payments made with a filing extension may be allocated between the spouses at their discretion.

To determine your portion of the total overpayment, which becomes the amount refundable, simply subtract your share of the joint tax liability from your contribution to it. For example, suppose your share of a $5,000 total tax bill is $2,000. Suppose you contributed $2,500 to the joint tax bill. Your share of the refund is $500 ($2,500 - your contribution, minus $2,000, your share of the tax bill).

The IRS actually figures the tax refund. It is supposed to use the procedures and formulas set forth in Revenue Ruling 85-70. However, you provide the underlying numbers through your allocation of income, deductions and payments. Despite the fact that IRS actually performs the refund calculation, you too should perform the exercise to double-check its work.

The Innocent Spouse

One of the most important and least understood provisions of the tax code is the "innocent spouse" rules. Expressed under code sections 63(c) and 6013(e), these provisions relieve a spouse of liability on a joint return in certain circumstances.

Generally speaking, to qualify as an innocent spouse, you must have signed a joint return and the liability must be the result of either unreported income or grossly improper tax deductions attributable solely to your spouse. Merely filing a joint return without paying the tax shown due does not create an innocent spouse situation.

In addition, you must be able to prove,

1. That you did not know or have reason to know about the unreported income or bogus deductions,

2. That you did not materially benefit from the unpaid tax, and

3. Taking into consideration all of the facts and circumstances, it would be inequitable to hold you liable for the debt.

In addition to these elements, there is an income test which you must meet to be an innocent spouse. It is described in *The Defense Manual*, chapter twelve.

When you establish these facts, you are entitled to a tax abatement. This stops enforced collection as to you and causes the IRS to re-direct its enforcement guns at the guilty spouse.

To establish your innocent spouse status, carefully follow the guidelines set forth in chapter eleven of *The Defense Manual*.

Conclusion

Enforced collection through liens, levies and seizures is always a risk when you owe the IRS. However, the tools described above allow you to neutralize, minimize and in some cases eliminate their ravages. Normally, one must act quickly and decisively when dealing with levies and seizures. Hesitation and inactivity only make matters worse. Therefore, it is always best to know *in advance* what to do if a given situation presents itself. That is how to survive enforced collection.

Chapman testifies to the effectiveness of knowing these procedures. His letter to me is short and simple. It reads,

> I ordered your tax publications a year or so ago and won release of lien in the amount of $18,739.12 for my fiancée. I am now in law school due to my interest in law tax work. Keep up the good work in this field.
> Signed: Chapman - Texas

"Even though I walk through the valley of the shadow of death, I fear no evil; for thou art with me; thy rod and thy staff, they comfort me."

Psalm 23:4

CHAPTER SEVEN
Dial 9-1-1--Emergency
Measures to Stop Collection

In September, 1997, the Senate Finance Committee held well-publicized hearings on the question of IRS abuse. The hearings came on the heels of the report of the National Commission on Restructuring the Internal Revenue Service. The report exclaimed, among other things, that the IRS must do more to ensure taxpayers' rights are protected in the enforcement process.

The nation was riveted to the television as about a dozen citizens told heart-rending stories of how the IRS ran them over in the collection process. Even IRS employees testified about the culture of abuse that permeates the agency. The employees testified while hidden behind screens with their voices electronically altered so as not to disclose their identity. It seemed more like a Mafia trial than a congressional hearing.

In a massive damage control effort following the hearings, the Treasury and Senate Democrats attempted to minimize the impact of the horror stories. They suggested that the leadership of the finance committee scoured the nation looking for horror stories but was able to unearth just the handful who actually testified. Their spin was that IRS abuse is an "isolated occurrence" and most people have a favorable experience with the agency.

In my own testimony, I documented thirteen specific ways the IRS abuses citizens in the collection process. I pointed out that revenue officers use tactics of bluff and intimidation, misinformation and disinformation and in many cases, they out-right lie to people concerning their rights and the agency's limitations. I proved that IRS abuse of citizens is a regular practice.

The hearings prompted the IRS to conduct two internal audits of its collection activity. The first audit, the results of which were delivered to the Senate Finance Committee on December 5, 1997, focused on collection actions within the Arkansas-Oklahoma district. The second report, issued on January 13, 1998, analyzed the collection function nationwide.

As a result of its reviews, the IRS itself concluded that the agency "has created an environment driven by statistical accomplishments that places taxpayer rights and a fair employee evaluation system at risk." IRS Fact Sheet, FS-98-4, January, 1998. In other words, the "effectiveness" of the Collection function is determined by how much money is collected--period. And while the 1988 Taxpayers' Bill of Rights Act prohibited the agency from using enforcement statistics in the evaluation of employees, that is exactly what the agency does.

Specifically, by ranking the districts in the order of their collection results, the IRS in effect gives more emphasis to "enforcement results without corresponding emphasis on case quality, adherence to law, policy and procedure, or taxpayer rights." Ibid, page 1. The result is citizens are routinely run over by the agency in its lust to build favorable statistics. As stated in the January, 1998, report, "This [collection] emphasis led to an environment that heavily focused on achieving enforcement results." Ibid, page 2.

What is troubling is the lack of management concern for the plain language of the Taxpayers' Bill of Rights Act. As noted, that law prohibits IRS managers from evaluating employees on the basis of enforcement statistics or "production quotas." Public Law 100-647, section 6231, November, 1988. Furthermore, the law requires each district director to "certify" in writing to the IRS Commissioner on a quarterly basis that his district is in compliance with the law. In reviewing these certifications, the January, 1998, report found, "The [certification] process practiced by districts is perfunctory in nature; group managers and/or branch chiefs initiate the process by self-assessing that violations have not occurred." FS-98-4, page 3.

What we see here is an apparent total lack of regard for the law. And what is more troubling is the fact that this takes place at the highest levels of IRS' district management. When management has no regard for the law, taxpayers rights or procedural restrictions and safe-guards, how can rank and file employees be expected to uphold them? I believe the answer is obvious and is expressed in the January, 1998, report:

Approximately one-fourth of the revenue officers and group managers stated that *they feel pressure* to achieve enforcement goals and take enforcement actions. Ibid, emphasis added.

Not only is collection action often improper, but it is often in error. IRS Publication 1500, Internal Revenue Research Bulletin, once reported that 25 percent of all outstanding balances on the agency's books exist because of "duplicate assessments or administrative error." That means about one in every four collection targets is an innocent citizen.

The combination of both the pressure on ROs to produce and outright assessment errors leads to substantial improper collection actions. And when they develop, citizens must know how to seek quick and effective help to stop the steam roller. I address those measures in this chapter.

An All New Right--The Collection Appeal

Historically, there was very little in the way of recourse for those caught in the Collection function. Even the prospect of court action against the agency is significantly tainted due to the so-called anti-injunction act. Code section 7421 (See chapter six of this book and *Taxpayers' Ultimate Defense Manual*). That statute deprives federal courts of jurisdiction to "restrain or enjoin the assessment or collection of taxes." Said another way, courts have little power to stop the IRS.

The biggest obstacle to collection justice or reasonableness is the fact that there has been no independent check or appeal process from the devastation of IRS' collection powers. True, one could always "appeal" to a manager for a second opinion, but that offered little hope and even fewer results. After all, the manager was often the one calling the shots. And as we know from the IRS' recent reports, managers have a vested interest in *pursuing* enforcement action.

However, new procedures offer new hope. Threatened by the Taxpayers' Bill of Rights Act 2, the IRS instituted collection appeal procedures in 1996. Designed to give the citizen an avenue of review, the collection appeal applies to liens, levies and seizures. The process does two important things. First, it freezes collection action pending review. Second, it provides up to two reviews. The first is handled by the RO's manager and the second by the Appeals Office.

The real promise lies with the Appeals Office. I am fond of saying that Appeals has as its function to *solve* problems, whereas other IRS enforcement divisions are more concerned with *causing* them. Nowhere is this more true than with Collection. Almost without exception, the most egregious cases of IRS abuse involve out-of-control Collection officers. The new collection appeal procedures promise some hope of changing that.

The collection appeal should be used in *any* situation where collection action is unreasonable, will cause serious financial hardship or loss or otherwise is contrary to the spirit of reasonable resolution of the case. A classic example is where the IRS intends to sell real property, such as a home, for a small fraction of its value, only to leave the citizen both destitute *and* still owing a tax debt.

In the collection appeal, be prepared to prove your assertions. If you owe the tax but contend that collection actions are harsh, inappropriate or will cause undue hardship, offer alternatives to resolve the situation. You must be clear and specific in defining both the potential harm and in proposing an alternative.

The collection appeal process is described in IRS Publication 1660, Collection Appeal Rights (for Liens, Levies and Seizures). See Forms Kit. Please review it carefully.

The two-page document expressly states that you enjoy the right to appeal *any* collection action. The important aspect of this procedure is that when you tell a Collection officer you wish to appeal his action, he must "honor your request" and refer you to a manager. If an amicable solution cannot be reached, you have the right "to have your case reviewed by an Appeals officer."

According to page two of Publication 1660, when you state the desire to appeal the decision, collection action *must stop*. However, you have just two days to submit Form 9423, Collection Appeal Request, with supporting documents. If you fail, collection resumes. Form 9423 is needed to carry the matter from the Collection manager to the Appeals Office. Form 9423 is reproduced in the Forms Kit.

File Form 9423 with the local Collection Division responsible for the action you intend to appeal. Remember, it must be received within two days of the conference with the Collection manager.

Form 9423 is quite simple. The key is in line 15 where it asks why you disagree with the collection action. It also asks for an explanation of "how you would resolve your tax problem." If necessary, attach documentation and further explanations to support your claims.

This pushes the case to the Appeals Office where you have a meeting with an Appeals officer. The Appeals officer has the authority to make rulings that bind the parties. Take notice of page two of Form 9423, where it states, "both you and the IRS are required to accept the decision and live up to its terms." This binds you administratively. That is, if you propose a $200 per month installment payment, *you must make the payment.* That is not to say you cannot re-negotiate the payment if your financial conditions change.

The Taxpayer Advocate and the Problems Resolution Office

The Taxpayer Advocate (TA) is intended to function as a liaison between the IRS' enforcement divisions and the citizen. Originally created as part of the 1988 Taxpayers' Bill of Rights Act, it has undergone some changes over the years. In 1996, TBR2 gave more independence to the office.

The TA operates through the IRS' Problems Resolution Offices (PRO). PROs are located in the various district offices and are responsible for handling cases when normal channels fail. The purpose of the Problems Resolution Program (PRP) is expressed by the IRS as:

> PRP is intended to assure that individual taxpayers have somewhere to turn when the system fails; someone who will step in and make sure that their problem is not lost or overlooked; someone who will assure that their rights are protected. PRP Handbook, para. 110(2) (5-27-92)

Language in the PRP Handbook makes it easy to understand why citizens generally have success using the TA to head off abusive collection action. In section 313(2)(a) of the handbook, under the heading, "Statement of Rights," it says, "It should be assumed that each taxpayer wants to comply, unless circumstances of the case indicate otherwise." This attitude is vastly different from the typical notion that delinquent citizens are mere "deadbeats."

The TA can often help hasten IRS' acceptance of installment agreements, win release of improper levies and otherwise assist in resolving general collection disputes. The TA has the ability to issue what is called a Taxpayer Assistance Order (TAO). The TAO is designed to prevent or correct IRS actions--or lack of actions--the effect of which is to cause a "significant hardship."

This authority gives the TA the power to intervene in installment payment negotiations and assist in arranging a workable plan. It gives them the power to stop threats of enforced collection, to reverse collection action, to release wage and bank levies when they create "hardship" and to order a refund under appropriate conditions.

IRS regulations define a "significant hardship" as a "serious privation caused or about to be caused to the taxpayer as a result of the manner in which the tax laws are being administered by the IRS." Revenue Regulation section 301.7811-1(a)(4). Mere personal or economic inconvenience does not rise to the level of "hardship." However, "significant hardship" created by wage or bank levies does.

Please note that the phrase "significant hardship" is highly subjective and what is considered hardship by one person may not be hardship to another. Therefore, the determination must be made on a case-by-case basis after careful consideration of the facts. The IRS must consider what its actions will do to *you* and not how somebody else might fare under identical circumstances.

The IRS' Penalty Handbook, Internal Revenue Manual Part XX, lists eleven elements to consider and provides a couple of examples of what constitutes significant hardship. They are:

1. Will the taxpayer be able to retain housing?
2. Will the taxpayer be able to obtain food?
3. Will the taxpayer be able to retain utilities?
4. Will the taxpayer be able to retain or obtain transportation to and from work?
5. Will the taxpayer be able to remain employed?
6. Will the taxpayer be able to obtain essential medical treatment and/or medication?
7. Will the taxpayer be able to obtain reasonable clothing and/or shoes?
8. Will the taxpayer sustain an avoidable loss of education?
9. Will irreparable damage be caused to credit rating?
10. Will the taxpayer be unable to meet payroll and/or be in imminent bankruptcy?
11. Is the hardship imminent?

Below are some examples of potential "significant hardship" cases.

(a) A wage levy that impaired the taxpayer's ability to purchase needed medication or medical care. The Service's lack of awareness causes an unintentional negative impact and qualify for an application for TAO if the employee contacted cannot or will not relieve the hardship.

(b) A payment is improperly applied to a taxpayer's account, thus blocking the taxpayer's receipt of a refund. After many contacts with the Service, substantiated with dates, the taxpayer is suffering emotional stress and files a Form 911 [Application for TAO] for relief. A TAO is appropriate to request action to substantiate the credit and authorize the refund. IRS Penalty Handbook, section (20)117.2(4) and (5) (7-15-96).

The chief way to bring your case to the attention of the TA is through the use of IRS Form 911, Application for Taxpayer Assistance Order. See Forms Kit. I provide much more detailed discussion of the Form 911 and PRO in chapter twelve, *Taxpayers' Ultimate Defense Manual*. Also, I address a caveat concerning Form 911 in chapter ten of this book. Please review it carefully before submitting a Form 911.

Releasing Wage Levies

I have found the fastest way to win release of a wage levy is to immediately contact your local TA. It is located in the same office as your district director. It is not even necessary to file Form 911 to accomplish it. In fact, given the negative aspect of the Form 911 discussed in chapter ten, it is desirable *not* to file the form.

Instead, send a certified letter to the TA explaining that you are under a wage levy and cannot pay your monthly living expenses. Explain that you cannot pay the tax in full and desire an installment agreement. If possible, submit Form 9465, Installment Agreement Request, with your letter. Your letter should include a brief worksheet showing current income and expenses to support your payment request. Also point out the monthly amount of the IRS levy.

State clearly that continuation of the wage levy will cause significant hardship by making it impossible to pay monthly living expenses. By showing your monthly expenses and how much you have left after the IRS helps itself to your pay, the TA can easily see that you are facing a financial crisis. Argue from the list of elements set forth above that the collection action is causing a serious hardship.

The TA's approach is generally to immediately assign the case to an RO. At that point, negotiate the installment agreement as outlined in chapter five. Under no circumstances should you permit a wage levy to continue without following these steps. If you do, the levy continues until all the tax, interest and penalties are paid in full. Before that occurs, you are likely to be financially destroyed. You can use these same procedures to challenge any improper collection action.

Property Exempt from Levy

In chapter four, I listed the various types and values of property exempt from levy. Perhaps the most important of these are the wage levy exemptions. The law exempts a minimum amount of wages from IRS levy. Unfortunately, it is common for revenue officers and ACS to ignore these exemptions. The result is nearly 100 percent of a person's wages are clipped in violation of the law. Code section 6334(d).

The wage levy exemption is based upon the standard deduction applicable to your filing status and the number of dependent exemptions you are entitled to claim on Form 1040. The value of those amounts is added and that total is divided by the number of weeks in the year. If paid monthly, the total is divided by the number of months in the year. The quotient constitutes the amount of your exempt wages.

For example, suppose you are married and have four children. Based upon 1997 tax tables, the married filing jointly standard deduction is $6,900. The value of one dependent exemption is $2,650. You are entitled to claim six dependent exemptions, one for yourself, your spouse and each of four children. The combined value of the exemptions is $15,900 ($2,650 x 6). After adding the standard deduction, your exempt wages are $22,800 ($6,900 plus $15,900).

When you divide $22,800 by 52, the number of weeks in a year, you arrive at $438. That is the amount you are entitled to earn weekly, free of levy. If paid monthly, divide the exempt amount by 12. Under our example, that entitles you to earn $1,900 per month free of levy.

To claim exempt wages, carefully complete the statement on the reverse side of Form 668-W. See Exhibit 4-4, page 64. Using certified mail, send the form to the RO or ACS office which issued the levy. Be sure to maintain a copy for your files.

If the RO or ACS refuses to honor the exemptions, contact the TA immediately. Send a letter as outlined above with a copy of your exemption statement. Communicate only through certified mail. Explain that you are being denied your right to exempt property and ask the TA to step in immediately and correct the injustice. At the same time, seek an installment agreement through the TA. If you proceed as illustrated, expect to win release of the levy and establish a reasonable installment agreement.

New Limitations on Levy and Seizure Power

With the revelation that IRS is enforcing collection merely to build revenue statistics, the Assistant Commissioner for Collection instituted new enforcement guidelines. By memorandum issued December 2, 1997, Assistant Commissioner Ronald S. Rhodes declared,

> Effective immediately, all Collection seizures will require a minimum approval level of the Collection Division Chief. A District Director will approve all seizure cases involving a taxpayer's principal residence, the contents of a principal residence (which includes items located in garages and other structures on the land on which the principal residence is located), or perishable goods.

This new directive places the decision to seize homes, etc., in the hands of higher level management officials. We can only hope this cuts the number of indiscriminate seizures. It can be truly effective, however, only if managers are relieved of the pressure to collect regardless of the propriety of their actions.

With respect to one's principal residence, it has long been the rule (see chapter six) that the signature of a district director is required before it can be seized. And while this may have cut down the number of residences seized, it has not reduced the bluff and intimidation routinely practiced by some ROs. One man told me the revenue officer declared that if he did not sign an unreasonable installment agreement "on the spot," he would begin enforced collection including, "the seizure of your home." The man did not understand that the RO did not have the independent authority to seize the home. Consequently, he was forced to live with an unreasonable installment payment for years.

If you are faced with demands backed by threats to pursue collection in a manner you know is illegal, do not hesitate to go over the RO's head. Proceed straight to the TA. Explain the situation and how collection action is sure to cause hardship. Document your claims.

Do not be afraid to go over the heads of unreasonable collection officers. You cannot make matters worse by involving the one office that can stop them. Remember what happened in Deb's case when we went over the head of that RO? She was no longer forced to contend with the irrational threats of a person who had no interest in seeing that justice was done.

Conclusion

When you are in trouble, dial 9-1-1. When dealing with the IRS, this means getting through to the Taxpayer Advocate who can help solve your problem. The Taxpayer Advocate is your voice in the IRS and I have used that office with great success by following the points outlined above. Do not be afraid to use it when the circumstances dictate.

Here is part of Marsha's story concerning how she obtained success after learning her rights:

> I just had to let you know how much you have helped my husband and me.
>
> Our tax problem began in 1990 and continued until 1992. We owed an excess of $25,000 plus penalties and interest. I remember hearing advertisements of your books on the radio in 1994, but initially thinking that your books could never work for us. Reluctantly, I withdrew your book "How to Get Tax Amnesty" from the library. After reading that book, I just had to purchase it. It gave me hope by showing me step-by-step how we could also be victorious. It was so refreshing to know that you had encouraging scriptures from the Bible throughout the book.
>
> I encourage people to employ the instructions/advice in your books. THEY WORK! We settled our case for just $4,600. And by doing it yourself, you see our process at work. You give simple step-by-step directions. And with as little as $150 investment you save money rather than paying an attorney $1,000 or more and not accomplishing anything.
>
> Your books/newsletters are phenomenal. Anyone can lick the IRS with a postage stamp. I am testimony to negotiating and winning with the IRS. It is all thanks to God and your books. Thank you ever so much for your wisdom and dedication to this field.
>
> Signed: Marsha - New Jersey

"...in any and all circumstances I have learned the secret of facing plenty and hunger, abundance and want. I can do all things in Him who strengthens me."

Philippians 4:12-13

CHAPTER EIGHT
How To Step Forward--
The Non-filer Program

If you are ever to experience the reward of tax amnesty, accept the fact that running and hiding must end. Up to this point, you were probably concerned that if you did step forward, the IRS would sooner make a statistic out of you as assist in solving the problem. Up to this point, you were probably right. However, with adoption of the Non-filer Program, that is no longer the case.

Former IRS Commissioner Shirley Peterson adopted the Non-filer Program in 1992. It is intended to offer non-filers an opportunity to get back into the system without being crushed. She recognized that most non-filers stopped filing due to traumatic situations which arose in their lives, not because they are tax cheats. Maybe they had a serious medical problem or accident, a failed business or marriage or some other good faith reason for the delinquency. Once they failed to file the first return, a pattern began and many ended up mired in inaction.

The Non-filer Program is essentially a carrot and a stick. The carrot is, "you file the returns and we will accept them without nit-picking and without criminal prosecution." However, the stick is, if you do not file them, as Mrs. Peterson declared, "we will use a more direct approach." By that, she means that repeated, aggravated non-filers will be targeted for prosecution. See chapter three.

Non-filers are often mired in inaction for two reasons. First, they do not have the money to pay the tax; the vast majority are not criminals, but they are broke. Secondly, they know that not filing creates a second problem, that of the failure itself--a problem they believe can land them in jail. And as long as the IRS is silent their fear and uncertainty lead them to continue doing nothing.

Unfortunately for non-filers, the reality is you cannot take comfort in the agency's lack of action. The reason is, when a return is not filed, there is no statute of limitations governing IRS' ability to assess a tax. Do not confuse this with the clear *criminal* statute of limitations discussed in chapter three. Though the IRS' ability to prosecute is limited, its capacity to get the money is not. This is referred to as the assessment statute of limitations.

When a return is filed on time, the IRS normally has just three years from the filing date to make an assessment. However, if no return is filed, there is no limitation. As many as twenty years may pass from the return due date and the IRS is nevertheless able to assess. Code section 6501(c)(3). This is why I recommend filing past due returns. For details on the assessment statute of limitations, see chapter seven of *IRS, Taxes and the Beast.*

Another important consideration is that generally speaking, tax amnesty is not available when past due returns remain unfiled. This chapter explores the manner in which delinquent returns should be filed when the IRS is not pressing for them.

Filing Past Due Tax Returns

I must begin this discussion with an important *caveat*. If you intend to pursue bankruptcy as a means of obtaining tax amnesty, *do not read* this analysis in a vacuum. Read it in conjunction with the discussion in chapters thirteen and fourteen. Furthermore, *do not act* on these suggestions without consulting experienced counsel.

Nobody wants to kick a sleeping lion. When the IRS is not pursuing you for back tax returns, it seems self-destructive to beckon its attention. That is especially true in light of all you learned thus far. But, to fully eliminate your problem, that is exactly what must happen.

Who is Required to File

I have talked with hundreds of non-filers. Nearly without exception, each believes all persons are required to file, *without exception*. This is not true. The obligation to file attaches to the receipt of taxable income. It exists only when taxable income is received in excess of the statutory filing requirement for the year in question.

Therefore, the first step to curing a non-filing situation is to determine whether you are required to file the return in the first place. I once worked with a man panicked by a pattern of non-filing stretching over a period of five years. After talking with him, I found that for three of those five years, he was unemployed. Living off the charity of his family, he earned no income during the three-year period. Therefore, he had no legal obligation to file.

Each year, the so-called threshold filing requirements change. These requirements refer to the minimum amount of income one must earn before being required to file. For example, in 1996, a single person was not required to file unless he earned at least $6,550. If you were entitled to file a joint tax return with your spouse, the filing obligation did not attach until joint income reached $11,800.

Because of the importance of this, I include a chart depicting the filing requirements for single, married filing jointly and head of household (for persons under 65) dating back to 1985. See the filing requirements chart.

FILING REQUIREMENTS CHART

YEAR	SINGLE	MARRIED JOINTLY	HEAD HOUSEHOLD
1985	3,430	5,620	3,430
1986	3,560	5,830	3,560
1987	4,440	7,560	4,440
1988	4,950	8,900	6,350
1989	5,100	9,200	6,550
1990	5,300	9,550	6,800
1991	5,550	10,000	7,150
1992	5,900	10,600	7,550
1993	6,050	10,900	7,800
1994	6,250	11,250	8,050
1995	6,400	11,550	8,250
1996	6,550	11,800	8,450
1997	6,800	12,200	8,700

These filing requirements cover most people. They are different, however, if your circumstances vary somewhat from those shown. For example, if you are over age 65, each of the threshold amounts jump slightly. The best advice is to consult IRS Publication 17, *Your Federal Income Tax*, for the year in question. That document contains a more detailed chart illustrating the filing requirements. If you are not required to file, your problem is solved! But be prepared to prove it if the IRS asks questions. My books *41 Ways to Lick the IRS with a Postage Stamp* and *IRS, Taxes and the Beast* will assist you.

How to File Delinquent Returns

If you find that a return is required, the next step is to prepare, *but not yet file* it. If you must file past due returns for several years, prepare *all* the returns first, before filing *any* of them. You may wish to use a professional return preparer to help with this project. Before embarking, carefully read chapter six of *IRS, Taxes and the Beast*. It illustrates exactly what records you need to accurately report income and deductions. It also illustrates how to reconstruct lost records if necessary. You should also consider audit-proofing your tax returns at the time of filing. This reduces the possibility of the IRS flagging the tardy returns for audit. See *IRS, Taxes and the Beast.*

Because the IRS does not archive tax return blanks for prior years, consult the library for copies. Alternatively, a company known as Dial-a-Tax-Form sells prior years forms and instructions of every description. Call 910-724-3978 to order.

After preparing the returns, sort them into two groups; those which show *no tax* owed (or a refund) and those which show *tax owed.* The returns showing no tax due, or a refund, should be filed first. Obviously, filing these returns creates no collection problem.

Please note that if the return is more than three years late, you waive your right to any refund. Therefore, if you believe the IRS owes you a refund on a tardy return, prepare and file that return *before* any of the others and if possible, before the three-year period expires. To illustrate how to compute the three-year period, suppose your 1994 return was due no later than April 15, 1995 (unless you filed an extension). If filed after April 15, 1998, you lose your refund.

After filing all returns showing no tax liability, begin to address those which do. There are two ways to approach filing these returns. Which method to employ depends upon your ability to pay the tax. Keep in mind that penalties and interest *at least* double the tax due.

Method One. The first method is to file all the returns at once. Do this only if there is no chance of paying the taxes, interest and penalties within a very short period of time. This may sound contradictory, but keep in mind that in order to achieve tax amnesty, you must file the returns. (The exception is discussed in chapter thirteen.) If there is no hope of paying the tax, you might as well file and get on with the business of winning amnesty. Be aware, however, that enforced collection begins after filing those returns.

Method Two. The second method is to file the returns at substantial intervals, perhaps as many as six months apart. Do this only if you are able to raise the money to pay the tax due on a given return *prior to* filing the next return. For example, suppose you owe $2,000 for each of three years. After securing the money to pay the first year, file the first return, together with payment. The IRS computes the interest and penalties within several weeks of filing and bills you. Pay these before filing the next return. File the second return only after you secure the funds to pay the tax for that year. Use this procedure for each return.

The advantages of doing this are substantial. First, by filing the returns one at a time, *with the money*, you never create a serious collection problem. Secondly, you cannot make matters worse by pursuing this tactic. The reason is, all failure to file penalties accrue within the first five months of the filing delinquency. Thereafter, no further failure to file penalties attach. Moreover, interest on the tax and the failure to pay penalty accrue whether the return is filed or not. Therefore, waiting to file does not increase those amounts. See chapter nine for a discussion on canceling penalties.

If you are able to successfully carry out method two, you accomplish two important goals. First, you cure your tax return filing and payment delinquencies. Second, you do so without ever exposing yourself to enforced collection activity. If you can accomplish this critical goal, you need none of the remaining information in this book!

Prior to exercising either method one or two, ascertain the amount of tax owed and whether it can be paid quickly. If it cannot be paid quickly, you must use method one. Otherwise, you diminish your ability to win amnesty under the programs discussed.

In any event, never send more than one tax return to the IRS in a given package. The IRS is notorious for failing to process anything beyond the first return when a group is submitted simultaneously. Be sure to send the individual returns via certified mail with return receipt requested. Keep copies of the returns, certified cards and postage receipts and *attach* the latter two to the file copy of your return should your filing be challenged.

How Far Back Should I go to Cure Delinquent Filings?

I often run across those who have not filed for eight years, ten years and longer. The tasking of preparing a single tax return is daunting by itself but the idea of preparing ten or more is overwhelming. Consider Deb who was called upon to prepare and file returns for eight years.

When a revenue officer is in your face demanding the returns, it is easy to answer the question, "How far back do I go?" The RO answers it for you. However, when the IRS is not in your face, the question can be difficult to answer if your omissions go beyond six years. Here are some guidelines, partially derived from experience and partially derived from the law and regulations. They help lead us to the answer.

The first guideline is Pilla's Rule of Loose Ends. I do not like loose ends. The whole idea of the amnesty programs is to tie up loose ends and solve problems, to put the delinquencies behind you and get on with your life. By *not* filing all delinquent returns, you leave loose ends. As such, the possibility exists--however remote it may be--that at some point, the IRS may come back and rub your nose in them.

The biggest loose end of all is the assessment statute of limitations. The IRS is *not* limited in its ability to assess taxes when a return is not filed. Therefore, you are *never* out of the woods on a non-filed return.

Moreover, generally speaking, the returns should be filed to take full advantage of the relief offered through the various amnesty options. Why, for example, would you attempt to resolve taxes for six unfiled years only to leave the seventh year off the table? The addition of the seventh year, by itself, does nothing to jeopardize the success of your efforts. On the other hand, if, after making a deal, the IRS turns up the unfiled year, it could kill the deal later. Therefore, all things being equal, file all delinquent returns whenever practical and possible.

The second guideline involves a delinquency duration of fewer than six years. In any case where the non-filing period is fewer than six years, *file all returns*, regardless of what the IRS demands. The reason is the criminal statute of limitations runs for six years from the due date of the return. See chapter three. Furthermore, the IRS has guidelines in its manual, indicating plainly that non-filers are expected to cure all delinquencies of six years or less.

The manual part I speak of is Internal Revenue Manual Policy Statement P-5-133. It provides guidance on how far back to go when the delinquencies stretch *more than* six years. The IRS says that normally, non-filers are not required to file more than six years worth of delinquent returns "without managerial approval." That means the IRS can require more than six years worth of returns but generally does not unless the facts and circumstances warrant.

According to the IRS, the factors to be taken into consideration include,

> Prior history of noncompliance, existence of income from illegal sources, effect upon voluntary compliance and anticipated revenue in relation to time and effort required to determine tax due. Consideration will also be given any special circumstance existing in the case of a particular taxpayer, class of taxpayer, or industry, or which may be peculiar to the class of tax involved.

Based on this, we may conclude that if you were self-employed during the delinquency period and earned substantial income and accumulated substantial assets, the IRS may likely require returns for all periods even if they go beyond six years. Likewise, if there is evidence of involvement in illegal activities the agency may likely require the filing of all returns.

Conversely, a wage-earner who underwent income tax withholding would likely not be required to file more than six delinquent returns. In addition, a self-employed person with little business success, living hand-to-mouth during the delinquency period, would likewise probably not have to file more than six returns.

Dealing with IRS-filed Returns

A common problem faced by delinquent filers is the IRS-filed return. We learned from Deb's experience that ROs often threaten to just "file the returns for you" if you fail to "cooperate." To do this properly, the IRS must make a determination of the tax liability, which it does based upon "available" information. That may be the information you provide or it may be the W-2s and 1099s in its possession. More likely, it is based on the fact you earned six hundred thousand dollars during the delinquency years and had no deductions.

From there, it must mail a report explaining how it arrived at its tax figures. You then have the right to appeal the determination before it becomes final. In the appeals process, you have the right to present documentation to show your correct income and deductions.

Too often, however, the IRS overlooks the pesky part about the appeals process. Instead, it just assesses the tax based upon what is called a "substitute for return" (SFR). The SFR is made under the authority of code section 6020(b). It allows the IRS to assess a tax where no return is filed based upon "available information." That return is considered correct for all legal purposes and the citizen has the burden to prove it is wrong.

Once the SFR is processed, enforced collection begins with notices from ACS. This is often the first word a non-filer hears from the IRS. He is also flabbergasted at the amount of tax the IRS claims is owed.

When faced with payment demands by an RO, the citizen exclaims, "I can't possibly owe that much." Sadly, however, the RO's only reply is "the tax is assessed and it's my job to collect it."

However, two new procedures *require* the RO to care. First, when collecting a tax based upon an SFR the citizen disputes, the RO is required to explain the right of "audit reconsideration." IRS Audit Reconsideration Reengineering Report, June, 1996. But do not hold your breath. The audit reconsideration is the process by which the IRS opens closed audit cases. And while you may never have appeared for an audit, the SFR is essentially the result of an audit.

You have the right to re-open such an audit when you can prove the tax assessment is incorrect. The details of this procedure are spelled out in chapter eleven of *IRS, Taxes and the Beast*. We have been very successful using this process to correct inaccurate SFR assessments.

Second, under procedures adopted by the IRS in December, 1997, the RO is instructed to be direct with the citizen about his rights to challenge SFR assessments. This change is the result of revelations of abuse brought forth in hearings conducted by the Senate Finance Committee in September, 1997, and by the IRS' own internal audit of its enforcement actions, reported on December 2, 1997.

When collecting a tax assessed via SFR, the RO must, upon contact with the taxpayer,

> [E]xplain to the taxpayer how the tax was computed and fully advise the taxpayer of the opportunity to correct the return with any appropriate expenses or deductions or other information to support a decrease in the assessed tax. The taxpayer must be given reasonable time to provide this information before collection actions begin. IRS Fact Sheet, FS-97-27, December, 1997.

Contrast these procedures and guidelines with the statements and demands Deb faced. As you can see, it is a new world but it remains your obligation to understand your rights or face the real possibility that you will not enjoy them. See *IRS, Taxes and the Beast*.

Get Off the Tax Debt Treadmill

Perhaps the greatest source of frustration for the delinquent citizen is that once behind the eight ball, he never seems to be able to get off the treadmill. The scenario goes something like this: April 15 arrives and with it, the horror of knowing you are not able to pay your taxes. In the best case, you file a return without the money and await the inevitable onslaught. In the worst case, you file no return--hoping against hope that the money materializes somehow.

The common belief is you will pay the tax out of current income. Though your earnings rarely change, you make every effort to commit all available funds to the task. However, penalties and interest accumulate at the staggering rate of about 20 to 22 percent annually. Considering the fact that many Americans live paycheck to paycheck, interest and penalties pose a substantial hardship, making it impossible to pay both delinquent taxes and necessary living expenses.

Over time, the IRS applies the payments to the *back* taxes. At the same time, current tax funds are often diverted to pay living expenses.

This creates a second problem. Not only does a liability exist for the first year, but now you are cultivating a liability for a second year.

By the time you file the return for the second year, you face two delinquent debts. This pattern generally continues for several years. At some point, you may eventually pay off the first year's taxes, but only after substantial penalty and interest assessments. As the pattern continues, tax liabilities multiply at the rate of one or two new years for each year paid. This is one reason many just stop filing altogether.

Given this demoralizing process, I have developed a very effective plan for bringing an end to the madness. This has to do with "getting current" with the IRS. This is mandatory if you are going to solve your problem. In fact, if you do not get current, there is no hope of being successful with the amnesty programs. This is what you must do to terminate your trip through the tax collection Twilight Zone.

1. Pay current taxes. Whatever you do, you must pay current taxes, that is, taxes for the *present* year. Do not allow yourself to utilize current tax revenue either to pay back taxes or to pay living expenses. Always remember Pilla's First Rule of Tax Debt Management: If you have money to pay the back taxes or money to pay the current taxes but cannot pay both, *NEVER PAY THE BACK TAXES!* The back tax debt can *always* be managed through one or more of the techniques discussed in this book. However, *NONE* of these techniques work if you are not current with your tax payments and filing obligations.

An essential element of working out of tax debt is to very carefully establish a monthly budget and stick to it. The budget must consider wage withholding for federal and state income and social security taxes. What you are left with is net income. That alone is what you must base your personal expenditures upon. Resist the temptation to adjust your withholding allowances to increase your take home pay. That does not solve a back tax problem but creates a current one.

If you are self-employed, you must use more caution and restraint with your budget because you do not enjoy the "benefit" of wage withholding. You must make quarterly estimated payments of your current taxes. Make the payments on IRS Form 1040 ES.

To avoid both another tax delinquency and the penalty for underpayment of estimated taxes, generally you must pay either 100 percent of your prior year's tax liability or 90 percent of the current liability, whichever is less. The best way to do this is to ascertain your "effective tax rate" and make estimated payments based on that. The effective tax rate is the percentage of your income you pay in total tax measured against your gross, *before deductions.*

To compute your effective rate, start by determining your total federal tax for the preceding year, say 1996. Your total 1996 federal tax liability includes social security and is the tax liability *before* applying payment credits. Suppose that number is $10,500. Divide that number into your gross receipts for 1996, *before* considering any deductions or expenses whatsoever. Suppose your gross receipts were $60,000. By dividing $10,500 into $60,000, you arrive at a fraction, which is .175. Thus, .175, or 17.5 percent, is your effective federal tax rate. It means that 17.5 percent of *every dollar* goes to federal taxes.

After finding your effective federal tax rate, do the same for state income taxes. Suppose your state effective tax rate is 7 percent. You must now set aside a total of 24.5 percent (17.5 federal plus 7 percent state) *of every dollar* to cover your income tax burden. If you earn $60,000 gross, your monthly income is about $5,000. At 24.5 percent, you must set aside $1,225 ($5,000 x .245) to cover your *current* federal and state income and social security tax debt. On a quarterly basis, send a payment to the IRS equal to three monthly estimates using Form 1040 ES, the payment coupon. Make a similar payment to the state using its coupon.

I recommend you establish a separate bank account to handle the estimated taxes. That way, the money is not co-mingled with business or personal operating funds and you are less likely to spend it. In addition, you get into the habit of writing a monthly check for taxes. That way, they become a real part of your budget.

If you are a wage earner, check your wage withholding using the same procedure. Be sure that enough withholding is taken to cover your debts. However, do not over-withhold. That just gives the IRS another asset to take from you when you file your return.

2. Establish a manageable installment payment. Using the techniques and strategies discussed in chapter five, negotiate a reasonable installment arrangement that takes into consideration necessary living expenses and current taxes. Making payments to the IRS beyond your means translates to financial problems elsewhere, usually with current taxes. Remember Pilla's First Rule of Tax Debt Management. *Do not* propose a payment or allow yourself to be forced into a payment in excess of your "disposable income," as explained in chapter five. Such an arrangement cannot help you or the IRS.

If you have no disposable income either because you are unemployed or under-employed, push hard for uncollectible status. See chapter eleven for details. When classified as uncollectible, the IRS pushes the hold button on the collection machine, giving you an opportunity to either get back on your feet or otherwise use one of the amnesty programs to handle the debt.

3. Request abatement of all penalties. Many tax delinquencies can be solved through the cancellation of penalties. When the IRS cancels penalties, it also cancels the interest on penalties (but not interest on the tax). This often cuts the debt by half and even more, depending upon its age. In any event, canceling penalties makes the debt more manageable. See chapter nine for more on penalty cancellation.

4. Consider a loan to pay the tax. It is much cheaper to borrow money from a bank or third party than it is to borrow from the IRS. There are several reasons for this.

First, interest paid to the IRS is considered personal interest and is not tax deductible. However, interest on a home equity loan or refinance is likely deductible. Handle tax liens standing in the way of a refinance as outlined in chapter six.

Second, personal loans from a bank or third party carry a fixed interest rate and no penalties. IRS charges penalties and interest until the tax is paid in full. Furthermore, the interest rate is subject to change twice per year based on prevailing market rates. Lastly, the IRS compounds interest on the entire unpaid balance on a *daily* basis, meaning that over time, you pay interest on taxes, interest on penalties and interest on interest.

Third, loans from banks and third parties are generally amortized over a long period of time. This reduces the monthly installment payment compared to what the IRS might otherwise expect.

Fourth, short of getting forgiveness of the debt, paying the tax you owe in full is the only sure way to avoid enforced collection action.

5. Use the tax amnesty programs if necessary. If you are unable to secure funds from an outside source or are otherwise unable to liquidate the debt, turn to one of the amnesty programs discussed in this book. Do not be concerned that your bill may be escalating while you make small installment payments or are deemed uncollectible. The IRS cannot chase you forever. Eventually, you *will be* in a position to eliminate the bill somehow, if through no other way than with the expiration of the collection statute of limitations. See chapter ten. And while the bill sits with little or no collection results, you heighten the IRS' willingness to negotiate the debt.

As long as you *get and remain current* with income return filing and payment obligations, it is unlikely you will force the IRS into irrational collection action before your case is ripe for settlement through one of the amnesty programs.

Conclusion

The best time to step forward is when you are not under fire. That way, you enjoy the luxury of handling the problem on your own terms and within your own timetable. This is particularly true if you are able to secure the money to pay the tax over a fairly short period of time.

By filing past due returns as shown here, you very possibly may lick your tax delinquency problem before it becomes a threatening monster. You would be surprised to learn how many citizens are in a tax debt prison of their own making. In most cases, the citizen himself holds the key to the jail cell door. All he needs is simple instructions on how to work the lock.

I began this chapter by saying that if you ever hope to solve your problem, the running and hiding must end. And while I know that directive creates a great deal of apprehension, listen to what happened to Jim when he did just that:

> I want to write this note to thank you for your help. I got myself into quite a mess a number of years ago. Through fear and ignorance, I didn't meet the problem head on and actually tried to hide from it. But as the song says, "Nowhere to run, nowhere to hide." Anyway, I came across your books and talked to you personally. After completely understanding my rights as you so clearly state in your book and then talking to you personally to clarify a few details, I now have a workable plan to get myself out of this mess. Outside of doing your homework, it dawned on me what a difference you have made in keeping the government honest. Some of the changes that you have made are incredible. Most of us believe that one man cannot beat city hall, that we should accept whatever injustice is done to us because there's nothing we can do anyway. Well sir, you are proof that one man can make a difference and you are doing it. Keep up the good work. You will never really know how much you are appreciated.
> Signed: Jim - Indiana

"More than that, we rejoice in our sufferings, knowing that suffering produces endurance, and endurance produces character, and character produces hope, and hope does not disappoint us, because God's love has been poured into our hearts"

Romans 5:3-5

CHAPTER NINE
Forgiveness of Penalties

Rare is the tax bill which does not include an assessment of one or more of the nearly 140 penalty provisions of the Internal Revenue Code. Every act or failure to act, including failure to file, is punishable under the code. Penalties exist for not filing timely, negligence, underpaying taxes, for overstating deductions and so on. The punishment appears in the form of civil *ad valorem* penalties. An *ad valorem* penalty is one based upon a percentage of the tax.

Penalties are insidious because they often increase the tax beyond what can be paid. After adding interest, the bill doubles, triples, even quadruples. This strips even the most desirous citizen of not only the *capacity* to pay, but the *will* to pay. I have been told a thousand times, "I can pay my *taxes*, it's the interest and penalties I can't pay. And with the bill constantly going up, there's no point."

Without question, penalties often account for up to 50 percent or more of a given tax bill. That being the case, if one could eliminate the penalties, he would be half-way home. My guess is a good number of those in trouble with the IRS could put the matter behind them once and for all if they could only be rid of the penalties.

Can it be done? The answer is yes. And the procedure is not as complicated as you might think. The problem, however, is the IRS regularly lies to the public concerning the ability to cancel penalties. While a guest on one radio show, I spoke with a listener who received a notice demanding about $1,000 in penalties. He explained he called the Austin, Texas, Service Center which issued the penalty and asked whether it could be canceled. He explained he did not feel the penalty was appropriate and would like to seek its reversal. He was told there was nothing he could do about it. He would just have to pay it.

Later, after hearing one of my diatribes concerning the right to cancel penalties, the man wrote a letter to Austin in the fashion I suggested. He gleefully reported that this simple letter met with success. He canceled nearly $1,000 in penalties with just one letter.

If he were thrilled to win a $1,000 cancellation, how much more so for the citizen who owes $10,000 or even $50,000, in penalties alone? No matter what the amount, the procedures are the same and the chances of winning something are substantial. In fact, of all the procedures discussed in this book, cancellation of penalties is perhaps the one area we have the most consistent success.

Penalty assessments are often arbitrary and issued without regard to the facts of the case. The purpose of the penalty provisions of the code is to punish wrongdoers, those who have no regard for the law or who deliberately turn their backs on the requirements of the law. Penalties were never intended to apply to the ignorant or the one who, in good faith, misunderstands the law. Yet the IRS bashes those people with penalties to the tune of billions of dollars every year.

As I point out in the opening chapter, the IRS is finally listening. After years of complaining, thousands of radio shows, and tens of thousands of citizens demanding their rights, the IRS has relented. In May of 1992, the agency issued a revised Policy Statement on penalty assessment and abatement procedures.

In the revised Policy Statement, the IRS confirmed my long-stated contention that improper penalty assessments do nothing to encourage compliance with the tax laws. The IRS observes,

> Penalties support the Service's mission *only if* penalties enhance voluntary compliance. Even though other results such as raising of revenue, punishment, or reimbursement of the costs of enforcement may also arise when penalties are asserted, the Service will design, administer and evaluate penalty programs *solely on the basis* of whether they do the best possible job of encouraging compliant conduct. IRS Policy Statement P-1-18, May 19, 1992; emphasis added. See also IRS Penalty Handbook, IRM Part XX, section (20)123 (7-15-96).

This is an incredible admission. All along, I claimed penalties were nothing more than a means of raising revenue, having little to do with creating deterrence to non-compliance. Here, we see the IRS finally admitting that while such a practice occurred in the past, *it must end.*

The statement goes on to describe what the new penalty system is to achieve. It is designed to "ensure consistency." Under the prior program, the IRS cared little whether its assessment practices were consistent from one case to another or from one district to another.

The system is designed to "ensure accuracy of results in light of the facts and the law." A system with no concern for accurate results is the nature of the system we were forced to live with for decades.

The system is designed to "provide methods for the taxpayer to have his or her interests heard and considered." The mere admission of this right is a *major* attitude adjustment.

The system is designed to "require impartiality and a commitment to achieve the correct decision." If the new system is to be impartial and strive for correctness, it naturally follows that the old system was devoid of such basic, fundamental characteristics.

The system is designed to "allow for prompt reversal of initial determinations when sufficient information has been presented to indicate that the penalty is not appropriate." The old system, following the lack of partiality and regard for accuracy, often required appeals to cancel inappropriate assessments.

Lastly, the system is designed to "ensure that penalties are used for their proper purpose and not as bargaining points in the development or processing of cases." One of my hottest criticisms of penalties is IRS regularly threatens penalty assessments against those who do not accept audit decisions. In my experience, I can say with certainty that nary an audit goes by without some kind of warning from the auditor that the citizen is in jeopardy of increased penalty assessments if he "doesn't sign now."

How to Cancel Penalties

Every penalty provision of the code contains a good faith or reasonable cause provision. It means simply that a penalty does not apply when the citizen acted in good faith and based on a reasonable cause for his actions. Its purpose is to ensure penalties are issued only to the deliberately negligent citizen or he who takes affirmative steps to improperly avoid paying the correct tax.

The citizen bears the burden to prove the penalty does not apply. To meet the burden, provide a sworn statement to establish all the facts of the case. Offer sufficient detail to support the contention you acted in good faith and based upon a reasonable cause for your actions and not out of a deliberate attempt to cheat, deceive or mislead the IRS. The facts should contradict the legal presumption that the penalty applies. Make sure your abatement request provides details.

Examples of good faith and reasonable cause can include, but are not limited to,

a. Adverse financial conditions brought on by circumstances beyond your control;

b. Medical factors leading to an inability to meet your tax obligations;

c. Reliance upon the advice of qualified counsel or the IRS which turned out to be wrong;

d. Reliance upon IRS statements or publications which turned out to be wrong; or

e. Simple ignorance of the law or requirements in a particular area, where you can demonstrate you made at least minimal efforts to ascertain your responsibilities.

These ideas are not intended to be exhaustive. The concept of good faith is entirely subjective and turns on the facts of a given situation. What may seem reasonable to one person may not to another. Therefore, present your good faith argument based upon what you knew or believed, not what somebody else knew or believed.

The letter seeking abatement must be signed under penalty of perjury. That transforms the mere statement into *sworn testimony*. Mail the letter to the service center responsible for your account. If your case is handled by a revenue officer, submit the claim directly to the RO. Bear in mind any initial decision denying the request *is not final*. Whether issued by the RO or the service center, the decision may be appealed to the Appeals Office. There, it receives a fresh review by persons better trained to consider your facts and apply the law.

Chapter six of my book, *41 Ways to Lick the IRS with a Postage Stamp* is the most thorough, definitive discussion ever written to the public on techniques for winning abatement of penalties. Because of that exhaustive analysis, I elect to be more brief here. Anyone setting out to challenge tax penalties does himself a disservice if he does not read that discussion. In addition, my "Penalty Special Report," published in connection with the *Pilla Talks Taxes* newsletter, has numerous excerpts from the IRS' Penalty Handbook. These give dozens of ideas on effective arguments.

Conclusion

Forgiveness of penalties constitutes amnesty in the true sense of the word. This is because in most cases, the absence of penalties opens the door to a final resolution to an otherwise uncontrollable tax problem. Just do not look for the IRS to mail any notice suggesting you seek abatement of penalties as a means of solving your tax delinquency. You must take the initiative.

Eileen's letter explains how important the penalty abatement procedure can be.

My ex-husband and I owed IRS $15,566 which represented taxes for four years, plus penalties and interest. Payment of $400 per month had been worked out with them in early 1990. In the fall of '92, I heard you on KVTT [Dallas] and ordered *41 Ways to Lick the IRS*. Yeah! It only took two licks!

Using your model letters, on November 17, I sent off my request for abatement of penalties and interest. On January 4, I received the denial. I was discouraged, re-read the chapter and you said "no" is never final. I appealed on January 20.

On February 1, I was notified that all penalties and interest on the penalties had been abated! Dan, you saved me $9,066. That credit brought the total down to approximately $3,000, which we were able to pay off almost immediately. Thank God for the Christian radio program which invited you to air your knowledge and I thank Him for your willingness to share your valuable knowledge with the public. I will pray for your safety as you travel to tell others.

Please encourage listeners to go for it and for them to never underestimate their individual case. I prayed over both letters before mailing them to the IRS and put the matter in God's hands. It felt so great to have that burden off my shoulders and I thank you a million times for being instrumental in helping me be where I am today financially with IRS--debt free!!

Signed: Eileen - Texas

"Who shall separate us from the love of Christ? Shall tribulation, or distress, or persecution, or famine, or nakedness, or peril, or sword?* * *No, in all these things we are more than conquerors through him who loved us."

Romans 8:35, 37

CHAPTER TEN
The Collection
Statute of Limitations

Please go back to the end of chapter one and review Jon's letter. Jon's friend Gene was the direct beneficiary of the collection statute of limitations. That is the law capping the amount of time a debt is permitted to linger. When the collection statute of limitations expires, the IRS' right to collect dies with it.

Whether learning the details of the collection statute of limitations means as much to you as it did to Jon and his friend Gene, I do not know. I do know that countless citizens face grim prospects for their financial future due to unpaid tax bills which mount year after endless year. You may be surprised to learn that the enjoyment of your rights under the collection statute requires no formal letters or convoluted tax forms. In many cases, all it takes is the affirmative declaration that the statute has expired.

How the Collection Statute of Limitations Operates

The general rule establishing the collection limitation period is set forth in code section 6502. Section 6502 reads in pertinent part,

> Where the assessment of any tax imposed by this title has been made within the period of limitation properly applicable thereto, such tax may be collected by levy or by a proceeding in court, but only if the levy is made or the proceeding in court begun --
> 1) within 10 years after the assessment of the tax, or
> 2) prior to the expiration of any period for collection agreed upon in writing by the Secretary and the taxpayer before the expiration of such 10-year period.

Note that the IRS has at least ten years in which to collect taxes after making the assessment. The manner of achieving an assessment is described in chapter four under the heading, *What to Expect From Enforced Tax Collection.* The ten-year rule was established in November, 1990. Prior to that, the IRS had just six years from the date of assessment in which to collect.

The ten-year rule operates this way. For assessments made *after* November 5, 1990 (the date of enactment), the IRS has ten years in which to collect or commence a proceeding in court for collection (more on that later). For assessments made *on or before* November 5, 1990, the rule *extends* collection from six to ten years if the tax was collectible on November 5, 1990.

To illustrate this, suppose a tax was assessed against you on November 1, 1984. Assuming you did nothing to extend the statute of limitations, the collection statute expiration date (CSED) was November 1, 1990. On November 5, 1990, the day the act was passed extending the statute, your collection case was *closed* because six years expired. Therefore, the new law does not affect you.

On the other hand, suppose a tax was assessed against you on November 6, 1984. The six-year statute expired on November 6, 1990. However, at the time the new law was passed (November 5, 1990) your collection case was *open.* Therefore, the statute adds *another four years* to the time in which the IRS may collect.

How to Compute the Collection Statute Expiration Date

In dealing with any collection problem, the first order of business is to determine the CSED. Do this by referencing your Individual Master File (IMF). You obtain an IMF by making a written request under the Freedom of Information Act (FOIA) to the service center where you file your returns. Ask for the IMF for the year in question. Chapter three of *Taxpayers' Defense Manual* provides more details.

The IMF contains a transaction code (TC) showing the date of the assessment. Taxes assessed by filing a return are shown with a TC 150. If the IRS filed the return for you, the IMF makes reference to an SFR, then the assessment. Taxes assessed pursuant to an examination of your return or through other administrative action are shown with a TC 300. The six-digit number adjacent to the TC is the actual assessment date.

Tax liens state the assessment date on their face. See Exhibit 4-3, page 62 for an example. I like to cross-check this with master file data to ensure I have the exact CSED.

The next step is to count forward six years from the assessment date. If that date falls on or before November 5, 1990, and you did nothing to extend the limitations period (discussed below), the statute is expired. The IRS is no longer at liberty to collect. However, if by counting forward six years you are taken beyond November 5, 1990, your collection statute does not expire until ten years from the date of assessment. It may be longer if it were extended.

IMF printouts often show the collection statute expiration date in encrypted fashion. Look for the letters "CSED," followed by a six-digit number. The number is a date code. That is the date on which the statute expires.

It is always important to know when the statute of limitations expires to determine the appropriate course of action. This is evidenced by Jon's letter. Had Jon's friend Gene elected to come forward without knowing the statute expired, he could have paid taxes he had no longer owed. On the other hand, if he continued to run and hide, limiting his potential in the underground economy, he would have done himself and fellow citizens a great disservice. Instead, just by learning that the statute expired, Gene went from "rags to riches" in the carpet business.

Knowing the expiration date can save untold levels of hassle and hardship. This is best illustrated by the case of a lady with whom I talked some time ago. She explained that a revenue officer demanded that she sign IRS Form 900, Tax Collection Waiver. She wondered whether she was obligated to do so.

I asked her, "What is the expiration date of the statute?"

She did not know off hand, so I asked her to read from the tax lien she had in front of her, which she did. I then asked whether she previously signed a waiver or did anything else to extend the statute of limitations (see list below). She assured me she did nothing. I therefore concluded that the statute expired prior to the RO's request. As such, she was under no obligation to sign Form 900.

Upon further questioning, she explained that the demand to sign Form 900 came out of the blue. There was no other IRS action pending. A revenue officer simply appeared on the scene making demands and issuing threats if she refused. It was plain to me that the revenue officer attempted to coerce her into signing the form in a pathetic attempt to breathe life into an already dead collection case.

Of course, the RO did not explain that the statute was already dead. Nor did it matter that the law plainly holds Form 900 extends the CSED only if signed *prior* to the statute's expiration! He merely huffed and puffed, issuing demands with accompanying threats.

Obviously, somebody in the Collection Division, probably that very revenue officer, fell asleep at the switch and allowed the statute to expire. In an effort to rectify his own non-feasance, he attempted to browbeat a citizen into signing a waiver after the fact. Had the woman not known the case was closed, signing Form 900 would no doubt have been a perceived license to begin enforced collection.

Extending the Collection Statute

The CSED can be extended in a number of ways. You should know the conditions that extend the statute and avoid them if possible. We already discussed the congressional extension from six to ten years. Let us now examine other means by which the CSED is extended.

The Voluntary Extension

The most common way the collection statute is extended is by voluntary waiver. Form 900, Tax Collection Waiver, is used for this purpose. Form 900 is presented to the citizen when the circumstances make it plain the IRS cannot collect the full amount within the statutory collection period. An example is where the citizen negotiates a long-term installment agreement under which he makes a small monthly payment. A signed Form 900 is generally a prerequisite.

The first question one asks when presented with a Form 900 is, "Should I sign?" That question is sometimes difficult to answer but at times, the RO makes the decision easy. If you refuse to sign, he explains, the agency has no choice but to carry out enforcement action to maximize collection before the statute expires. In other words, if you do not sign, liens, levies and seizures surely follow in full force.

Still, one should never sign a Form 900 purely on the basis of statements and demands of an RO. As we saw from the above case study, their representations are not always factually pure. In one case, the RO presented the Form 900 saying, with all sincerity, "If you sign this form, you'll get extra time to pay if you need it." Sure.

Before signing, carefully consider all the facts and circumstances of your case. Most importantly, know your CSED. If the statute does not expire for several years, signing Form 900 probably does not hurt you. This is especially true if, after stabilizing the collection situation, you move right into using one of the amnesty programs. However, if the statute is to expire within a short period of time, it may be financially better to endure enforced collection than to extend the CSED.

Form 900 can be written as either an open-ended extension, with no set date for expiration or it can be a fixed date extension, set to expire on a specific date in the future. Under no circumstances can I imagine an open-ended extension benefiting the citizen.

The Offer in Compromise

The Offer in Compromise (OIC) is the means by which the citizen offers the IRS a lesser sum of money than is due in satisfaction of an outstanding liability. The offer process is the heart of the tax amnesty program and is discussed at great length in chapter twelve.

By signing Form 656, Offer in Compromise, you extend the CSED. It is tolled for the period of time the offer is pending, *plus one year*. Therefore, in determining when your collection statute expires, ascertain whether you *previously* filed an OIC. If so, add to the ten-year period the amount of time the offer was pending, plus one year.

Citizen Outside the United States

When a citizen is outside the United States for a continuous period of at least six months, the collection statute is tolled during his absence. Code section 6503(c).

Judicial Actions

Under some circumstances, judicial actions commenced by a citizen or the government can toll the collection statute of limitations. Three situations come to mind.

Bankruptcy. Section 6503 of the code provides that the period of limitations on collection is suspended during the period of time the IRS is precluded by law from making an assessment or collecting taxes, plus six months. Code section 6503(b) specifically states when the assets of the citizen are in the custody or under the control of a court, such as occurs when one files bankruptcy, the statute is tolled during such period, and for six months thereafter.

If you filed a bankruptcy any time during the collection process, the CSED is extended for a period equal to the time in which your case was pending in bankruptcy, plus six months after the case is closed. Naturally, those taxes which are discharged by the bankruptcy are no longer subject to collection regardless of the statute of limitations. That is another of the amnesty programs we address in chapters thirteen and fourteen.

Civil actions by the United States. Code section 6502 expressly provides that the normal ten-year period of limitation is extended if, prior to that time, the government commences a suit in court for collection of the tax. Such a suit is contemplated under Code section 7403. That section permits the government to sue the citizen to reduce its tax lien to a judgment. It also permits the IRS to seek judicial approval to execute that judgment against property owned by the citizen. Once a judgment is in place, it is good for whatever period governs civil judgments under state law.

If you are on the threshold of the statute expiring and the IRS asks for a signed Form 900, you must consider the chances of its filing a suit in court if you refuse to sign the form. Two considerations are critical. First, do you have any assets it could reach if it obtains a judgment? If you own a home with equity or a substantial retirement fund, chances are the IRS may file the suit. In that case, you may be better off to sign the Form 900 and attempt a settlement under one of the amnesty programs. If you have no assets, it is unlikely the IRS will pursue court action.

The second consideration is the amount of time before the statute in fact expires. If you are several months away from the actual expiration date, the agency may have time to consider its options and paste together a court action. Conversely, if the statute is weeks from expiring, it is unlikely the agency can move before its expiration.

Also take into consideration the cost of your actions. By that I mean, balance the cost of signing the form, measured in terms of the monthly payment the IRS might receive beyond the normal expiration period, against what it might get if it files suit.

The wrongful levy. A wrongful levy exists when the IRS seizes the property of one citizen in an effort to satisfy the tax liability of another. We have all heard of cases where the IRS seizes Junior's bank account because Dad owes taxes. That is a typical wrongful levy case.

Code section 6503(f) provides that the collection statute is tolled from the period of time beginning when the IRS receives the wrongfully levied property (including money) until the agency either returns the property or the citizen obtains a judgment against the IRS under code section 7426, the wrongful levy statute. However, this extension applies only to the portion of the assessment *equal to* the money or value of property returned by the IRS.

Application for Taxpayers' Assistance Order.

Submitting a Form 911 to the TA suspends the running of the collection statute of limitations. Code section 7811(d). The suspension is effective beginning with the date one submits Form 911 and continues to the date of the decision disposing of the application. *It does not matter* whether the TAO is granted or not. Also, the TA may specify additional time in which the statute is tolled.

You might have noticed that in chapter seven, I recommended sending a *letter* to the TA seeking help, *rather* than submitting Form

911. In addition to this process being faster, it *does not* toll the statute. If at any time you submitted Form 911, add to your collection statute the time it was pending.

Canceling Expired Assessments

If you believe the collection statute has expired, send a certified letter to the IRS' Special Procedures staff seeking abatement of the tax and release of the liens. The letter should follow the outline of IRS Publication 783, How to Apply for Certificate of Discharge of Federal Tax Lien. See Forms Kit and chapter six.

Point out that the collection statute of limitations has expired. Provide whatever proof you have, including lien documents and IMF printouts. Demand that IRS abate the outstanding tax liability. If any liens are in effect, they must be released once the tax is abated. See chapter six for details on removing liens.

Conclusion

You should never pay a dime to the IRS unless you are certain the statute of limitations has not expired. My experience proves time and again that the IRS lies or deliberately misleads citizens concerning this right. When you can prove the statute has expired, or can hold on until it does, you are *free, free, free* of the IRS' claim. What is that, if not amnesty?

Judy operates a professional tax service in south Texas. She worked with a client who received a bill from the Austin Service Center in the amount of $5,845. The bill, dated *April 3, 1991*, demanded payment of taxes for the year *1979*. The client could not understand how the IRS could legally chase her for an eleven-year old tax debt. As you might imagine, the IRS refused to breathe a word about the collection statute of limitations.

I worked with Judy suggesting ideas and procedures to force the issue on the statute. Judy followed up with the client. Then after several months, she wrote me this letter:

Dear Dan:

I called you recently to ask for your advice on a collection attempt by the IRS which appeared to be outside the statute of limitations period. I say "appeared" because my client and her husband had been divorced in 1981. My client never signed a return for the year in question but her ex-husband provided a copy to the court in the divorce proceedings and declared under oath that the return had been filed. Your advice to me was to assume the return was actually filed and demand proof that the IRS was within the statute of limitations period.

Interestingly, my client was writing to her congressman before she came to me, so the response letter went to him. Notice that your advice did two things:

1. Made the IRS admit to expiration of the collection statute of limitations; and

2. Revealed the date the statute actually expired.

So, this was a fun case and the client is delighted.

Signed: Judy - Texas

By doing nothing more than enforcing the statute of limitations, a citizen under attack walked cleanly away from a $5,845 tax debt which, because of her financial condition, she could not pay.

"Blessed is he whose transgression is forgiven, whose sin is covered. Blessed is the man to whom the Lord imputes no inequity, and in whose spirit there is no deceit."

Psalm 32:1-2

CHAPTER ELEVEN
Tax Amnesty Program Number One
--The Life Jacket

The purpose of a life jacket is to prevent disaster. It is certainly not the greatest thrill in the world to float freely in the deep blue sea but at least with a life jacket, you can hang on until a rescue ship arrives. In the context of the IRS, our life jacket is known as "uncollectible status."

Beginning with this chapter, drawing upon the delinquency profile provided in chapter two, I preface the discussion of each Tax Amnesty Program with a statement of who that program can most likely benefit. As you read chapter two, you know doubt identified with one or more categories of delinquent citizens. Now, expect to learn how your particular problem can be treated to tax amnesty.

Uncollectible Status
WHO CAN BENEFIT?

Anyone with so little disposable income or assets that any payment whatsoever is impossible. This person is either unemployed or under-employed and his personal living expenses meet or exceed his income. A gainfully employed person also benefits from uncollectible status if his fixed monthly living expenses for health and welfare items consume his income.

My good friend Pat is a seasoned tax attorney. While working together in a seminar, Pat and I answered tax collection questions for the public. One man announced that he owed the IRS $20,000. He explained he had no assets and was out of work. He wanted to know how he could solve his "tax problem." Pat's answer was inspired, articulating a principle I have acted on for years. He said, "You don't have a $20,000 tax problem unless you have $20,000."

In other words, unless you have something the IRS can take, you have no problem. I already proved in chapter three that you are not going to jail just because you owe the IRS. The reality is, unless you can pay, the IRS is powerless to do anything.

You are likely recoiling from this statement. Pointing to the agency's awesome enforcement power, you may suggest that while you do not have savings piled up, the IRS certainly has ready access to your paycheck or checking account, however modest they may be.

Despite the power to collect, a citizen is entitled to enjoy "uncollectible status" when his financial statement shows the inability to make payments. To illustrate, I point to Steve's case. Steve made payments to the IRS of about $260 per month for some time. He could not afford it, but he made them because he was told by an RO he must. In the meantime, Steve fell behind on other debts. His rent was late, all recreational activity was eliminated and he was living off credit cards.

Finally, Steve stopped paying the IRS. Within just a short period, it threatened a wage levy. That is when Steve phoned me. He lamented that he simply could not continue paying. His monthly income and personal living expenses were such that there just was no money available to meet his IRS obligation.

How to Achieve Uncollectible Status

I explained to Steve that the first move was to submit a Form 433-A. Form 433-A is the personal financial statement for individuals. See Forms Kit. I told him to pay close attention to Section V, which lists current monthly income and monthly living expenses. The difference between the two figures is "disposable income." That is "at least" the amount the IRS wants as a monthly installment payment. Details of how to figure disposable income are presented in chapter five.

In Steve's case, there was precious little difference between monthly income and living expenses. In fact, the difference was under $20. Steve presented the financial statement to the RO along with documents to verify expenses, including canceled checks, invoices, etc. We argued the maximum he was able to pay was less than $20.

After carefully reviewing the financial statement and the supporting documents, the RO explained it was not worth her time to write an installment agreement. She agreed to classify Steve as "uncollectible." Under that classification, Steve is required to make no monthly payment. At the same time, the wage levy was released and there exists no further risk of a levy as long as "uncollectible status" remains in effect.

The key to attaining uncollectible status is to painstakingly prepare the financial statement. Before beginning the process, go through your checkbook and record your expenses for the past twelve months on a separate sheet. This helps you recall all the expenses you face but which do not necessarily recur each month. An example is medical insurance. If, for example, you pay $600 in medical insurance quarterly, divide $600 by three to determine the monthly expense. Make an entry of $200 per month for medical insurance on Form 433-A. Repeat that process for each expense that constitutes an allowable expense for purposes of determining the installment agreement amount. Review chapter five, under the heading, *How to Establish the Installment Payment Amount.*

As a result of the National Standards (NS) and Local Standards (LS) for expenses, ROs look for ways to squeeze money into existence when it may seem to a reasonable person that none exists. For example, in finding you spend $500 per month on food for a family of six, the RO may demand that you cut the expense to $200 and pay the remaining $300 to the IRS. After all, "what do you need food for?"

One key to establishing uncollectible status remains to *document* all necessary personal living expenses and expenses necessary to earn income. As we learned in chapter five, expenses necessary to earn income *are not* subject to the IRS' arbitrary NS and LS figures. They not only must be allowed, but are somewhat subjective in that different people incur different expenses in the process of earning income.

Furthermore, what may be considered a reasonable expense in one situation may not be in another. For example, a person who rides the bus to work every day faces trouble arguing that his car is necessary to earn income. However, a copy machine service rep with the job of driving from office to office repairing copy machines certainly can argue that his auto is necessary to earn income. As such, it is not a personal expense subject to NS and LS limitations.

Another key is to push hard on the idea that NS and LS expenses are *guidelines*. As stated plainly by A. Zack, Chief, Collection Division, in St. Paul, Minnesota, they are merely "a guide and may be adjusted based on the circumstances of each individual case." Revenue Officers in the field do not like to accept this reality, but that is exactly what it is--*reality!* The IRS manual makes this clear, but even if you cannot trust my reading of the manual, the import of Zack's letter is *undeniable*. NS and LS guidelines are just that--guidelines.

Ask yourself, what are the cogent and compelling reasons why your circumstances take you outside the scope of IRS' standards? State your case clearly and document your claims to the fullest extent possible. If you argue a medical condition exists, provide a statement from the doctor, insurance company, etc., to support your claim.

Also keep in mind unreasonable demands for installment payments can be appealed using Form 9423, Collection Appeal Request. See chapter seven. Use caution, however, because the collection appeal process involves an agreement to be bound by the decision of Appeals. Note however, that such an appeal does not preclude the other options talked about in chapters twelve, thirteen and fourteen.

When your necessary and allowable living expenses and expenses necessary to earn income approximately meet or even exceed your monthly take-home pay, you are considered uncollectible. In Steve's case, the $20 per month the IRS would receive was not worth the effort to complete the paperwork.

Living with Uncollectible Status

Once classified as uncollectible, the IRS reviews the file periodically to determine whether to alter the status. There are two ways the review process occurs. The first is on a calendar basis. The IRS pulls the file every twelve or twenty-four months. It requests an updated 433-A and once more undertakes the process of determining an installment amount. If circumstances have not substantially changed, uncollectible status remains in effect. If there were changes, the installment agreement is fixed based upon current conditions.

The second method is based upon current income tax returns. The IRS reviews current tax returns to ascertain the level of income reported. When income exceeds a certain, predetermined level, a review takes place. The income level at which the review occurs is determined by the revenue officer based upon your financial statement. If, for example, you earn $26,000 per year but cannot afford a payment, the RO may decide to call for a review as soon as your income reaches $28,000.

Uncollectible status is the truest form of life jacket. It places you into a position where you can at least survive. If your financial picture does not improve, there is no reason the uncollectible status must change. Bear in mind the statute of limitations on collection eventually expires. If your circumstances never improve, the statute could expire without the IRS collecting. This is why you must be careful when signing Form 900 since it *extends* the CSED.

I worked out uncollectible status for a citizen in a case where the RO pointedly stated, "I have no illusions that this guy will ever pay a nickel of these taxes." In effect, he conceded the past due liability. He was insistent, however, the citizen absolutely not revert to the pattern of non-compliance that caused the delinquency in the first place. If he did, the RO's full collection wrath would be visited upon him.

I then worked hard to persuade the citizen that all quarterly tax payments must be made on time and all tax returns must be filed timely and accurately. See chapter eight, under the heading, *Get Off the Tax Debt Treadmill.* I also persuaded the RO that the citizen learned his lesson and backed up my statement by submitting the quarterly payments and tax returns to the RO personally.

Under uncollectible status, the liability remains in existence, but the citizen is not faced with levies. In fact, after negotiating uncollectible status, the RO released the seizure he executed against the citizen's home. Now he can at least survive, earn a living and have a place to lay his head. Beyond that, he will eventually be in a position to use one or more of the other amnesty techniques discussed in later chapters.

You should note that while deemed "uncollectible," tax liens remain in effect and penalties and interest continue to accrue. That is why this program is generally used in connection with others discussed later.

Conclusion

Uncollectible status can keep you afloat until help arrives. In fact, if you can wait out the collection statute of limitations, it can lift you out of the sea of financial disaster. In any event, it plays a fundamental role in winning forgiveness of tax debt. By winning uncollectible status, you take much of the risk out of dealing with the IRS. This is important because so often, simple fear keeps people from acting. Consider Bill's story:

> About two years ago on a dark, cold, winter night I was making the trip home from work drowning in my despair as I have since 1985 due to a serious federal tax debt that had my life handcuffed. It was then that I heard an obscure radio commercial for your book *Tax Amnesty*, which I ordered the next day.
>
> After reading your book cover to cover, I realized that you really had the solution to my tax problem and probably many other taxpayers.
>
> I proceeded on a mission to negotiate. Dan, I can't thank you enough for your motivational words and accurate assessments on dealing with the IRS. Your inexpensive book

has turned out to be the best investment I've ever made. A little over a week ago, I walked out of my local IRS office with lien releases for all of my back taxes. I was able to negotiate an $18,000 settlement for my $83,000 debt and I truly believe it was because of the confidence installed by you and your book! My wife and I are so happy to be able to return to a normal life without the burden of an insurmountable tax debt.

You truly are a savior to people like ourselves.

Signed: Bill - Maryland

"Comfort, comfort my people, says your God. Speak tenderly to Jerusalem, and cry to her that her warfare is ended, that her iniquity is pardoned"

Isaiah 40:1-2

CHAPTER TWELVE
Tax Amnesty Program Number Two
--Cents on the Dollar
The Offer in Compromise

Does the IRS ever agree to accept less than full payment of an outstanding debt? Yes! The procedure is known as the Offer in Compromise (OIC). Early in this book, I quoted a statement from former IRS Commissioner Peterson in which she remarks, "you can't get blood out of a turnip and if we're dealing with turnips, then we're better off cutting our losses and moving on." This was directed squarely at the IRS' Offer in Compromise policy.

In the past, the IRS was hesitant, *at best*, to discuss the process. In fact, at one time the manual instructed ROs to "consider" an OIC if the facts dictated but provided no directive to *discuss* the process. This accounts for the fact that so few people know of or use the right.

Thankfully, the IRS rewrote the book on OICs. Revenue officers are now expressly instructed to discuss "the possibility of an offer in compromise" with the citizen. The discussion is mandated when the financial statement (Forms 433-A or B) indicates "a tax liability cannot be realistically collected in full." See IRM, chapter 5700, 57(10)5.1.

More importantly, the manual reflects a "new attitude" which has led to the acceptance of far more offers. In 1991, of the millions of people suffering with tax collection problems, just 8,711 filed OICs. And of those, just 1,955 were accepted. That is barely a 22 percent acceptance rate. Those are *not* good odds.

However, with the IRS' change in attitude and the release of the first edition of this book in 1992, both the number of offers filed and those accepted exploded. By 1996, there were 60,893 OICs filed and 27,673 accepted. That acceptance ratio is in excess of 45 percent, more than double that of the 1991 rate.

Even more impressive is the rate of settlement of the actual tax. In 1991, the average settlement was about 26 cents on the dollar. Each year thereafter, the average has fallen steadily. In 1994, it was 17 cents on the dollar. And by 1996, it had fallen to just 13 cents on the dollar.

I believe this "new attitude" was at least partially forced upon the agency by citizens utilizing their rights in greater numbers than ever before. The IRS has no choice but to accept reality due to the various factors discussed in chapter one, especially *The Education Factor*.

We examined in chapter one the memorandum issued to revenue officers. It led the way to the formal Policy Statement covering OICs. Released in February, 1992, the statement knocked my socks off. In it, the IRS makes the following observation:

> The ultimate goal [of the OIC] is a compromise which is in the best interest of both the taxpayer and the Service. Acceptance of an adequate offer will also result in creating, for the taxpayer, an expectation of a *fresh start* toward compliance with all future filing and payment requirements. IRM 57(10)1.1; emphasis added.

In the past, the IRS expressed little concern with the "interest of the taxpayer." Nor did it care whether the citizen could ever look forward to a "fresh start." Instead, its sole concern was whether it could achieve "maximum collection with the least possible loss or cost to the government." Revenue officers were told plainly, "get all you can get."

Furthermore, I am particularly intrigued by the IRS' use of the phrase "fresh start." It rose from the page to hit me in the face because the entire premise of our *bankruptcy laws* is to provide a "fresh start" to those subsumed by debt.

What we see here is the manifestation of the fruit of my labor since 1988 in the area of taxes and bankruptcy. Since *How Anyone Can Negotiate with the IRS and Win!* was released in 1988, countless millions of dollars in federal income taxes, interest and penalties have been discharged in bankruptcy. There is no way to know how many lawyers and accountants were educated by that book and what that led to in terms of canceling tax debt.

I also know the book had a profound impact on how the IRS handles delinquent tax cases. Having read the IRS' new OIC policy statement and other pronouncements we examine later, I know the impact has extended to the highest levels of the IRS. More and more, citizens are resorting to bankruptcy to discharge their tax debts, a right the IRS lied about for over twenty-two years. The result is, the agency was forced to rewrite its offer policy in an effort to prevent the wholesale discharge of delinquent taxes.

Let us now explore the nature of an offer in compromise and the manner in which it operates to achieve forgiveness of tax debt.

Who Can Benefit from an Offer in Compromise?

Section 7122 of the code allows the IRS to "compromise" or reduce, any civil or criminal tax liability on two grounds. They are:

1. There exists doubt as to one's "liability" for the tax assessed; or
2. There exists doubt as to the government's ability to "collect" the tax assessed.

The beneficiary of this amnesty program is any person able to demonstrate that the *amount* of the assessment is improper or he is unable to *pay* the tax.

An offer in compromise based upon *doubt as to liability* helps any person who,

• Accepted an audit determination he knows to be incorrect but *never appealed* the decision;

• Was unable to file a Tax Court petition within the ninety-day grace period, thereby preventing judicial determination of his tax liability;

• Failed to file tax returns, but against whom the IRS determined a tax liability without considering his proper deductions, allowances, credits, etc. (i.e., the SFR);

• Is an innocent spouse and is left with unpaid tax bills attributable to her husband.

An offer in compromise based upon *doubt as to collectibility* helps any person whose assessed tax bills exceed their capacity to pay, considering equity in assets and ability to make an installment payment.

Submit the OIC on IRS Form 656. See the Forms Kit. When the offer is based upon doubt as to liability, provide detailed explanations and supporting documents to prove there exists doubt as to whether you indeed owe it. When the offer is based upon doubt as to collectibility, provide a full financial profile. Include a current financial statement (Forms 433-A and if necessary, 433-B). As we address each aspect of the offer, I describe the nature of the material needed to support it.

Special Conditions of the Offer in Compromise

The most important special condition to consider before submitting an offer is the fact that Form 656 extends the collection statute of limitations. The CSED is extended for the period of time the offer is pending (or the period during which installment payments are to be made under the offer if accepted), *plus one year.* Whether or not accepted, the extension operates for the period the offer is pending.

This waiver is profound. For this reason, take care to ascertain the CSED prior to submitting an offer. Do not risk submitting an offer if the collection statute is about to expire.

Next, when your offer is accepted, you must file your tax returns and pay all your taxes *on time* for the next five years. If you fail in this charge, your offer is reneged and the tax reinstated.

Do not allow the negative aspects of the OIC to color your judgment. Minimizing the effects of tolling the statute, for example, is merely a matter of timing. If the statute is to expire within an acceptable period of time, consider waiting it out. (See chapter ten.) If not, you generally do not prejudice yourself by filing the offer. The important thing is to be aware of what you are doing. Moreover, as I pointed out earlier, you cannot hope to fix your problem unless you get and stay current on your filings and payments anyway.

How To Submit an Offer in Compromise

In this section, we first discuss the offer to compromise a tax based upon doubt as to liability. Next, we discuss the offer based upon doubt as to collectibility.

Questioning Liability.

One example of a successful "liability" offer involves Gerry and his wife Judy, a couple who filed a petition in the United States Tax Court. Due to certain procedural failures on their part and because of submitting untenable legal positions, they lost the case. The court assessed both a sizable tax and imposed a penalty of $5,000 for maintaining a "frivolous" Tax Court. Code section 6673.

When the IRS began collection, Gerry and Judy *both* were presented with separate bills. Each bill was $5,000 above the tax determined by the court. The additional $5,000 purported to cover the penalty. The RO insisted it was assessed against *each person.*

We objected to the second $5,000 penalty. I maintained the Tax Court assessed just one penalty against both persons, not one penalty against each. In responding, the RO pointed only to the assessment certificate as her proof of two assessments.

We countered that code section 6673 permitted just one penalty per case. Despite my presentation, the RO would not budge.

To end the stand off, we filed an offer in compromise challenging the validity of the second $5,000 assessment. The offer was based upon doubt as to liability. To prove it was improper, we submitted a copy of the Tax Court's opinion and judgment as well as the statute. The language of the opinion and the statute clearly stated that just one $5,000 penalty was to be assessed. As such, Gerry and Judy would be separately responsible to pay a maximum of $2,500 each.

The IRS abated the second $5,000 penalty. The OIC saved Gerry and Judy not only $5,000, but the interest and additional penalties.

Earlier, I listed other specific circumstances in which an offer based upon liability may be beneficial. We submitted such an offer in an innocent spouse case. There, the wife faced huge tax assessments as a result of joint tax returns filed with her husband. For several years, their joint returns understated the husband's income. He earned income from his own business. His wife had no control over the business and she did not participate in any way. For more details on the innocent spouse defense, its elements and necessary proof, see chapter six.

The IRS commenced two cases against the couple. The first involved three tax years. Hal and Faye were represented by counsel who knew little about the IRS. As a direct result, Faye agreed to accept liability for her husband's failings. The ensuing assessment was staggering and there was no hope of paying it.

The second case involved two later but successive years. That is when I got involved. I was successful in proving Faye had nothing whatsoever to do with the business. Consequently, under the innocent spouse law (code section 6013(e)), she could not be held accountable for the tax. After several discussions with an Appeals Officer, Faye was completely absolved of any liability for those years.

An important consideration, however, is that the facts of the latter years were precisely the same as in the earlier years. If Faye were entitled to relief in the second case, she should be entitled to the same relief in the first case. However, Faye was stuck because of the agreement she signed. Or was she?

After finalizing the decision relative to the latter years, we submitted an offer in compromise based upon doubt as to liability with respect to the earlier years. We submitted the same documentation to support our claim as was submitted to the Appeals Officer. This, of course, is the key to success with any such offer. You must prove the existence of bona fide doubt about a question of law or fact addressing the merits of the liability. When you are able to prove the existence of such doubt, the IRS recognizes there is room for "mutual concession."

To increase the degree of doubt, present all definitive information available when making the offer. You must document your claim, either factually or legally, that the assessed liability is "incorrect." Provide proof as attachments to Form 656.

IRS generally does not accept vague or undefined claims of error in connection with an offer. Expect it to presume the assessment is correct. Your burden in a "liability" offer is to take it by the hand and prove otherwise.

Please note that such offers are generally rejected when the question of liability was already ruled upon by a court. The IRS looks at such a ruling as conclusive. Therefore, you must look to other avenues to win relief if the courts declared you owe the tax.

Also note that when you challenge an improper assessment because IRS failed to consider all deductions, allowances, exemptions and credits to which you are entitled, the matter is handled as a routine audit. At the point of filing the offer, the matter is handed to the Examination Division. A tax auditor is assigned to review your documents to determine your correct liability. When the examination is complete, a recommendation is made to the Collection Division.

Going into the examination, be sure to have all documents necessary to prove your correct tax. These include records pertaining to both your income and deductible expenses. Do not count on the ability to gather these records after the examination begins. Have a complete file *before* making the offer. For more information on the type of records needed, see chapter six, *IRS, Taxes and the Beast.*

Questioning Collectibility.

The second ground for an OIC is based upon doubt as to the "collectibility" of the tax. Offers accepted on this ground were once quite rare for a number of reasons. Not the least of these was the fact that ROs rarely ever discussed the OIC. Under the now policy, however, that has changed. Both these facts are evidenced by the OIC statistics mentioned above.

In the past, offers were rarely granted because the agency was loath to forgive a dime. It would rather chase the citizen for years in the hope of collecting the entire debt. As it turned out, most were never collected as citizens went underground to avoid enforcement action.

A major difference in the "new attitude" is reflected in the manual statement describing what constitutes an "adequate offer." Under the new guidelines, an offer is adequate if it "reasonably reflects collection potential." IRM 5700, 57(10)(10).1 (2-26-92). Collection potential is determined by figuring your equity in assets and the IRS' ability to collect from your future income. These elements are explained thoroughly below.

Determining asset values. In determining whether an offer "reasonably reflects collection potential," much attention is paid to asset values. Generally, the IRS expects one to pay at least the amount it could expect to realize through the forced sale of assets.

Problems arise in this area because what one person considers an asset's value is not necessarily the value ascribed by the IRS. Indeed, when the IRS is to sell an asset, it sets a criminally low value. Yet, when it considers the same asset in the context of an OIC, the value sails like a helium balloon.

Suppose your car is worth $10,000. If the IRS were to sell it at auction, expect it to capture just a fraction of its value, say $2,500. Yet, under an OIC, the IRS claims the vehicle is worth the full $10,000 and demands at least that amount to fund the offer.

Consequently, the citizen is trapped in a pincer movement. In the OIC, the IRS considers a person's ability to pay to be much greater than does the citizen. The difference is always due to the IRS' perceived value of your assets. As a result, the offer is rejected. In the same breath, it then seizes those very assets and sells them for *half the amount* it would have realized had it accepted the offer. Go figure.

Finesse in connection with a collection offer begins with understanding how the IRS values assets. Here I introduce you to three terms used in valuing assets. They are:

(1) "forced sale value"--the amount the IRS could obtain from a distraint sale of the asset. This is the *lowest* possible valuation;

(2) "fair market value"--the amount agreed upon between a willing buyer and a willing seller. This is the *highest* possible valuation; and

(3) "quick sale value"--a compromise between "forced sale value" and "fair market value." It is the *negotiated difference* between the highest and lowest valuation.

Each of these values plays a role in determining whether an offer "reasonably reflects collection potential." Note however, that quick sale value (QSV) shapes the IRS' thinking. Consider with me the following manual language:

The starting point in the consideration of an offer submitted based on doubt as to collectibility is the value of the taxpayer's assets less encumbrances which have priority over the federal tax lien. Ordinarily, the liquidating or quick sale value of assets should be used. Quick sale or liquidating value is the amount which would be realized from the sale of an asset in a situation where financial pressure causes the taxpayer to sell in a short period of time. *It should be recognized, however, that the acceptance of an offer serves the best interest of the government.* Therefore, it would not be unreasonable in a given case to use *forced sale value* in determining collection potential. Additionally, since valuations of property, except cash or cash equivalents, *are not* scientifically exact, care should be exercised to *avoid* inflexible, non-negotiable values. IRM 5700, 57(10)(10).1(2) (2-26-92) (emphasis added.)

The guidelines go on to declare that,

Rejection of an offer solely based upon narrow asset and income evaluations *should be avoided.* The Service should attempt to negotiate offer agreements which are in the best interest of *all parties.* Included in determining the government's interests are the costs of collection. If an offer is rejected because more can be collected than is offered, it is generally expected that the amount determined to be collectible *will actually be collected.* Ibid (emphasis added.)

Let us put this very important manual language into perspective. When OICs are rejected, it is almost always because the IRS believes it can collect more, either through forced sale of assets or through future earnings.

As we learn here, however, "inflexible" property valuations are not to stand in the way of reaching an acceptable offer. As a matter of fact, the manual goes on to say, "Because asset values are generally not carved in stone, offer examiners should remain flexible towards negotiating an offer that, considering all factors, would be in the government's best interests." Ibid.

Also note that the manual plainly admonishes offer examiners, declaring, in essence, "if you believe we can collect more money than is offered, then you better make sure we actually collect *more* money." Why the admonition? Because the agency is tired of chasing financial ghosts. ROs regularly demand more than is offered but never stop to think of where that money will come from. Stated another way, the

IRS recognizes the reality that a bird in the hand is worth (considering the costs of bureaucracy) about three-and-half in the bush.

Another important point is that IRS officers are instructed to negotiate the specific question of asset value. Such values are, after all, "not carved in stone."

There is yet another major element to the new procedures. The manual declares that, "it would not be unreasonable in a given case to use *forced sale value* in determining collection potential." Please recall that forced sale value is the *least amount* the IRS can expect to realize through sale of property.

Under the old manual, the IRS was absolutely forbidden to use forced sale value in compromise negotiations. The manual stated such a value did "not represent any concession" on the part of the citizen. Why not? Simply by seizing the assets, the agency can collect the amount offered.

How then does one capitalize on this information? Recognize plainly:

•   That asset values, the premise of all compromise discussions, are entirely negotiable and are "not carved in stone;"
•   That the *fair market value* of your assets *is not* the starting point for determining the amount of the offer. Rather, the starting point is *quick sale value;*
•   That any offer which serves the interests of all parties and affords a meaningful opportunity for a "fresh start" is an acceptable offer.

Asset value is not the only issue considered. The IRS also considers the citizen's "future earnings." In this respect, information about one's age, education, profession or trade, experience, health, past and present income is evaluated. I present more details on this later, under the heading, *How Much Should I Offer?*

The financial statement. Any offer based upon collectibility which does not present a financial statement is summarily rejected. The reason is the IRS must consider all assets which the citizens owns when deliberating the offer. Disclose assets on Forms 433-A and B. They include cash, securities, life insurance, pension and profit sharing plans, furniture, fixtures and personal effects, machinery, equipment, trucks and cars, inventory, receivables, business licenses, the value of an ongoing business and real estate.

Collection personnel evaluate assets to determine whether you presented an acceptable OIC. Generally, you are afforded an opportunity to meet with Collection to discuss your offer. Be prepared to discuss and negotiate asset values based upon the principles outlined above. Do not be afraid to use the manual language itself to communicate your points. Often, that is helpful to move an RO off an unreasonable negotiation position. More details on the negotiation process are presented later.

How Much Should I Offer?

The textbook answer is, offer an amount reflecting your maximum ability to pay, but which affords you an opportunity for a fresh start. Your OIC must offer the most amount the IRS can reasonably expect to collect in the shortest possible time. For more tangible guidance, let us examine the two elements that come into play when answering this question. The first is your equity in assets and the second is your current income. I address each in turn.

Equity in Assets. The starting point for valuing your offer is your equity in assets. Remember, for purposes of the OIC, equity is figured based upon the property's quick sale value (QSV), not fair market value (FMV). An offer presenting at least the QSV of assets is the foundation of an acceptable offer. However, the IRS may accept less than QSV. Therefore, a particularly desperate citizen could structure an offer based upon forced sale values. More on this later.

How to figure QSV. Let me illustrate the principle of quick sale value. Suppose you have a tax bill of $45,000 and your only asset is the family homestead. Its fair market value is $120,000. The home has a mortgage of $70,000. The mortgage pre-dates the tax assessment so it enjoys "priority" over the IRS' claim. The mortgage must be paid before the IRS realizes any proceeds from a forced sale. Your maximum equity, based upon fair market value, is $50,000 ($120,000 minus $70,000).

Because the mortgage ($70,000) must be paid before other creditors, the property must sell for more than $70,000 to benefit the IRS. However, it is unusual for IRS to sell assets for much more than mortgage value. It is not unusual to see property sell for just 25 percent or less of the owner's equity. That means the $120,000 home is sold for $82,500. And since $70,000 must be paid to the bank, the IRS is left with just $12,500 against the tax.

In our example, the citizen is not only left homeless, but faces a remaining balance in excess of $32,000. Obviously, the government's purpose of collecting revenue is not served. The sale collected just 27 percent of the debt and the citizen owns no other assets. The remainder of the debt is now largely uncollectible.

Following the above facts, the citizen could have offered the IRS a full 50 percent ($25,000) of his equity. If accepted, the IRS would have realized twice as much as it would under forced sale conditions. This would not only have saved the citizen $20,000 in taxes (the difference between the total owed and the amount offered), but most importantly, it would have saved his home!

Report asset values on Form 433-A (individuals) and 433-B (businesses). Be aware that neither form mentions QSV as the starting point for asset values. In fact, both forms ask for the "market value" of assets. Forms 433-A, Section IV, and 433-B, Section II (see Forms Kit). It is a *mistake* to use fair market value in these forms. QSV is the starting point for all asset values.

Virtually all IRS districts have established arbitrary methods of valuing assets. Most use a fixed 80 percent rule for QSV. That is, QSV is fixed at 80 percent of fair market value. For example, if your home would sell for $100,000 on the open market, its QSV is $80,000.

This practice of using hard asset values is expressly forbidden in the manual. The applicable language states, "Since valuations of property. . .are not scientifically exact, care should be exercised to avoid inflexible, non-negotiable values." IRM 57(10)(10).1(2). The only hard and fast rule expressed in the manual states, "QSV is defined as value greater than forced sale value with forced sale value defined as no less than 75 percent of fair market value." Ibid, (3).

Suppose your home has a fair market value of $100,000. For OIC purposes, the value may be set at somewhere between $75,000 and $100,000. Generally, QSV falls somewhere in the range of 75 to 80 percent of FMV. Suppose further your mortgage balance is $60,000. If the QSV is 75 percent of market value, this fixes your equity at $15,000 ($75,000 QSV minus $60,000 mortgage balance).

Other factors should be taken into consideration when determining QSV. First, what is the current market for the *type* of asset in question? A hotter market might indicate a slightly higher QSV, while a sluggish market points to a lower value.

The condition of the asset is also very important. An asset that is depreciated or run down fetches less in the marketplace than one in better condition. The cost of selling an asset also comes into play. In the case of real estate, costs include repairs necessary to bring the property up to code or salable condition, sales commissions, appraisal costs and the cost of necessary title work. All of these costs bring down QSV.

How to figure forced sale value. It is worth noting that the manual allows one to use the "minimum bid" price or forced sale value to establish equity in assets. The minimum bid is the value used by ROs in determining the amount to ask when selling seized property. It is generally the *lowest* of all property valuations. Minimum bid is ascertained using rules expressed in IRM 56(13)5.1.

The first step is to determine the property's fair market value. Apply a reduction not to exceed 25 percent to determine forced sale value. In our example of the $100,000 home, the forced sale value could be as low as $75,000. The precise percentile reduction from fair market value is determined based upon "past experience" or on a "case-by-case basis." There is no guideline carved in stone.

Upon ascertaining forced sale value, two further steps follow. First, reduce forced sale value by 20 percent, or less depending upon the facts of the case. Then, "reduce this figure by the verified balance due on prior encumbrances, if any, to arrive at minimum bid price." Ibid, (2).

The equation shapes up this way, using our $100,000 home with a bank note of $60,000. The starting point is fair market value of $100,000, less, up to 25 percent depending upon condition of property, market conditions, etc., to arrive at forced sale value of $75,000 ($100,000 minus 25 percent = $75,000). Next, reduce that figure by up to 20 percent based upon facts and circumstances. In this example: $75,000 x .80 equals $60,000. Now subtract verified prior encumbrances, such as balance of bank note, in this example $60,000. Result is minimum bid price or equity in property for OIC purposes. In this example, the equity works out to zero. See IRM 56(13)5.1 and 57(10)(10).1(3).

These two valuation alternatives give us much flexibility in determining the amount of an acceptable offer. The manual says "the range of alternatives from quick sale to forced sale to minimum bid are acceptable options." IRM 57(10)(10).1(3). While the IRS expresses willingness to accept forced sale value in special circumstances, it does not explain what those circumstances are. I have determined that forced sale value is probably acceptable in cases involving aged citizens, serious medical or other physical problems or those whose earning potential is seriously impaired for any other reason.

Use this process to figure your equity in all assets. Equity is then reflected as a total in line 30, Form 433-A and line 27, Form 433-B. A successful offer must present an amount at *least equal to* or greater than the equity shown in lines 30 and 27, respectively.

The impact of current income on collection potential. The second element to consider in determining ability to pay is your current income. According to the IRS' guidebook on the OIC, "If the taxpayer has the ability to enter into an installment agreement, the present value of the those payments will be considered as an asset." IRS Document No. 7917, *Highlights of the Offer in Compromise Program*, page 19. This is called the "future income" asset.

The value of the future income asset is based upon either (1) the time remaining on the collection statute of limitations or (2) five years, *which ever period is shorter.* Let me illustrate. Suppose you can pay the IRS $200 per month and your collection statute of limitations expires in thirty months. The projected value of the future income asset is therefore $6,000 ($200 per month x 30 months). The procedures for determining the collection statute of limitations are explained in chapter ten.

On the other hand, suppose your collection statute expires in seven years. Under that scenario, the installment payment is projected for just five years. Remember, the rule is sixty months or the time remaining on the statute, whichever is *shorter.* Therefore, the projected value of the future income asset is $12,000 ($200 per month x 60 months).

A successful offer must include the *present value* of the current income asset. We all know that money paid over time is worth less than the month paid today. The IRS also knows this and therefore reduces the projected value of the future income asset to its *present value.* The manual has this to say about valuing installment payments:

> In cases where it is determined that the taxpayer can make installment payments, the Service normally considers that any agreement that requires more than five years to complete has a high probability of not being completed. The Service must then determine the "present value" of those five years of payment. Manual section 57(10)(13).(11).

IRS determines "present value" by applying an interest rate factor to the time payments. It came up with a chart showing reductions in the projected value of the future income asset based upon interest rate assumptions. The higher the prevailing interest rate, the greater the reduction to arrive at present value. The chart provides a multiplier to use against the monthly installment amount to arrive at present value.

Exhibit 12-1 is a portion of the IRS' Present Value Table, reproduced below. It covers installment periods of between four and five years. Please locate the five-year level shown in the middle of the exhibit. Move to the right, locating the column for the seven percent interest rate. There you find the multiplier of 50.76. Let me illustrate how this operates. A five-year, $100 per month installment payment has a projected value of $6,000 ($100 x 60 months). However, its present value at seven percent interest is $5,076 ($100 x 50.76 months). This has the result of reducing the projected value of the installment payment by 15 percent.

The multiplier at eight percent interest is 49.64. Thus, at eight percent, a $100 per month five-year installment payment has a present value of $4,964 (100 x 49.64), a 17.3 percent reduction.

Exhibit 12-1

YEARS & MONTHS	12%	11%	10%	9%	8%	7%
4 YEARS	38.41	39.07	39.75	40.45	41.18	41.93
1	39.04	39.72	40.43	41.18	41.91	42.69
2	39.67	40.37	41.10	41.85	42.64	43.45
3	40.28	41.01	41.77	42.55	43.36	44.20
4	40.89	41.65	42.43	43.24	44.05	44.94
5	41.50	42.28	43.09	43.92	44.78	45.69
6	42.10	42.91	43.74	44.60	45.50	46.42
7	42.70	43.53	44.38	45.27	46.20	47.16
8	43.29	44.14	45.02	45.94	46.90	47.89
9	43.87	44.75	45.66	46.61	47.59	48.61
10	44.25	45.35	46.29	47.27	48.28	49.33
11	45.02	45.95	46.92	47.92	48.96	50.05
5 YEARS	45.59	46.54	47.54	48.57	49.64	50.76
1	46.15	47.13	48.15	49.22	50.32	51.47
2	46.71	47.72	48.77	49.86	50.99	52.18
3	47.26	48.29	49.37	50.49	51.66	52.88
4	47.80	48.87	49.97	51.12	52.32	53.57
5	48.35	49.44	50.57	51.75	52.98	54.27
6	48.88	50.00	51.16	52.37	53.64	54.96
7	49.41	50.56	51.75	52.99	54.29	55.64
8	49.94	51.11	52.33	53.61	54.94	56.32
9	50.46	51.66	52.91	54.21	55.58	57.00
10	50.98	52.20	53.48	54.82	56.22	57.67
11	51.49	52.74	54.05	55.42	56.85	58.34

PRESENT VALUE TABLE
INTEREST RATE

Present Value Table
Exhibit 5700-19 Cont. (2)
5700 Special Procedures
SM 3-92
Special Procedures
7509

This valuation process poses a substantial problem for a person with the ability to make a respectable monthly payment but who has no cash. Suppose for example you can pay $400 per month and have at least five years remaining on the collection statute. The projected value of the payment is $24,000. At seven percent, the present value is $20,304 ($400 x 50.76).

In order to present an acceptable OIC, you must offer at least $20,304, *plus* the QSV of equity in assets. Even if you own no other assets, $20,000 is a lot of money. If you are unable to borrow the money, it seems the prospect of settling through an OIC may be remote. To solve the problem, you must negotiate the future income asset.

Negotiating the future income asset. Negotiating the future income asset begins with understanding the manner of determining your ability to make payments. Too often, ROs make arbitrary determinations of one's ability to pay. This is done by hastily disallowing payments for necessary living expenses and using the often-harsh NS and LS expenses. On paper, this increases the funds available to pay the IRS. In turn, the projected value of an installment payment agreement increases.

The manual states that future income must not be determined arbitrarily. At section 57(10)(13).(10)(1), it states that "the issue is how much of the taxpayer's income is or will be *realistically available* to pay the delinquent taxes." (Emphasis added.) An arbitrary determination of your expenses certainly makes more money available *on paper*, but most such determinations are simply unrealistic and do not lead to increased collections.

Demanding an installment payment that leaves the citizen unable to pay necessary living expenses is *not* realistic. One of the reasons so many citizens face the need for tax amnesty is because the IRS forced them into a situation where exorbitant installment payments left them without the ability to provide for their families.

Another important consideration is that often, revenue officers jack up the installment payment at the expense of current income tax payments. A citizen must be allowed sufficient revenue to pay current taxes or he will never solve his problem. When negotiating an installment agreement, be sure there is adequate accommodation for payment of current taxes. For more on this, see chapter eight under the heading, *Get Off the Tax Debt Treadmill.*

So the first key to reducing the present income asset is to be sure to list every necessary living expense you incur. Take great pains to pore through your records to locate those expenses which might not readily present themselves. Be prepared to deal with NS and LS expenses and be sure to show your current taxes in these calculations. These procedures are explained in chapters five and eleven.

Ideally, you should achieve *uncollectible status* in your payment negotiations before making the OIC. When your living expenses meet or exceed your take-home pay, there is no money available to pay back taxes. Thus, there is no monthly installment payment. It follows that the present value of such an agreement is zero. That of course means an offer covering the QSV of any assets should be sufficient to settle your case.

If the present value of your installment agreement represents a substantial amount of money, the IRS has the authority to accept monthly payments over time in the context of the OIC. The key is to structure the offer properly. Here is an example.

Suppose the QSV of equity in your assets is $5,000. Suppose you can make a payment of $200 per month. The present value of that installment payment at seven percent is $10,152 ($200 x 50.76). An acceptable offer must present at least $15,152 ($5,000 + $10,152). An acceptable offer could present $5,000 in cash and $200 per month, beginning thirty days after the offer is accepted and continuing for five years.

Often, local IRS personnel state that installment payments on an OIC are not acceptable. They often state you must liquidate an offer with cash. That is just not true. What is true is that it is *best* to liquidate with cash when possible. It is true that the *best* hope of getting a deal is to liquidate in cash. But that is not the *only* hope.

IRM section 57(10)6.4 discusses the terms of payment. It states the offer should "be paid as quickly as possible." It describes a cash payment as one made "within 90 days of acceptance" of the OIC. However, it goes on to state that "a longer or shorter period of time may be acceptable" if the circumstances dictate and are documented in the case file. Furthermore, section 57(10)6.4(3)(1) expressly states that individual IRS regions or districts "*may not* establish a general rule to require payment within a specified period of time" (emphasis added).

If you propose to liquidate your offer over time, three things are important. First, you must clearly state the terms of the payment plan in your offer, showing (1) the amount of the payment, (2) the day of each month the payment will be made (i.e., mo/dy/yr), and (3) the duration of the payment terms (i.e., "twenty-four months, with the final payment made on or before mo/dy/yr"). Secondly, you must pay interest on the amount over the period of the payment terms. Interest is calculated on the compromised amount, not the original debt but is compounded daily on the unpaid balance. Third, in all events, the payment terms cannot exceed five years.

The IRS may oppose this offer, suggesting the payments do not present more than it could otherwise collect because it could collect the payments anyway. This, however, is not true if, in addition to the payments, you offer the QSV of your equity in the form of cash. By tendering the QSV of your equity, plus the payments over time, the IRS does indeed net more than it would otherwise collect. This is true because if it were to enforce collection against your assets, it would realize only forced sale proceeds, substantially less than quick sale proceeds.

Based on the above, the second element of a successful offer is to keep the installment payment as low as possible by proving the existence of personal living expenses, etc., which must be funded ahead of the IRS. The higher these expenses, the less that is available for an installment payment. Hence, the lower the value of the current income asset. Finally, the less that must be offered in settlement.

Another consideration bearing upon future income is the age of the citizen, his health and capacity to earn future income. An elderly citizen with poor prospects for future income sufficient to pay the tax weighs in favor of a low offer. A young citizen with little or no skills or one employed in a highly capricious industry such as construction, may stand a better chance of selling a low offer than would a corporate executive only temporarily out of work.

It is very important to communicate to the RO your good faith and sincere desire to resolve the situation. If the RO believes you are stalling or otherwise not attempting to negotiate in good faith, your offer could be summarily rejected. On the other hand, if the RO takes you seriously and works with you to prepare an acceptable offer, you achieve two very important goals. First, enforced collection action is postponed while the offer is pending. Secondly, the RO becomes somewhat of an ally working with you to have the offer accepted. For these reasons, the offer must be sufficiently high to avoid being perceived as "frivolous" and summarily rejected.

Other Factors Which Make a Successful OIC

There are several other factors that make a successful OIC which we examine here.

The bankruptcy factor. The well-crafted OIC must address the question of what is reasonably collectible in the shortest period of time. As such, the issue of whether the taxes you seek to compromise are dischargeable in bankruptcy becomes important. Among the arguments which may prove persuasive in convincing the IRS that the amount offered is all that is reasonably collectible is the fact that your tax bill is dischargeable in bankruptcy.

Of course, to make the argument plausible, you must be able to prove your assertion. I suggest a careful analysis of the facts surrounding the discharge issue to ascertain whether you can indeed achieve the goal. See chapters thirteen and fourteen for the discharge rules. Your offer may be quite attractive if the IRS believes a bankruptcy leaves them with less than your OIC would fetch.

This is an important factor when negotiating the future income component of your collection potential. For example, suppose the collection statute of limitations does not expire for six years. In that case, the IRS expects you to pay the present value of five years worth of installment payments. However, suppose your tax bill is ripe for discharge in bankruptcy in just three years. Under these circumstances, the IRS cannot reasonably expect five years worth of payments if you can discharge in bankruptcy after three years. This fact has the impact of *reducing* the duration of installment payments and hence, the present value of the future income asset.

The key in all of this is negotiation. The purpose of the offer in compromise is to provide the citizen an opportunity for a fresh start and to permit the IRS to collect as much as possible in the shortest period of time. All negotiations should be centered around this premise. If the agency demands large sums of money paid in cash merely because of the present value of an installment agreement, that may well defeat the purpose of the OIC program.

The IRM makes the following statement regarding bankruptcy and the OIC:

> In evaluating an offer from a taxpayer with dischargeable tax liabilities, where the taxpayer is actually threatening to file bankruptcy, *the amount of the offer may be negotiated.* IRM 57(10)(13).(12)11(4); emphasis added.

This is a remarkable statement coming from an agency which, just a few years ago, categorically denied taxes were even dischargeable in bankruptcy. In negotiating the offer, the IRS is called upon to weigh two conflicting factors. First is the extent to which a citizen may indeed discharge his taxes, taking into consideration that a tax lien remains in effect as to equity in assets and exempt property. See chapter thirteen. Second, is the fact that *"rarely would the Service be better off* in bankruptcy because the costs connected with filing and administration frequently absorb a large portion of the available assets." Ibid, (2); emphasis added. The manual section concludes by saying,

> It is within this framework that negotiations should be conducted. Acceptance of an offer in compromise from a taxpayer who is using the possibility of bankruptcy as leverage should be a calculated business decision, rather than capitulation. Ibid, (5).

There are two elements to consider when negotiating a reduction of your future income asset based upon the bankruptcy factor. The first is whether the tax is dischargeable at the time of filing the OIC. If so, the future income asset has a practical value of zero. If the IRS rejects an otherwise reasonable offer in an effort to force the issue on the future income asset, you have the right to pursue bankruptcy immediately and discharge the debt. That means the IRS cannot collect anything from the future income asset. Your offer must present an amount equal to what the IRS would otherwise get if you filed bankruptcy.

The second is where your case is not ripe for discharge at the time of making the offer. Suppose you must wait twenty-four months before you can discharge and you can pay $400 per month. The IRS calculates the future income asset at $400 per month for sixty months, or $24,000. However, the true value of the future income asset is $400 for twenty-four months, or $9,600, which is itself subject to a present value reduction depending upon prevailing interest rates.

Some time ago, I worked with an elderly lady who owed the IRS $40,000 for taxes dating back several years. She was contemplating bankruptcy but we decided to give the new offer in compromise procedures a try.

Vivian offered the IRS $5,000 to satisfy the debt. She explained to the RO she would have to borrow the money from her son. As a result, she had nothing the IRS could collect. In response, the RO reported that there was good news and bad news. The good news was the offer was accepted. The bad news was the IRS wanted $8,500, not $5,000. Vivian phoned me asked what to do.

I asked a question to which I knew the answer. "Vivian," I said, "do you have $8,500 to give them?"

"No," she replied without hesitation.

I then instructed her to phone the RO and explain that $5,000 was all she could come up with. I instructed her to explain that if the IRS rejected the offer, she would have no choice but to file bankruptcy. If she did, the agency would get *nothing* since even the $5,000 was borrowed money. In other words, Vivian said, $5,000 is all there is. Take it or leave it. If you leave it, you get nothing. After politely relaying the message, Vivian hung up the phone.

The RO called her back less than three hours later. "It's a deal," she said. "When can you get us the money?"

The bottom line is a dischargeable tax liability forces the IRS to the table. It forces the agency to make intelligent decisions based upon reality and not fantasize about collecting taxes from non-existent revenue sources. Chapters thirteen and fourteen discuss the bankruptcy rules in detail. You must understand them before negotiating based upon the bankruptcy factor.

The "public policy" factor. The IRS has expressed a clear desire to utilize the offer process as a means to accomplish more than just collecting revenue. Certainly that is the heart of the process, but it goes beyond that. A successful offer incorporates these policy issues. By doing so, you allow the IRS to conclude that acceptance of your offer is consistent with the IRS' overall attitude. The following issues are considered the public policy aspects of the OIC program.

OIC promotes voluntary compliance. The IRS has finally recognized that squeezing one for funds only makes matters worse. Furthermore, under even the best of circumstances, heavy handed collection creates a pattern of delinquencies even if it does not drive one into hiding. The IRS has observed that through the offer process, it can encourage a citizen to file future tax returns and pay future taxes in a timely manner. This has the effect of "rehabilitating" the delinquent citizen, affording him a fresh start.

In a written explanation attached to Form 656, make a point to emphasize that acceptance of the offer *ends all delinquencies*. Point out that at the time of filing the OIC, you are current with tax return filings and payments and will not fall behind in the future. Affirmatively accept the requirement set out in Form 656 (see Forms Kit) that you timely file future returns and pay future taxes when due. A successful OIC must illustrate how acceptance "rehabilitates" you and leads to future return filings and tax payments, thus having a positive impact on voluntary compliance.

OIC resolves the case. The IRS has plainly expressed the desire to use the OIC program as an alternative to reporting cases as "currently not collectible" or to a protracted installment agreement. IRS Document 7917, page 2 and National Office Memo, Exhibit 1-1, page 14. Too often, such agreements do not even pay accumulating interest and penalties. Such agreements generally only make matters worse for both the IRS and the citizen.

In one successful OIC, Richard explained that on three previous occasions dating back many years, his file was closed as "uncollectible." So, while Richard was asked to pay nothing, the interest and penalties continued to climb, putting the bill further out of reach each day. Richard's offer of $5,000 against a $114,000 debt presented a viable alternative to once again putting the matter on the back burner. The IRS accepted it without question.

Therefore, a successful offer presents an alternative to uncollectible status or protracted installment payments that do not even pay penalties and interest. The former means no revenue for the IRS and the latter means the bill only gets larger and the citizen is likely to become delinquent in the future.

OIC provides revenue IRS cannot otherwise reach. Both Vivian and Richard offered $5,000 to settle their accounts. With letters attached to the offer documents, they pointed out that the money was coming through a loan from third parties. In his written explanation, Richard emphasized that if the offer was rejected, the funds would simply not be available to the IRS. The agency certainly has no right to levy his son's money. The letter explained the funds would be made available within forty-eight hours of the IRS accepting the offer but only if payment constituted full and complete settlement.

Therefore, another key to a successful offer is to fund as much of it as possible with revenue from an outside source. Such revenue cannot be attached by the IRS should it refuse the offer. This provides strong encouragement to accept the OIC.

IRS' duty under OIC policy. The IRS' policy under the OIC program states, in part, "The success of the compromise program will be assured only if taxpayers make adequate compromise proposals consistent with their ability to pay and the IRS makes *prompt and reasonable decisions*." IRM 57(10)1.1 (emphasis added).

Richard affirmatively stated in writing that the offer was his best, good faith effort to resolve an otherwise unmanageable tax debt. He offered an amount that represented his ability to pay. He tenderly reminded the IRS in his written statement that rejection of the offer would be contrary to the policy mandate that IRS make "reasonable decisions" in these matters.

Therefore, another element of a successful offer is to remind the IRS that the OIC policy cannot be carried out successfully if offers are rejected arbitrarily or without reasonable foundation.

The Document Submission Package

By now you have guessed that a successful OIC presents much more than just Forms 656 and 433-A. I recommend an impressive package to present all the above ideas in a logical and organized fashion. The package consists of,

1. Form 656--Offer in Compromise (latest version) prepared consistent with the instructions on the form;

2. Form 433-A--Collection Information Statement (Form 433-B is required if self-employed) prepared as discussed above and in chapters five and eleven. When making an offer based upon doubt as to liability (as opposed to collectibility), you do not have to submit financial statements;

3. Written explanation of OIC--provided as an adjunct to Form 656 describing in detail the reasons why the OIC should be accepted. The explanation should encompass all the points outlined above and argue for acceptance of the offer. Explain clearly why the IRS cannot collect more than your offer. In the case of offers based upon doubt as to liability, attach all documents needed to verify your claim that you do not owe the amount assessed;

4. Individual Master File for years in question--especially important to show that required rules are met for discharge of taxes in bankruptcy;

5. Copies of relevant tax liens--to aid IRS research and make release of liens more prompt when OIC is accepted; and

6. Letter to IRS from person agreeing to make loan to fund offer upon acceptance. Letter should state that loan will not be made if OIC is rejected.

As you analyze your situation, do not be afraid to provide such additional documentation you feel necessary and desirable to establish the elements of a successful offer.

Securing Future Income

A major aspect of prior offer in compromise rules required the citizen to submit a collateral agreement before IRS accepted the OIC. A collateral agreement is an agreement to pay a percentage of future income in exchange for a concession of the outstanding tax balance. The form used to accomplish this is Form 2261.

The old manual language stated, "In return for this abatement [upon acceptance of the offer], it is reasonable to expect that the taxpayer will agree to pay additional sums from future income . . ." In other words, even though your offer was accepted, the debt was not fully forgiven because you were expected to commit a certain amount of future earnings to the IRS.

Under new procedures, the IRS trashed the requirement for a collateral agreement. The new language reads:

> Collateral agreements should *not be routinely secured* but secured only when a significant recovery can reasonably be expected. For example, a future income collateral agreement would be appropriate where it is reasonably expected that the taxpayer will be receiving a substantial increase in real income. A collateral agreement *would not* be entered merely on unfounded speculation about real increase in income.* * **Securing a collateral agreement should be the exception and not the rule.* IRM 5700, 57(10)(15).1(2) (2-26-92); (emphasis added).

This language evidences the true spirit of amnesty, or forgiveness. After all, if the IRS is willing to accept the offer, it should not do so with strings attached.

Deposits Submitted with the Offer

While it is not required, the recognized practice is to submit a deposit against the amount offered. For example, an offer to pay $10,000 may be accompanied by $1,000, or a ten percent deposit. This demonstrates good faith and your sincerity in making the offer.

If the offer is rejected, the IRS is required to refund the deposit in the absence of an agreement to apply it to the tax.

A Processable Offer in Compromise

Unless your offer is in *processable* form, it is summarily rejected. It is not processable if,

1. It does not identify the citizen;
2. It does not list the tax years, type of tax and total due;
3. The amount offered and the terms of payment are not clear;
4. Form 656 is not signed;

5. A financial statement is not provided, unless the OIC is based upon doubt as to liability;

6. The amount offered does not equal or exceed equity in assets as shown in your financial statements, Forms 433-A and B; or

7. You use an obsolete Form 656.

When the Answer is "NO"

If your offer is rejected, you may appeal to the Appeals Office. The procedure is to submit a written protest letter within thirty days of the IRS' rejection letter. IRS Publication 5 (see Forms Kit) explains how to draft a protest letter. The protest must be in writing and submitted on time. While the letter must set forth seven elements, two are vital. You must explain what part of the decision you disagree with and why it is incorrect. See Publication 5 for details. Also, *IRS, Taxes and the Beast* has much on the appeals process and negotiating with Appeals Officers. Address your letter to the Chief of Appeals for your district and send it via certified mail, return receipt requested.

The appeals process affords you the right to present your arguments to a fresh face. The Appeals Office is far more reasonable than other IRS divisions. In fact, while other divisions principally *cause* problems, it is the Appeals Office that *solves* them.

Conclusion

The offer in compromise is the epitome of amnesty in the administrative context. While the IRS is reluctant to publicize this procedure, those who use it properly often meet with great success. Since my first treatise on the offer process was published in 1988, times have changed incredibly. With the guidance provided in this chapter, tens of thousands of citizens nationwide have profited immeasurably from the OIC.

What you have just read is, without a doubt, the most thorough analysis of the offer process ever written to the general public. It may be the most thorough analysis available anywhere. After reading this, you are better equipped than most tax professionals to handle the OIC. Following these procedures, you can achieve tax amnesty and set yourself free of oppressive debt.

Sherry and Rich fell into a non-filing pattern for several years after Rich lost his job. With interest and penalties building, the IRS debt soared to over $126,000. Sherry grew increasingly despondent as she struggled to deal with the RO. In their regular meetings, she cried out for help and guidance and the RO responded simply by saying, "Pay it, you have no other choice." It got to the point where he threatened to seize their home, which would have left their children homeless. Sherry said she become so depressed, she was prepared to "blow up the house--with myself in it!"

Then Sherry heard me on the radio talking about tax amnesty. She got the book and followed the OIC procedures to offer $15,000 in settlement of the debt. When it was over, she wrote me saying,

> On March 12, 1996, we received in the mail the letter of acceptance of our Offer. We are going to pay $15,000 and we are told that the liens will be released as soon as we do. I think that the total debt at this point is well over $130,000. It was $126,000 in March, 1996.
>
> Thank you Dan Pilla for your work. I would like to encourage those who feel hopeless. This has been a learning process for us in many ways, but our weight has been lifted. We PRAISE THE LORD!
> Signed: Sherry - Texas

"And do not seek what you are to eat and what you are to drink, nor be of anxious mind. For all the nations of the world seek these things; and your Father knows that you need them. Instead, seek his kingdom, and these things shall be yours as well."

Luke 12:29-31

CHAPTER THIRTEEN
Tax Amnesty Program Number Three
--Wage-Earner's Repayment Plan

At the beginning of this treatise, I offered to prove there is no such thing as a hopeless tax case. I hope by now you have concluded that there are many more opportunities to manage your problems than you realized. But there is more. The programs discussed in chapters thirteen and fourteen are the essence of the "fresh start" principle. They are intended for those whose debts are so far beyond reach, there seems no way of living a normal life. They are designed for those unable to find relief due to unreasonable IRS demands or unrelenting collection action.

Though others have tasted success with the programs previously discussed, there is no absolute guarantee of success in every case. The success or failure of a given technique depends, in large part, upon the facts of each case. However, for those unsuccessful, there is an important alternative that for many years, was relatively unknown.

At the time of this writing, nearly 15 percent of our working population suffers from some form of tax collection ill. At the end of 1997, there were approximately 13.5 million citizens with delinquent tax accounts. In addition, the IRS estimates as many as seven to ten million have stopped filing altogether. Each year, about three million more are added to these roles.

As citizens sink deeper into tax debt, many turn to public support for their daily bread. Worse, they run for cover in the underground economy. This places dangerously negative pressure on public programs and disrupts the private economy. Because of that, it is time to welcome home those lost in debt, for their loss is our loss.

The loss we suffer goes well beyond the fact of their inability to be productive elements of society. It must also be measured in human terms. These millions of citizens are unable to earn a living in many cases. They cannot provide for their families. They are desperate and usually without hope.

Brenda, for example, a housewife, was stuck by her ex-husband with *$1.5 million* in tax debts that grew out of *his* illegal business. All Brenda had to show for her years of marriage was the debt and three children. With an $18,000 per-year job, how do you suppose she fixed her chances of ever living a normal life?

Jack was a retired fireman. Lost in a pattern of non-filing, he faced tax assessments far beyond what he could pay, even if he lived to be ninety-five. The IRS began seizing his pension, leaving him just $325 per month. Even if Jack went back to work, there was no hope of paying the tax.

Don was a truck driver. He was persuaded to invest a small sum in a tax shelter program he was assured was perfectly legal. In 1983 and 1984, Don's investment saved him a few thousand in taxes. But by the time the IRS' attack and ensuing litigation ended unfavorably many years later, he faced over $57,000 in tax assessments. Don's hope of resolving the problem ended when the levies began.

Marilyn was a victim of her husband's passion. Mike was an adamant tax protester and persuaded Marilyn that she too should carry the banner. The eventual assessments against Mike drove him underground and he was unable to support his family. The strain of the continual hiding, the financial strain caused by living hand-to-mouth (and other unknown elements) led to a divorce. After the split, Marilyn stepped forward to reverse a stance that she was never comfortable with from the start. The IRS, however, was more interested in wringing a pound of flesh from a former tax protester. Suddenly, Marilyn faced tax assessments in excess of $35,000. On a teacher's salary, what do you suppose her confidence level was that the debt would ever be paid?

The most tragic of all our losses occurs when those trapped in debt abandon all hope, then turn their desperation and depression inward. The most famous story is that of Alex Council, the North Carolina resident who committed suicide so his wife could collect the insurance money to resolve their IRS problem. But the IRS seized the insurance proceeds. In Houston, a young couple shot themselves on the front lawn of their home as IRS sold it to the highest bidder. In Orlando, a fourteen-year-old shot himself as a result of depression caused by the IRS' unmerciful, five-year pursuit of his parents over fabricated tax debts. In Phoenix, a man exploded his home just prior to being evicted by the IRS. He was inside at the time. He committed suicide over a $15,000 tax bill.

Common sense and sound judgment dictate that in the United States of America, there must be some way to avoid this kind of suffering, hopelessness and tragedy. Take heart--there is.

As you read the next two chapters, think of these programs as the end of the journey. While you may have been wandering in the wilderness of debt for years, you may now return home to satisfy your hunger. These programs offer the means by which you may cross the river into the promised land of financial liberty, *free at last* from the oppression of unyielding tax debt. To those of you who hunger and thirst for liberty, I say, welcome home!

Who Can Benefit from the Wage-earner's Repayment Plan?

Any person with *steady monthly income* may benefit from this program. To optimize success with this program, one should have sufficient income after paying all monthly living expenses (*without* regard to the IRS debt) to enable payment of a "dividend" to the IRS. The overriding potential benefits of this program are:

- Reduce or eliminate prior penalty assessments;
- Reduce or eliminate further accumulation of penalties;
- Eliminate further accumulation of interest;
- Reduce or eliminate sufficiently aged tax debts, including penalties and interest, which cannot be repaid.

The wage-earner's repayment plan is administered by the Federal Bankruptcy Court. It is commonly referred to as a Chapter 13 repayment plan. Under Chapter 13 of the Bankruptcy Code (Title 11, United States Code), a person with regular income and debts within certain limits may propose a repayment plan to creditors, including the IRS. A properly drafted plan accomplishes the four points just mentioned.

Please Note: Unless otherwise indicated, all references to "the code" in chapters thirteen and fourteen of this work are to the United States Bankruptcy Code (Title 11, United States Code). Where reference is made to the tax code, such distinction is clearly indicated.

Common Concerns About Filing Bankruptcy

For most citizens, the "B" word is a horrible prospect. It represents many things, not the least of which is embarrassment, failure and abandonment of financial responsibilities. While the feelings are certainly legitimate, the truth is, the perceptions are not. Let me address those concerns.

"Bankruptcy is a Way of Cheating"

The ability to discharge lingering, unmanageable debt in bankruptcy is a right protected by the United States Constitution. Article I, sec. 8, clause 4. It is no more legally or morally correct to suggest one is a "cheater" simply because he filed bankruptcy than it is to suggest he is an anarchist by voting to unseat an incumbent president. The rights and protections expressed in the Constitution were not placed there by our wise and divinely guided forefathers for the benefit of criminals, cheaters or malcontents. They are intended to ensure the continued political and *economic freedom* of all citizens, rich or poor. Continual, unmanageable debt is one of the oppressive conditions from which we were set free.

The first bankruptcy law in the Unites States was passed in 1800. It was patterned after the English law which dated to the time of Henry VIII. For the first time, however, the United States' law extended protection to debtors and expanded their rights substantially. In England, bankruptcy statutes functioned primarily to the benefit of creditors. However, drawing upon the insight and wisdom of the great English jurist William Blackstone, our founding fathers broadened bankruptcy to benefit debtors as well.

At the behest of Blackstone, the bankruptcy process was established as a means of humanely resolving creditor/debtor relations. Principally, it was offered as an alternative to "jail-for-debt," a practice regularly utilized in eighteenth century Europe.

Beginning with the act of 1841, rehabilitation of the debtor was an object of increasing concern to Congress. With that legislation, the idea of a voluntary petition filed by the debtor himself was introduced into our society. The concept of debtor rehabilitation is now embodied in the phrase, "fresh start." It is the promise of a fresh start that drives most citizens to bankruptcy, not the desire to "cheat" creditors.

We all recognize that those lost in debt are of no real service to society. This is particularly true when such debt is so debilitating it drives the citizen underground. Now he is not only in debt, but unproductive to himself, his family and society. Not only does he fail to pay his back taxes, but he fails to pay current taxes as well.

"Filing Bankruptcy will Ruin My Credit"

This common sentiment is worthy of some attention. Certainly, the fact of filing bankruptcy follows a person for some time afterward.

Without question, it impacts his "credit worthiness." One man I spoke with about bankruptcy voiced a strong objection on this ground. He owed thousands to the IRS and it was threatening to levy his paycheck.

I asked him several questions.

"Sir, how much do you presently owe the IRS?" He indicated the total was in excess of $40,000.

"Can you pay the bill?" I asked.

"Not a chance," he said, as I expected.

"Can you get a loan to pay?" I inquired.

"No way," he chirped.

Though I knew the answer, I asked my next question anyway. "Why not?"

He explained the tax lien scared all banks away from lending to him. "As soon as they discover the tax lien," he said, "they run."

"Let me put this all into perspective," I said. "You owe the IRS $40,000 you cannot possibly pay. The tax lien prevents you from getting any kind of loan to pay it. Because of interest and penalties, you can make monthly payments for the rest of your life and owe more when you're dead than you do now. And to top it off, the IRS is presently on your doorstep threatening to levy and seize everything you own. Is that about right?"

"It sure is," he moaned.

Then I said, "I have just one more question, what *credit* are you talking about!?" He slowly nodded his head in agreement.

The cold reality is, by the time you reach this stage, IRS has long since settled any questions about the viability of your credit. The answer is, *you have no credit a bankruptcy can ruin!* You must recognize that the IRS does far more to ruin your credit and your life than any bankruptcy *will ever do.* Furthermore, the negative effects of the IRS' actions potentially linger much longer than those of a bankruptcy. This is especially true if you signed a Form 900, Tax Collection Waiver.

However convenient a line of credit may be, face the facts. The lack of it cannot destroy you. On the other hand, the IRS' actions--actual and potential--*can destroy you*--and not just financially!

"I will Lose Everything in Bankruptcy"

In the first place, if you do not seek the protection of the bankruptcy court in the appropriate circumstances, be assured the IRS will see to it that you do "lose everything." The true hardship occurs when the IRS sells your property for a fraction of its value, then leaves you with a remaining, unpaid debt. Not only are you dispossessed of your assets, you are faced with a huge tax bill and no way to pay!

Secondly, both Congress and the various state legislatures have passed "exemption" statutes permitting a debtor in bankruptcy to retain certain assets. The exemptions vary widely from state to state but all generally permit a debtor to retain his personal belongings such as clothing, furniture, an automobile (within a certain value), tools and equipment necessary to earn a living (within a certain value) and other property.

One is generally *not* "wiped out" and left as poor as a church mouse when bankruptcy is complete. In a Chapter 13, depending upon the facts of the case and in light of the manner in which the program operates, one need not lose *anything* to emerge free of IRS debt.

"But I Thought Taxes Were Not Discharged in Bankruptcy!"

The best kept legal secret in the country is that federal income taxes are dischargeable in bankruptcy. Not only are they dischargeable, *they have been since 1966!* In 1966, Congress passed the Bankruptcy Reform Act, Public Law 89-496. One purpose was to "make dischargeable in bankruptcy debts for taxes." U.S. Code Congressional and Administrative News, Vol. 2, page 2468 (May 12, 1966).

Because we have all been told that federal income taxes are not discharged in bankruptcy, you may still be questioning the validity of this startling revelation. Justifiably so, because there was a time when this was true. However, after a congressional investigation in 1966, *the law was changed.* Senate Report No. 1158 accompanying Public Law 89-496 points out that Congress discovered two specific problems created by the fact that taxes were, at the time, non-dischargeable. The first problem was,

> Frequently, the [non-dischargeability] prevents an honest but financially unfortunate debtor from making a fresh start unburdened by what may be an overwhelming liability for accumulated taxes. The large proportion of individual and commercial income now consumed by various taxes makes the problem especially acute. [Keep in mind, this was written in 1966.] Furthermore, the non-dischargeability feature of the law operates in a manner which is unfairly discriminatory against the private individual or the unincorporated small businessman. Although a corporation is theoretically not discharged, the corporation normally ceases to exist upon bankruptcy and unsatisfied taxes, as well as other unsatisfied claims, are without recourse even though the enterprise

may continue to operate in a new corporate form. Ibid, Vol. 2, page 2471.

The second problem involved the fact that federal taxes were given a "priority" over other debts. That is to say, taxes were always the *first* debts paid with assets obtained from the debtor. Many times, this left precious little or nothing for other creditors. Congress observed,

> The result has frequently been that tax collectors, assured of a prior claim on the assets of a failing debtor and assured of the non-dischargeability of uncollectible tax claims, *have allowed taxes to accumulate and remain unpaid for long periods of time.* With the proliferation of new taxes and the increased rates of old taxes, often nothing is left for distribution to general creditors who provided goods and services to the bankrupt." Ibid; emphasis added.

If this problem were bad enough to require congressional action in *1966*, imagine the breath and scope of the problem today. Tax, penalty and interest rates are head and shoulders above the levels of that time. What has not changed, however, is the fact that most IRS employees continue to hold to the notion that taxes are not dischargeable. Consequently, we continue to see citizens suffer through collection problems they simply do not have to endure.

Journalists at every level add to the confusion by publishing reports propagating the lie. I have seen them in major, respected journals such as *Money Magazine, Woman's Day, Kiplinger's Personal Finance Magazine* and a host of daily newspapers throughout the country.

The ignorance reaches to the highest levels of expertise within the bankruptcy community itself. Some time ago, *Money Magazine* published a story claiming taxes were not dischargeable. After seeing it, one of my newsletter subscribers sent the reporter a copy of *How Anyone Can Negotiate with the IRS and Win!* and several of my newsletters on the subject. That book was the first place anyone disclosed the fact that taxes are dischargeable and how to do it.

The reporter read the material with much interest, then phoned me. He asked many questions and I gave him chapter and verse to support my answers. During the conversation, I stated, "There is not one lawyer in a thousand who knows this can be done." He responded by saying, "I know. I called all the major bankruptcy law firms in Manhattan. They all said you could not discharge taxes in bankruptcy." Despite my information, the editors at *Money* chose not to tell the truth about discharging taxes in bankruptcy.

Perhaps the reason for the widespread ignorance is that bankruptcy experts do not often concern themselves with tax laws and tax experts generally do not get involved with bankruptcy matters. A more likely explanation is that the IRS has published the false information for so long, very few bother to question it.

The Internal Revenue Service has a publication discussing the topic. It is Publication 908, Taxes and Bankruptcy. It is woefully deficient in its explanation of the laws and the rules under which one may discharge tax debts. On page two of the *1982* edition, under the heading "Discharge of Unpaid Taxes," the document read, "As a general rule, there is no discharge for an individual debtor at the termination of the bankruptcy case for any prepetition (those existing prior to filing bankruptcy) taxes."

This explanation clearly leaves the impression that tax liabilities are simply not discharged. Moreover, questioning most IRS employees usually leads to the same conclusion. While writing this book, I phoned IRS Taxpayer Assistance as I sometimes do when I need a laugh. I asked the "expert" whether unpaid taxes could be discharged.

"Absolutely not," she declared without hesitation.

"Not under any circumstances whatsoever?," I probed.

"Positively not," she reassured me.

After asking the same question using different words, she replied, "Taxes are absolutely, positively, definitely, metaphysically [whatever that means] not discharged in bankruptcy."

She went on to give me some advice. She explained that I should contact a bankruptcy lawyer because "the bankruptcy lawyer will verify that taxes cannot be discharged."

Sadly, that is the *only thing* she said that was correct.

The deliberately false information appearing in Publication 908 led me to blast the document in the May, 1988, issue of my newsletter, *Pilla Talks Taxes*. The article criticized it for "intentionally misleading the public." Just *one month* after that newsletter hit the street, the IRS issued an internal memorandum addressing the inaccurate publication. The memo, dated June 15, 1988, recalled and ordered *destroyed* all existing copies of the document. The reason given was that revisions to the law made the document "out-of-date and could be misleading to taxpayers." IRS Message 88-00967, June 15, 1988.

Misleading indeed! The publication was downright deceptive. But in light of the 1966 Bankruptcy Reform Act, why did the IRS wait until June of 1988--twenty-two years after the law was changed, but just one month after *Pilla Talks Taxes* printed the *truth*--to acknowledge that the information "could mislead taxpayers?" You can answer that question for yourself.

While the matter of revising Publication 908 was deliberated by the IRS, we went on the offensive. My long-time friend and associate, tax attorney Donald W. MacPherson, wrote a letter to the IRS' National Office. He pointedly told the IRS that Publication 908 was misleading and he demanded the revised edition tell the truth about federal bankruptcy laws. In early December, 1988, the IRS responded to Mac's letter. The language is dramatic and exciting. More than anything else I can say, it proves that taxes are indeed dischargeable in bankruptcy. In the letter, Michael R. Gallagher, Chief Technical Publications Branch, states,

> Because of your letter, we made additional clarifying changes to the publication's manuscript. We will soon make the revised edition of Publication 908 available to the public.
>
> In addition to the actions we have taken to update and revise Publication 908, the IRS' Taxpayers' Service Division, which provides walk-in and telephone tax assistance to the public, will soon remind their field personnel that *there can be a discharge in bankruptcy of Federal income tax debt*. That division will also cover this matter in future employee training courses. Emphasis added.

On February 17, 1989, long after its expected due date, IRS released the revised Publication 908. Despite the fact the authors made no effort to explain the potentially confusing discharge rules, the IRS nevertheless came clean. Now Publication 908 basically says that one can be discharged of income tax debts. The only question is whether citizens will actually get the picture through the maze of convoluted jargon used in its text.

In two paragraphs under the heading, "Discharge of Unpaid Tax," one finds the critical admission we beat out of the agency nearly one year earlier. It reads, "*However,* claims against you for other taxes pre-dating the bankruptcy petition by more than three years *may be discharged.*" Please note, *the emphasis is in the original!*

Yes Virginia, federal income taxes are indeed dischargeable in bankruptcy. We proved it and forced the IRS to change their false publication. Since the cat was out of the bag, the IRS was forced to adopt its "new attitude" on the OIC in order to prevent oppressed citizens in wholesale numbers from exercising that right. The agency's worst fear is that this news spreads far and wide. The "new attitude" is in place not because the IRS suddenly cares about you, but to keep you from turning to bankruptcy and preventing the agency from collecting.

You now know why I insist there is no such thing as a hopeless tax case. The bankruptcy law provides hope and a remedy. Americans no longer need be driven to suicide by the actions of their government.

The Rules for Discharging Taxes in Bankruptcy

The ability to discharge taxes in bankruptcy is entirely dependent upon timing, hinging upon various dates. For purposes of a Chapter 13, wage-earner's plan, these are the rules:

1. *The three-year rule.* The tax must be for a return (whether or not filed), which was due, including extensions, at least three years prior to filing bankruptcy. Code section 507(a)(7)(A)(i). For example, suppose you owe taxes for the year 1994. The due date of the 1994 return was April 15, 1995, unless you filed an extension. The three-year rule is met if the bankruptcy petition is filed *after* April 15, 1998. If you submitted an extension to file, the due-date was pushed to August 15, 1995. You therefore meet the three-year rule if you file bankruptcy *after* August 15, 1998.

2. *The 240-day rule.* The tax must be assessed for at least 240 days prior to filing in bankruptcy. Code section 507(a)(7)(A)(ii). The assessment date is the day on which an assessment officer signs an assessment certificate. That date is then recorded in the master file. It governs for bankruptcy as well for determining when CSED.

3. *The post-filing assessment rule.* The tax may not be assessed or assessable after filing the petition in bankruptcy. Code section 507(a)(7)(A)(iii). Any assessment meeting the 240-day rule naturally meets this rule. This rule refers to taxes not yet assessed, such as those pending in a current audit, appeal or Tax Court case.

When a tax debt meets these three rules, it is considered a "non-priority" debt under bankruptcy code section 507. The significance is that only *priority debts* are considered non-dischargeable. Non-priority debts are absolutely dischargeable, even if they are income tax debts.

Please note that in order to be dischargeable, a tax debt must meet *all three rules* expressed above. If any one or more of the rules is not met, the tax is considered a priority debt and is not dischargeable. The only exception is when no return is filed.

When returns are not filed, only the three-year applies. Code sections 507(a)(7)(A)(iii) and 1328(a). That is why I warned in chapter eight, *How to Step Forward*, that one must not consider filing past due tax returns in a vacuum. He must consider filing only after determining, with counsel if necessary, the desirability of filing a petition in bankruptcy.

If you are a non-filer wishing to pursue bankruptcy, you activate the 240-day rule by filing tax returns before filing a bankruptcy petition. By so doing, the IRS has 240 days, or eight months, to enforce collection before you can file bankruptcy.

How A Chapter 13 Operates

Chapter 13 is a form of reorganization available to the working man. Think of a Chapter 13 plan as a means to consolidate debts and pay creditors in installments over a fixed period. As a general rule, the debt does not bear interest but there are exceptions. While the plan is in effect, the protections of the bankruptcy court keep aggressive creditors such as the IRS, at arm's length.

A Chapter 13 plan is extremely valuable when a person owes priority tax debts the IRS is collecting or about to collect through wage levies or property seizures. You may recall that priority tax debts cannot be discharged in bankruptcy. Code section 507(a). However, they can be managed through a Chapter 13 plan. This is how it works.

Suppose you owe total taxes of $60,000. Of that, you have *non-priority* tax debts of $50,000. This includes taxes which 1) are at least three years old computed from the due-date of the return, 2) have been assessed at least 240 days, and 3) cannot be assessed after filing bankruptcy. See the three rules expressed above. Further, suppose $10,000 of the $60,000 represents *priority* tax debts. A priority debt is one which does not meet one or more of the three rules.

Under a wager-earner's repayment plan, you propose a plan to pay the IRS the priority taxes in full over a period of time, based on your financial condition. You submit a form disclosing your gross earnings and net earnings after subtracting all payroll deductions. From there, you submit a budget disclosing all necessary monthly living expenses. This is computed in much the same way as an installment agreement with the exception that the IRS does not have the authority to nit-pick your expenses or apply arbitrary standards to what you spend.

The difference between your monthly net income and the monthly budget is called "disposable income." Disposable income is the amount used to fund your payment plan. Under section 1322(c) of the code, plan payments cannot exceed five years. Ideally, they should not exceed three years unless outstanding priority debts and limited disposable income make a three-year plan impossible.

To illustrate this idea, let us suppose you have a gross monthly salary of $1,500 and payroll deductions of $350. Net monthly income is therefore $1,150. Let us further suppose your monthly budget is $800. This includes rent, auto payments, gasoline, insurance, medical bills, food, clothing, utilities telephone and other fixed or regularly recurring expenses which are "reasonably necessary to be expended for the maintenance or support of the debtor or a dependent of the debtor." If the debtor is engaged in business, allowed expenses include those incurred "for the payment of expenditures necessary for the continuation, preservation, and operation of such business." Code sections 1325(b)(2)(A) & (B).

The difference between $1,150 (net income) and $800 (the monthly budget) is $350. This is your disposable income, the amount available each month to fund a payment plan to priority creditors.

The priority tax debts in our example are $10,000. The non-priority, dischargeable debts are $50,000. To be acceptable, a plan of repayment must make provision to pay "in full" all debts entitled to "priority under code section 507." Code section 1322(a)(2). In addition, you must pay some, *but not all*, of the non-priority, dischargeable debts. Paying just a few percent of those debts is often acceptable. The partial payment is referred to as a "dividend."

Because distribution of funds to creditors in Chapter 13 is handled by a Chapter 13 trustee, the plan must provide for payment of the trustee's fee. The fee varies from district to district but is generally about 10 percent of the money handled under the plan.

From this we can determine how much to pay the trustee to complete the plan. If you make payments for the full five years, the plan's gross revenue amounts to $21,000 ($350 x 60 months). Because the trustee receives 10 percent of the funds, the amount remaining for distribution to creditors is $18,900 ($21,000 minus $2,100).

The trustee pays funds to creditors in the order of their priority. Under our example, the IRS must receive $10,000 as payment in full for the priority debt. That leaves $8,900 remaining for distribution to non-priority creditors. The IRS' non-priority, dischargeable debt is $50,000. Under our plan, it is paid a dividend of $8,900, or 18 percent of the total. If you have other non-priority creditors, such as credit cards, the available funds are distributed on a pro rata basis. That way, each creditor receives the same percentage of its total claim.

Upon completion of this plan, the court is required to "grant a discharge of all debts provided for by the plan." Code section 1328(a). The *only* debt not discharged by a successful Chapter 13 plan is one for alimony or child support.

Under this example, the citizen successfully pays the $10,000 priority debt and *discharges* $41,100 of non-priority tax. Perhaps more importantly, there are absolutely no further penalties and generally, no interest. This aspect alone makes the Chapter 13 substantially more attractive than an IRS installment agreement. Under an IRS installment agreement, the penalties and interest often cancel the impact of the monthly payment.

IRS Publication 908 states, at one point, that no discharge of tax is available when no return was filed, a late return was filed or a fraudulent return was involved. This is not entirely accurate. Those rules do not apply to a Chapter 13. (We discuss these elements further in chapter fourteen of this book.) In a Chapter 13, only *priority* taxes are not discharged. A priority tax, again, is one which,

1. Is fewer than three years old, computed from the due-date of the return (whether or not filed), including extensions, as of the date of filing bankruptcy;

2. Has been assessed for fewer than 240 days prior to filing bankruptcy; or

3. May be assessed after the petition in bankruptcy is filed, except when no return is filed. In that case, this rule does not apply. Just the three-year rule applies. Code section 507(a)(7)(A)(i)-(iii).

As you see, none of these rules require the filing of returns, timely or otherwise and they do not mention fraud. Even when no return is filed or one is filed late, a discharge is available. A late-filed return must, however, meet the 240-day rule. Just for the sake of clarity, let us examine how the rules apply to a given factual scenario.

All Returns Filed Timely--Tax Not Paid
All three rules must be met to discharge in Chapter 13. When they are, the tax is considered non-priority.

Returns Filed Late--Tax Not Paid
Again, all three rules must be met to discharge in Chapter 13.

No Return Filed as of Date of Filing Bankruptcy
Just the three-year rule must be met to discharge in Chapter 13. When the returns are not filed, the convoluted language of section 507(a)(7)(A)(iii) operates to eliminate the 240-day rule and the post filing assessment rule (rules two and three). Discharge is available as outlined, even if the IRS claims fraud applies in a given tax year.

Good Faith Required

The final element necessary to succeed in Chapter 13 is the requirement that the petition and plan of repayment be submitted in "good faith." Code section 1325(a)(3). The bankruptcy proceeding must be pursued solely to enjoy the statutory rights of reorganization and fresh start, not for any reason forbidden by law. When the actions of the debtor, taken as a whole, do not indicate an improper purpose, he meets the good faith rule and is entitled to a discharge.

The beauty of a successful Chapter 13 is best explained with the example of Jack, the retired fireman mentioned earlier. Jack did not file tax returns for several years and IRS assessed taxes based upon SFRs. It then levied Jack's pension. Jack and his wife were living on just $325 per month, forcing him to file a Chapter 13 petition.

Thanks to the so-called *automatic stay,* bankruptcy code section 362, the wage levy was released immediately. Jack had his pension to himself once again. The automatic stay is very important. I discuss it later in this chapter.

Jack owed a total of $40,003 in taxes. Of that, just $9,008 were priority. Jack submitted the necessary forms and proposed a plan of repayment. The plan was to fully satisfy the priority debt. He proposed a dividend of 2 percent, or $625, against non-priority assessments totaling $30,995.23. He also proposed to satisfy the trustee's fee.

After some procedural bantering, the plan was accepted and approved by the Court. At that point, he began monthly payments of $195. While the levy was in effect, Jack did not receive enough money each month to live. After filing the bankruptcy and proposing an acceptable plan, Jack was freed of the IRS levy and freed of $30,370 in taxes he could never pay.

Not all cases can be settled with as little as a two percent dividend against non-priority debts. Several factors apply, not the least of which is the amount of disposable income available to fund the plan. Normally, when disposable income is high, the dividend is high. When disposable income is low, the dividend is low. All the facts of the case must be considered before proposing a plan to the court.

The rules for discharging taxes in bankruptcy are the most convoluted statements of law I ever read. There is no doubt in my mind they are deliberately written to confuse citizens, steering them away from the potential benefits. However, we *cracked the code!* There is no question that tax debts can be discharged. If seeking counsel to assist in this process, be *sure, sure, sure* he has an intimate familiarity with these confusing laws. If not, *I promise*, you will come out of bankruptcy with the same problems you had going in.

Special Provisions of the Bankruptcy Code

There is more to the bankruptcy code than simply discharging taxes, though clearly that is the most exciting aspect. Two important sections of the code must be addressed. They are examined in turn.

The Automatic Stay--Return of Wages

Bankruptcy code section 362 is called the "automatic stay." Upon filing a petition with the bankruptcy court, the automatic stay immediately kicks into effect. It means, quite simply, that no creditor may initiate or continue any action whatsoever to "recover a claim against the debtor that arose before the commencement of the case." Code section 362(a)(1).

With respect to the IRS, it means wage levies and bank levies stop- -now! Upon filing a petition, most bankruptcy clerks provide a document entitled, "Notice of Commencement of Case." This simple form notifies creditors of the pending bankruptcy. After filing bankruptcy, provide a copy of it to the RO and your employer, as well as any others threatened with levy, such as your bank. It leads to an *immediate release* of levy.

Another remarkable aspect of the stay is it prevents the IRS from taking any "act to obtain possession of property of the (debtor) or to exercise control over the property of the (debtor)." Code section 362(a)(3). This means, not only can the IRS no longer seize wages or bank accounts, it cannot seize any other property, real or personal. Perhaps most significantly, even if it already seized property, *it cannot sell* that property. And to go even further, at the request of the citizen, it must return property it seized but did not sell. Code section 542(a) and *United States v. Whiting Pools, Inc.*, 426 U.S. 198 (Supreme Court, 1983).

Redetermining Tax Liability

You may know from your own experience that the IRS grossly overstates tax liabilities on a regular basis. An ignorant citizen is often at IRS' mercy when it comes to arbitrary tax determinations. If not properly challenged, the overstated liability becomes assessed and IRS makes every effort to collect it.

Among the numerous benefits of bankruptcy law, code section 505 stands out as perhaps the most compelling to a person taken unfair advantage of by IRS auditors. That section hands the bankruptcy court the authority to "determine the amount or legality of any tax, any fine or penalty relating to any tax, or any addition to tax, whether or not previously assessed, (and) whether or not paid."

The advantages of section 505 spring from the page in a flurry of renewed hope. If a person were denied the ability to contest an IRS determination, he is provided a fresh opportunity after commencing a bankruptcy. Even if the underlying tax is determined by the court to be non-dischargeable, priority debt, the assessment may nevertheless be modified to reflect the *correct* tax.

In one case, the benefits of section 505 saved thousands of dollars for a citizen. The IRS assessed taxes arbitrarily against Don for several years. By the time he filed a bankruptcy petition, the IRS demanded just over $69,000. Don did not legitimately owe more than $10,000. And he could prove it if only he could get a hearing. But Don missed the boat with his notices and never did have a hearing. That left section 505 and bankruptcy as his only hope.

By the time the dust settled in Don's bankruptcy, we reduced the $69,000 tax assessment to $8,557.40. Don then began making payments in the amount of $237.40 each month to a Chapter 13 trustee to satisfy the correct assessment. Don stood to lose his home due to a tax liability over eight times higher than what he truly owed. Section 505 prevented that disaster.

Bankruptcy and the Federal Tax Lien

A federal tax lien can have a profound effect on how tax liabilities are treated in bankruptcy. For that reason, I address two aspects of the tax lien.

Tax Liens and Secured Debt

There is a third category of debt which we must discuss in order to fully analyze the effects of a bankruptcy on taxes. We already identified priority and non-priority debts. The third category is *secured* debts. It is important to consider secured tax debts because they, like priority debts, *are not* discharged.

For a tax debt to be secured, *two* elements must be present. First, a federal tax lien must have been properly filed. The lien must be filed in the county where the property in which the IRS claims a secured interest is located. If no lien is filed, if the lien is filed improperly or if it is filed after the bankruptcy petition, it is invalid. Also, the lien must specify the particular tax debts in question.

The mere presence of the lien, however, is not by itself sufficient to create a secured debt. Many bankruptcy lawyers mistakenly believe it does. A security interest is created only when *both* essential elements are present.

The second element is the amount of your equity in assets owned at the time of filing bankruptcy. For example, suppose you owe the IRS $100,000. Suppose a lien is filed properly. Suppose further the total equity in assets you own at the time of filing is $20,000. This includes equity in your home and the value of other personal and real property, including exempt property.

The presence of the lien secures the debt, but *only* to the extent of your equity in assets owned *at the time of filing*. Code section 506(a). Based upon this simple example, the *secured* tax debt is just $20,000 (the value of equity in the property), making the balance of the tax debt ($80,000), entirely *unsecured* and dischargeable. This is true regardless of the amount stated on the lien.

An acceptable Chapter 13 plan must provide for payment of all secured and priority debts within the allotted time. The secured debts must receive interest at the current applicable rate. However, the interest charged under bankruptcy law is not compounded daily, as is IRS interest and no penalties apply.

The Future of the Tax Lien

I stated in chapter four that the tax lien attaches to all real and personal property owned *at the time* the lien is filed and all property acquired by him *after* the lien is filed. One of the most important provisions of bankruptcy law is that it destroys the tax lien's ability to encumber "after-acquired property."

After-acquired property is property the debtor acquires after filing the bankruptcy petition. Though the tax lien remains effective as to any property he owned *prior* to filing, it cannot attach to property acquired later. Code section 522(c). This includes wages.

Hence, for all practical purposes, the filing of a bankruptcy kills the tax lien from that day forward. This allows the debtor to purchase property after commencement of the case which is not subject to any tax lien filed prior to commencing the case.

Employment Taxes and Chapter 13

Often, it is employment tax liabilities, not income taxes, that drive a citizen to the doors of the bankruptcy court. Replete throughout this text is the point that the IRS is extremely aggressive, sometimes to the level of ruthlessness, when it comes to employment taxes. If you face employment tax assessments or the Trust Fund Recovery Penalty, there are important aspects of these assessments with which you must be familiar.

First, please recall the difference between trust fund employment taxes and non-trust taxes. I discuss it at length in chapter five under the heading, *Employment Taxes and the Installment Agreement.* Please review it now if you cannot recite the difference between trust and non-trust employment taxes.

Under code section 507(a)(7)(C), the trust portion of employment tax assessments is considered priority debt. The statute speaks to "employment taxes required to be collected or withheld and for which the debtor is liable in whatever capacity." Clearly, this refers to trust fund taxes.

There are no circumstances under which trust taxes are transformed into non-priority debts. Therefore, as priority debts, trust assessments are never discharged. The non-trust portion, however, is a different story. Non-trust taxes are addressed in code section 507(a)(7)(D). It provides that an "employment tax on a wage, salary, or commission," as opposed to withheld taxes, are considered non-priority--and hence dischargeable--when the three-year rule is met. Employment taxes on wages you pay are assessed in the form of FICA (employer's matching funds) and FUTA taxes.

The tax is considered non-priority and is dischargeable when you meet the three year rule. Again, this rule states that the tax must be for a period which is more than three years old as of the date of filing in bankruptcy, computed from the due date of the return (whether or not filed), including extensions. Interestingly, code section 507(a)(7)(D) imposes no requirement to meet either the 240-day rule or the post-petition assessment rule before a non-trust assessment is considered a non-priority debt.

Therefore, when considering a bankruptcy involving employment taxes, separate the assessment into trust and non-trust liabilities. Trust liabilities must be paid in full as priority debt. Non-trust taxes may be discharged under applicable Chapter 13 procedures.

The Final Analysis

Through all of this, you may be asking, "Do I qualify for a Chapter 13?" This question can be accurately answered only after a full evaluation of all facts and circumstances. However, here are some firm guidelines to follow to help you make that determination.

1. Separate your tax debts into the three categories discussed above. They are priority taxes, non-priority taxes and secured taxes.

Be sure to pay close attention to the rules for determining priority and non-priority tax debts for filers and non-filers. Also review the process of determining what is and is not a secured tax debt. Determine the total amount in each category.

2. Prepare a monthly budget taking into consideration all mandatory payroll deductions and required monthly living expenses. The difference between monthly income and living expenses is disposable income.

3. Disposable income must provide for full payment of all priority and secured debts within sixty months. Remember to take into consideration the 10 percent fee charged by most trustees. Disposable income must also "provide for" non-priority, unsecured debts. Such provision may be as little as two percent. If necessary, you may consider the income of your spouse in determining disposable income, even if that spouse does not have any tax liabilities.

If, after this basic analysis, you are able to fund a plan, pursuing a Chapter 13 may be worthwhile. Bear in mind my caution regarding bankruptcy counsel. Not one lawyer in a thousand even knows this can be done, never mind how to do it! Be sure to find counsel capable of pulling it off.

Conclusion

In conversation with Jim several years after he filed bankruptcy to stop relentless collection action, he explained, "It was like I died and went to heaven!" The IRS just disappeared. The automatic stay *chases* it away and a proper plan of repayment *keeps* it away!

The results are profound. Even if you are a non-filer, this program could have far-reaching benefits for you. If more citizens understood they have the right to a repayment plan free of crippling interest and penalty charges, I dare say there would be no more tax motivated suicides in this country!

Some time ago, while a guest on a Houston radio talk show, Bob's wife heard me discussing taxes and bankruptcy. Their desperate tax problem eventually led them to file a Chapter 13. Later, Bob wrote this letter to Roger Grey, the host of the show.

Dear Mr. Grey:

Last week I walked out of a Houston Division, United States Bankruptcy Court leaving behind me several years of difficulty with the Internal Revenue Service. I had some major financial problems in the past several years but the one with the IRS seemed insurmountable.

I was on the verge of losing what I had left and then becoming a literal slave to the IRS for many years to come. It would have meant that my children could not receive any assistance from me in going to college. It would have meant a type of life, a future I was not willing to live.

My wife heard Mr. Dan Pilla, a guest on one of your programs, discuss how to negotiate with the IRS and under what circumstances taxes could be discharged. We ordered his two books which were promptly sent. I read the books. I subscribed to his newsletter which included one hour of consultation by phone. The one hour was quickly used. Arrangements were made with Dan for additional hours of consultation. I desperately needed them.

My lawyer told me it was impossible to discharge taxes in bankruptcy court. The taxes must be paid! Because I was out of town frequently, I needed a lawyer to handle my case while I was gone. I called other lawyers. I had previously retained, for a brief time, a tax consultant (former IRS agent). It quickly became evident that he only knew what the IRS taught him. I could not afford to have him on my side, even if he had been free. I could not find ANY legal counsel who knew what Dan Pilla knew. I even looked out of state.

One highly recommended tax attorney was shocked when he learned I had paid an author of a book (Dan Pilla) for assistance. He told me I had been taken. When I walked out of his office thirty minutes later, I realized I *had* been taken. The tax attorney had 75 of my dollars and all he could do was "stand by" me while he threw me to the "mercy" of the IRS wolves. And at the rate of $150 per hour, of course!

I decided to try to educate my board certified bankruptcy lawyer on bankruptcy law. The lawyer refused to read Dan Pilla's book, so using the book as a guide, I went to a local law library and copied the pertinent sections of the Bankruptcy Code. Using some material Dan sent to me, I wrote my own papers to present to the court and gave them to my lawyer.

My lawyer told me what I was trying to do was not possible. I pulled out my photo copies of the bankruptcy code and argued my case, point by point. He called in reinforcements. I found myself sitting at a conference table facing two board certified bankruptcy lawyers. They made statements but could not back them up by the code. They were relying on their "many years of experience," not the law. I had page number and paragraph reference for everything I said. The court date was two days later so there was no time to lose. The second lawyer ended up supporting my argument and convincing my lawyer that Dan Pilla was correct after all.

It is bad enough to have to pay lawyers who already have an education. But to have to pay them while YOU are giving them their education is intolerable.

The net result is that it will take me the next three and a half years to pay the IRS a small percentage of what I owed in taxes and penalties. The balance was discharged! After that, I will be free. I am not happy I had to go this route. However, bankruptcy court was established for those who, under unfortunate circumstances, find it impossible to pay what is owed.

Mr. Grey, please do not underestimate the power and influence you have in the lives of your individual listeners. The airing of Dan Pilla's interview has literally changed the rest of my life and the life of my family. Mr. Grey, there are many more people in the Houston area who desperately need to hear what Dan Pilla has to say. *Please* help them! Please help them as much as you can.

I will be eternally grateful to you and Dan.

Signed: Bob - Houston

"...for he has said, 'I will never fail you nor forsake you.' Hence we can confidently say, 'The Lord is my helper, I will not be afraid; what can man do to me?'"

                                                    Hebrews 12:5-6

CHAPTER FOURTEEN
Tax Amnesty Program Number Four --The Fresh Start

The principle of a *fresh start* is embodied in the very spirit of the bankruptcy laws. The IRS has, as least in part, adopted that philosophy in its "new attitude" because of its raw experiences with these laws. Amnesty program number four takes the principle of a fresh start one step further. Many citizens faced with IRS debt cannot solve their problem with a wage-earner's plan. Those with few assets to protect or whose debts are beyond the possibility of repayment may seek relief through this program.

Under the Fresh Start program, qualifying tax debts are simply eliminated. The citizen comes away with a clean slate and the opportunity for a new beginning.

Who Can Benefit From the Fresh Start Program?

This program is designed for those with little to lose and much to gain by exercising the right to wholly eliminate staggering IRS debts. Those who have endured enforced collection over a prolonged period are often ripe for this program. The reason is the IRS has generally helped themselves to most assets, leaving the citizen nearly destitute.

Some time ago, I spoke with a lady particularly distraught over the problem she and her husband faced. Jane explained her assessments ranged in the neighborhood of $500,000. She was not sure because the problem persisted for so long and the IRS had previously seized much in assets and cash. The IRS refused to provide a meaningful statement showing assessments and payments.

When I spoke with Jane, the IRS seized and was preparing to sell her home--for the *second* time. That's right! The first time occurred in late 1990. After it was sold, Jane's tax counsel persuaded her to "redeem" the property. Seized property is redeemed by paying an amount equal to the value realized through the sale, plus interest.

When the agency sold their home, it did so for the ridiculous price of $7,000. It seemed a simple matter to redeem it. They borrowed $7,000 from relatives, paid it to the IRS and soon, the home was released back to them.

However, $7,000 did not come close to satisfying the debt. Consequently, after the property was redeemed and once again was owned by Jane and her husband, it was re-exposed to seizure and sale. And that is exactly what the agency did. It seized the home a second time. After the second sale, the redemption amount was $15,000.

Jane and her husband were victimized by a phenomenon I addressed in chapter thirteen. It is the overwhelming level of ignorance, even among tax professionals, of the ability to discharge taxes in bankruptcy. In Jane's case, the ignorance of her counsel transcended even the subject of bankruptcy. His ignorance went to the core of basic procedural tax matters.

How the Fresh Start Program Operates

The program is administered under Chapter 7 of the bankruptcy code. It is often referred to as a liquidation or straight bankruptcy. The term "liquidation" is the source of much consternation for many citizens. However, for those such as Jane facing liquidation at the hands of the IRS or who have already suffered that fate, Chapter 7 can represent a long-awaited drink from the cup of forgiveness.

Filing a petition under Chapter 7 creates a legal entity known as the "bankruptcy estate." The estate is comprised of all property owned by the debtor at the time of filing, less any exempt property. Code sections 541 and 522. The estate is administered by the trustee for the benefit of creditors. The trustee liquidates the estate's property and distributes the proceeds to creditors in accordance with bankruptcy law.

All non-priority, unsecured debts not paid by the proceeds of liquidation are discharged. This is true whether or not the debt is for income taxes. Contrary to Chapter 13 rules, one need pay no dividend against those debts or otherwise make payment arrangements to win a discharge.

For example, suppose you own no assets other than the clothes on your back, some personal furniture and an automobile worth $5,000. Let us further say you owe $50,000 in non-priority, dischargeable taxes. In the Chapter 7, the trustee sells your non-exempt property and pays the proceeds to the IRS. Assuming your personal vehicle is not exempt (state and federal law determine exemptions) and assuming the trustee sold the car for $5,000, you discharge $45,000 in taxes.

Generally, however, it is not quite that simple. The reason is because almost every state enforces laws *exempting* a vehicle and other assets in some amount. Therefore, the trustee in our example is not free to sell it outright. Rather, he offers to sell the non-exempt portion *back to the citizen*. It is this aspect of the Chapter 7 that often prevents the absolute stripping of all one's assets.

To illustrate, I point to the federal automobile exemption provided for under code section 522. At the time of this writing, that exemption is worth $1,200. In our example, the vehicle exceeds the exemption amount. Therefore, expect the trustee to sell the vehicle to *you* at a negotiated price somewhere between the exemption amount ($1,200) and its declared value ($5,000).

Usually, a citizen is able to purchase property from the trustee at rates approaching 50 percent of the declared value. In this case, 50 percent of the difference between the exemption ($1,200) and the declared value ($5,000), is $1,900. That means for the sum of $1,900, you purchase the vehicle from the trustee. Because wage levies or your installment payment to the IRS cease the day of filing bankruptcy, funds to purchase the vehicle could come from that source. Borrowed money can also aid in purchasing assets.

The beauty of recovering assets in this fashion is two-fold. First of all, in addition to what I said in chapter thirteen of this book, this process defeats the notion that you "lose everything" in bankruptcy. Secondly, when you purchase the property from the trustee, you purchase it *free of the tax lien*. This is a wild contrast from what Jane did in her case. When she redeemed her home, she did it *subject to the tax lien* and you saw what happened.

Please recall our earlier discussion in chapter thirteen of this book concerning the tax lien. I declared that the lien does not attach to after-acquired property. When you purchase property from the trustee, such property is considered acquired after you filed bankruptcy. The reason is simple and perfectly logical.

When you filed bankruptcy, your property ceased to be yours. At that moment, it became property of the estate. Legal title passed from you to the estate. Paying funds to the trustee to purchase that property is no different than if you ran down to the local car store to buy another auto. Since the new car is after-acquired property, the lien does not attach to it.

At the time of purchasing property from the trustee, title passes to you free of the tax lien. You continue to drive the vehicle but you do so without the risk of the IRS seizing it at any moment. The same result can be achieved with real property, such as your home.

The Rules for Discharging Taxes in Chapter 7

Shortly after filing bankruptcy, the court issues a general discharge order. The order is vague. It does not expressly state which debts are and are not discharged by the order. It states merely that all debts "dischargeable" are "hereby discharged." One must look to the code to determine which debts are and are not discharged.

This leads to much confusion. IRS is often of the opinion that the bankruptcy has no impact on tax debt because of the mistaken notion that taxes are "not dischargeable." For this reason, it is necessary to communicate with IRS after the discharge to prove the tax debt was indeed canceled. Therefore, it is mandatory that you understand the rules for discharging taxes in Chapter 7.

In order to be dischargeable in Chapter 7, each of these rules must be met:

1. The three-year rule. The tax must be for a return (whether or not filed), which was due, including extensions, at least three years before you file bankruptcy. Code section 507(a)(7)(A)(i).

2. The 240-day rule. The tax must be assessed for at least 240 days prior to filing in bankruptcy. Code section 507(a)(7)(A)(ii).

3. The post-petition assessment rule. The tax may not be assessed or assessable after the petition in bankruptcy is filed. Code section 507(a)(7)(A)(iii).

You no doubt recognize these three rules as those required to determine a priority tax debt as discussed in chapter thirteen of this book. Thus, for a tax to be discharged in Chapter 7, it must be a non-priority debt. Remember, priority debts are not discharged. In addition, it is necessary to meet two further tests, bringing to five the total number of rules governing Chapter 7 discharges. The two additional rules are:

4. The return filed rule. A return *must be filed* for the year in question. *If filed late*, it must be filed at least two years prior to filing in bankruptcy. Code section 523(a)(1)(B)(i) and (ii). Hence, a non-filer cannot be discharged in Chapter 7. He is nevertheless able to discharge in Chapter 13 as already explained.

5. The no fraud rule. The tax must not be the result of a fraudulent return or an attempt to willfully evade or defeat payment of the tax. Code section 523(a)(1)(C). Any claim of fraud *proven* by the IRS

defeats a discharge under Chapter 7. It does not, however, prevent discharge in Chapter 13.

As you plainly see, each of these rules (with the exception of rule five) is *time-sensitive*. The critical point I made in chapter thirteen holds true here. The ability to discharge taxes in bankruptcy is *entirely dependent upon timing*. You cannot expect to meet with success if you do not understand and apply all the rules to the facts of your case *before you file bankruptcy!*

Permit me to illustrate exactly how effective a Chapter 7 can be under the appropriate circumstances. Virginia owed the IRS $57,662 as a result of tax shelters claimed for 1981 and 1982. The shelters were simple and sold as perfectly legal investment vehicles intended not only to save taxes, but also to earn a profit.

The IRS disallowed the investments. By late 1989, it was collecting the assessment through wage levies on Virginia's paycheck. This case illustrates how wildly a tax bill can grow. When the IRS first figured the bill in 1983, it found she owed $12,487 for 1981 and $9,504 for 1982. By the time it commenced collection in 1989, the agency demanded over $57,000.

Virginia worked part-time at a supermarket as a checker and drew a small pension. Her total monthly income was $1,700. There was no way she could pay the debt. After paying her normal monthly living expenses, she had just a few hundred dollars available each month to throw at the problem. At that rate, interest and penalties would keep the bill growing until the day she died.

In November, 1989, Virginia filed a Chapter 7 bankruptcy. Upon receiving the discharge order, she wrote a certified letter to the IRS Special Procedures staff for her district. Special Procedures handles bankruptcy matters for the IRS, including the processing of all relevant forms.

The letter explained she met each of the required five rules. She asked for an abatement of taxes for 1981 and 1982. After providing all appropriate documents to verify the bankruptcy, her letter was met with approval. The format of the letter is the same as that shown in IRS Publication 783, governing applications for certificate of release of federal tax lien. See chapter six and the Forms Kit.

When Virginia walked out of the bankruptcy court, she left behind the mistakes of her past. She walked into a fresh start occasioned by a slate wiped clean through a Chapter 7 discharge.

Special Provisions Relating to Chapter 7

In chapter thirteen of this book, I discussed two special provisions of the code and how they relate to tax cases. One was the automatic stay, section 362 of the code, which immediately halts all IRS levy and collection action. The automatic stay applies to Chapter 7.

After filing the petition, the IRS must cease and desist all enforced collection action. Wage and bank levies must stop and if a lien has not been filed, one may not be filed. This is important because the presence of a lien may give rise to a secured debt.

The second important special provision is section 505 of the code. It enables a person to win a hearing on the propriety of a tax assessment not previously determined by a court. This section is very important to those dealing with bogus tax bills. It enables one to submit the question of the legality of the assessment to the bankruptcy court for determination. If found improper, the court may order the IRS to abate the assessment.

The Federal Tax Lien

The federal tax lien has the same impact in Chapter 7 as it does in Chapter 13. A tax lien gives rise to the claim that the tax debt is "secured." A secured debt, like a priority debt, is never discharged. However, before a tax debt is secured, not only must the lien be properly filed *prior* to filing bankruptcy, but you must own equity in assets at the time of filing bankruptcy. The tax debt is then secured but only to the extent of your equity in those assets. Please note, however, the level of security is *reduced* in direct proportion to the non-exempt assets sold by the trustee.

For example, suppose you have $25,000 equity in all your assets at the time of filing bankruptcy. Of the $25,000, $10,000 represents exempt assets, such as furniture, equity in your home and a car. The remaining $15,000 represents non-exempt assets, such as a non-homestead parcel of real estate. Assume your tax debt is $100,000.

At the time of filing bankruptcy, the secured debt is $25,000 (the value of all equity). The unsecured, dischargeable debt (assuming all five rules are met) is $75,000. The secured debt is *reduced* when the trustee liquidates the non-exempt assets because the proceeds of the liquidation are designated to the secured debts. Therefore, in this example, the secured tax debt is reduced from $25,000 to $10,000 after sale of the non-exempt asset.

All assessments in excess of your equity are considered unsecured. Hence, they are subject to discharge in Chapter 7 if they meet all five rules.

What Happens if My Equity is Substantial?

As you know, the federal tax lien is not affected by the discharge. Code section 522(c). However, the lien exists only as to property owned at the time of filing bankruptcy. After-acquired property is not subject to the lien. This can create a problem for a citizen seeking discharge in Chapter 7. The problem may be exacerbated if his equity is substantial. There are two factors causing the problem.

First, when IRS recognizes that substantial equity in exempt assets exists at the time of filing, it does not release its tax lien upon discharge. Second, because secured debts are not discharged, one may face renewed enforced collection after the bankruptcy. For example, if your bankruptcy documents reveal you have $20,000 equity in your house, the IRS may very well pursue the house through enforced collection once your bankruptcy is closed. Having just passed through bankruptcy, it is unlikely you would have $20,000 in cash to pay the IRS. This places your home at risk.

Under this circumstance, we have effectively utilized a procedure informally termed a "Chapter 20." A Chapter 20 is a combination of a Chapter 7 followed immediately by a Chapter 13. There is no prohibition against this procedure. Most people believe you can file just one bankruptcy every seven years or every ten years. The truth is, you are entitled to one discharge in *Chapter 7* every *six* years. Code section 727(a)(8).

Let me illustrate how this works. Suppose you owe $100,000 in taxes. Your only asset is your homestead. It is exempt. The equity in the home is valued at $20,000. The IRS has a valid tax lien. The lien creates a security interest equal to your equity of $20,000. Your tax assessment meets *all five* rules expressed above.

Upon discharge, you eliminate $80,000 in taxes. That is determined by subtracting the secured debt (the amount not discharged) from the total tax bill. After receiving the discharge, you in turn file a petition under Chapter 13. In the Chapter 13, you disclose total tax debts of $20,000 and classify them as "secured."

You then propose a plan to pay the secured debt in installment payments. Remember, in Chapter 13 you must pay the trustee a 10 percent fee to administer the plan. In addition, secured creditors must receive interest. Under this example, $20,000 amortized over five years at 10 percent interest equals $25,496.45. Add the trustee's fee and the total becomes $28,045. Based upon that figure, you pay $467.42 per month for sixty months.

At the conclusion of the sixty-month plan, you receive a "completion discharge." Your IRS problem is behind you. At the same time, you retain your home and successfully keep the IRS from seizing wages, bank accounts or any other asset while carrying out your plan.

Contrast this approach with a payment plan administered by the IRS under which you pay penalties and compound interest. Under such a plan, you must pay about $350 per month just to *stay even* with the interest and penalties. Paying the IRS at the rate of $467.41 per month, the amount under our hypothetical Chapter 13 plan, it takes about 180 months--more than *fourteen years*--to satisfy the $20,000 debt. And during this period, you face a threat of enforced collection, are subject to IRS whim and the interest rate is subject to change twice annually.

The Final Analysis

As I declared in chapter thirteen, an accurate analysis of whether and to what extent this procedure can benefit you can only be determined after an evaluation of all your facts and circumstances. As I did in the last chapter, however, I provide some firm guidelines to get you close enough to warrant further consideration.

1. Separate your tax debts into the three categories of debt we identified. They are priority debt, secured debt and non-priority debt. Be sure to pay close attention to the rules of determining priority and non-priority debts. Also review the process of determining secured debt. Ascertain the total amount in each category.

2. With respect to the *non-priority* debt, determine whether those taxes are dischargeable in a Chapter 7. In order to be discharged, they must meet the return filed rule and the no fraud rule.

3. After determining the amount of tax discharged by the Chapter 7, ask yourself whether it is worth filing bankruptcy to win amnesty with respect to that amount.

4. You must then ascertain the amount, if any, of priority and secured debts remaining after the discharge. If full payment of those amounts is not possible, a Chapter 13 may be necessary to fully resolve your tax problem.

5. To determine whether the Chapter 13 can be effective, please refer to chapter thirteen of this book under the heading, *The Final Analysis*.

Planning For Bankruptcy

Nobody wants to file bankruptcy unless there is no other option. More than that, the IRS does not want you to file bankruptcy. It is as afraid of the "B" word as you are. The reason is, in most cases, the IRS gets nothing when one files bankruptcy, especially a Chapter 7.

Therefore, I say the best way to *avoid* bankruptcy is to carefully plan to *execute* a bankruptcy if necessary. Walk softly, but carry a big stick--the "B" stick. If the IRS proves uncooperative, unreasonable or unwilling to make concessions, use it. Hit it over the side of the head-- hard! Believe me when I say the IRS has already been stunned by thousands of citizens who have done the same thing.

The following steps should be taken while negotiating with the IRS under any of the other amnesty programs discussed in this book. Taking these steps puts you into position where you can negotiate the best possible solution to your case, possibly without having to file bankruptcy.

FIRST. Obtain a copy of your Individual Master File (IMF) for each of the years you owe taxes. That document is the IRS' computerized statement of your account. It reveals all pending assessments for tax, interest and penalties for each of the years in question. It shows the return filing date and the assessment date, etc. It also shows whether a civil fraud penalty has been assessed.

SECOND. Utilize the IMF to determine priority and non-priority debts. It is the only way to be certain of return filing dates and assessment dates. Also determine whether the fraud penalty is assessed.

THIRD. If you are presently under an installment agreement with the IRS, immediately begin designating all installment payments to *priority* taxes. This step is important because, as I explained in chapter five, undesignated payments are applied in a manner that best suits the IRS. In the typical case, the IRS applies those payments to the *earliest* tax year in question, then works its way forward as the liabilities are paid in full.

However, by applying the partial payment to the *latest* tax year-- the priority year--you accomplish two goals. First, because interest assessments are smaller in the later years, more of the payment applies to tax. The tax is satisfied faster. Second, because the priority years are not dischargeable, they must be paid. By applying payments to the dischargeable years, they are, in effect, wasted. By applying them to priority, non-dischargeable years, you work steadily to reduce the amounts that must be paid anyway.

IF YOUR DEBTS ARE FOR EMPLOYMENT TAXES, be careful to designate all payments to the trust fund assessments. Remember, trust fund liabilities are not dischargeable--period.

For the manner in which to designate payments, please see chapter five, under the heading, *Special Considerations for Employment Taxes*. Use the letter discussed there to designate income tax payments as well. Simply rephrase it to cover the tax year in question.

If your employment tax debts are relative to an operating corporation, consider terminating operations immediately if you cannot accomplish the goals stressed in chapter five, under the heading, *Stop the Bleeding*. By terminating operations, the trust liabilities do not grow worse. Also, when corporate operations are terminated, the IRS assesses the Trust Fund Recovery Penalty against the responsible officers. However, that assessment *may not include* non-trust taxes. Therefore, you effectively reduce the tax bill by as much as 25 percent, considering penalties. The remainder of the trust taxes are subject to repayment in a Chapter 13 if that becomes necessary.

FOURTH. Utilize the "new attitude" expressed in the penalty policy statement to pursue abatement of penalties. See chapter nine. By winning abatement of penalties and the interest on the penalties, you may eliminate the need to file bankruptcy.

FIFTH. Consider filing an offer in compromise prior to filing bankruptcy. Given the "new attitude" driving the offer policy, you are likely to meet with some success. However, pay *close attention* to this word of caution. If possible, file the offer only *after* your taxes are ripe for discharge in bankruptcy under the rules we studied. That is, file it when your taxes are considered non-priority debts.

There are two very important reasons for this strategy. First, by filing the offer before the taxes meet the 240-day rule, you toll that time period. The 240-day period is tolled for the length of time the offer is pending, plus thirty days.

To illustrate, suppose your tax has been assessed for six months. If you submit an offer at that time, the 240-day time period *stops running*. Suppose the offer is rejected one year later. Before meeting the 240-day rule, *ninety days*, not sixty, must pass from the date the offer is rejected. The poorly timed offer exposes you to enforced collection for a longer period than is otherwise necessary. It may not seem like much now, but it could seem an eternity while suffering under a wage levy.

The second reason for the timing strategy is that it is much easier to prove doubt as to collectibility when the tax you propose to compromise is already dischargeable in bankruptcy. Please recall the cases of both Richard and Vivian's offer in compromise, discussed in chapter twelve. They were successful with the "take it or leave it" offer because the IRS knew their taxes were dischargeable. As I outlined in chapter twelve, *prove* your taxes are dischargeable when making the offer by illustrating that the assessments meet the required five rules. By providing proof with an offer, you greatly increase the prospect of a negotiated settlement that is reasonable under the circumstances.

Do not be afraid to use the offer process as a means of canceling *all penalties and interest.* A so-called "tax only offer" is not uncommon. If accepted, it might eliminate the need to file bankruptcy. A tax only offer is one which proposes to pay just the tax without regard to penalties or interest. Because the penalties and interest may triple a tax bill, this relief alone can be very important.

Moreover, you should know tax penalties are dischargeable in bankruptcy even when the underlying tax is not. Two of the more convoluted bankruptcy code sections dealing with taxes and penalties are sections 523(a)(7)(A) and (B).

After carefully tracing the quadruple negative used in these sections, I conclude that a penalty is dischargeable when it relates to a transaction or event occurring at least three years *before* filing in bankruptcy. Thus, for example, if you are charged with the penalty for failure to pay on a tax due more than three years before you filed bankruptcy, the penalty is dischargeable even if the tax is not.

This rule applies equally to the fraud penalty. When fraud is imposed with regard to a particular year, the no fraud rule expressed in section 532(a)(1)(C) prevents discharge of the tax. However, the fraud penalty itself, assessed at the rate of 75 percent of the tax, is dischargeable under 523(a)(7)(B), provided it meets the rule I just articulated. For more guidance on discharge of the fraud penalty, see *Byrum v. Internal Revenue Service,* 92-1 USTC 50,275 (D.C. Cal. 1992).

The one sure way to guarantee success in any negotiation is to negotiate from a position of strength, not weakness. Do not perceive the need to file bankruptcy as a weakness. When dealing with the IRS, unmanageable tax debts and potentially uncooperative collection officers, the ability to file bankruptcy is a compelling strength. By maneuvering yourself into a position to strike quickly, you very well may eliminate the need to ever use it!

And the reason you did not have to use it is because you found tax amnesty through one or more of the other means addressed in this book. The important thing is to be sure your options are open. You must always consider the long-term implications of your actions.

Never employ any tactic without regard to its impact on your overall goal--to win amnesty.

Conclusion

The right to discharge taxes in bankruptcy is the tool that brought the IRS to its knees. It is, more than anything else, what forced the issue on the "new attitude." Beyond the fact it can save you a fortune in taxes, it can force the IRS to deal with you more reasonably, more realistically and in good faith.

In 1990, I received a letter from Larry explaining his experience with the IRS and Chapter 7 Bankruptcy. The letter reads,

> Dear Dan:
>
> Last year about this time my wife heard you on the Point of View Radio program on KVTT in Dallas. She ordered your book about how to defend yourself against the IRS and later received the book and your newsletter. The newsletter laid around the house for about two months before I actually sat down and read it cover to cover. There was an article in there regarding the abatement of income tax owed to the government after filing Chapter 7 Bankruptcy. In the article, you said that under certain conditions taxes could be abated but that most IRS personnel were not aware of this.
>
> I had declared bankruptcy in July, 1988, and at that time, owed the IRS $175,000. I went to the Fort Worth district office of the IRS and inquired about abating the taxes in January, 1990. They said there was no way to get out of paying these past due taxes even if I had declared bankruptcy.
>
> I asked them about provisions outlined in IRS Publication 908, Bankruptcy and other Debt Cancellation. Not one IRS agent or officer I spoke with knew anything about this publication. I then contacted the Special Procedures Branch in Dallas and the officer I talked with was familiar with the law. He said I was eligible to have the taxes abated and after researching my file, the IRS abated all taxes owed from 1980 through 1984, in the amount of $175,000.
>
> It took the IRS several months and a lot of very persistent phone calls on my part but I was finally given the releases for the liens which had been filed against me.
>
> Needless to say, I am very appreciative of the information that I found in your newsletter.
>
> Signed: Larry - Texas

Another example is Gary's case. After he successfully discharged thousands in taxes he could not pay, he received a letter from the IRS and shared a copy with me. Please see the letter reproduced as Exhibit 14-1 below. Read it, then tell me whether you still believe taxes cannot be discharged in bankruptcy.

"There's no such thing as a hopeless tax case."

--Daniel J. Pilla

Exhibit 14-1

INTERNAL REVENUE SERVICE   DEPARTMENT OF THE TREASURY

District
Director   310 W. Wisconsin Avenue
                                  Milwaukee, WI 53203

Gary E. & Sheila███████████   Person to Contact:
████████████████████████   Frank Cox
                                  Telephone Number:
            .   414-297-1948
                                  Refer Reply to:
                                  C:SPS FC
                                  Date:
                                  January 17, 1992

Dear Mr. & Mrs. █████

Pursuant to your request dated December 31, 1991 we have reviewed our record of your Chapter 7 bankruptcy, Case Number████████. We have concluded that your liabilities on Forms 1040 for the years 1985, 1986 and 1987 were dischargeable in that proceeding. We have therefore requested abatement of all remaining tax, penalty and interest on those accounts. We have also requested a suspension of collection activity on those accounts pending the completion of the abatements. Please advise this office at telephone number 414-297-1948 if any further collection action is taken. We would immediately reverse any such action.

We regret any inconvenience which the issuance of billing notices on these accounts may have caused.

Sincerely,

J.T. Cox

Frank Cox
Advisor, Special Procedures Staff

"The Spirit of the Lord God is upon me, because the Lord has anointed me to bring good tidings to the afflicted; he has sent me to bind up the brokenhearted, to proclaim liberty to the captives, and the opening of the prison to those who are bound."

Isaiah 61:1

Glossary

AD VALOREM: Based upon a percentage. Tax penalties are usually ad valorem penalties, based upon a percentage of the tax.

AFTER-ACQUIRED PROPERTY: Property acquired after the occurrence of a specific event. As used here, it refers to property acquired after the filing of a notice of federal tax lien or after the filing of a petition in bankruptcy. See CHAPTER 7 and CHAPTER 13.

ANTI-INJUNCTION ACT: Section 7421 of the tax code. It prevents the federal courts from issuing an order, known as an injunction, stopping the IRS from taking action.

APPEALS OFFICE: An IRS division established to negotiate settlements in unresolved cases.

ASSESSMENT: The act of recording a debt on the IRS' accounts. A valid assessment requires a signed assessment certificate, usually IRS Form 23C. See DEFICIENCY PROCEDURES and NOTICE OF DEFICIENCY.

ASSESSMENT STATUTE OF LIMITATIONS: The legal period of limitation in which the IRS may assess a tax. Taxes pursuant to a filed return must ordinarily be assessed within three years of filing.

AUDIT RECONSIDERATION: The formal procedure for re-opening a closed audit file. This is used to correct improper or erroneous assessments where no previous appeal was taken or available.

AUTOMATED COLLECTION (ACS): The Automated Collection System is a collection function designed to collect unpaid assessments as quickly as possible through an automated process. See COLLECTION DIVISION.

AUTOMATIC STAY: Section 362 of the federal bankruptcy code. It takes effect immediately upon filing a petition in bankruptcy and prevents creditors, including the IRS, from commencing or maintaining any action to collect a debt while the bankruptcy is pending. See CHAPTER 7 and CHAPTER 13.

BANKRUPTCY CODE, The: Title 11, United States Code. This is the body of law which sets forth all bankruptcy rules, procedures and statutes. See UNITED STATES CODE.

BANKRUPTCY COURT: The portion of the federal court structure which administers bankruptcy filings and related litigation. See CHAPTER 7 and CHAPTER 13.

BANKRUPTCY ESTATE: The legal entity created upon the filing of a bankruptcy case. The debtor's NON-EXEMPT PROPERTY is transferred to the estate upon filing bankruptcy. See EXEMPT PROPERTY.

BURDEN OF PROOF: The legal requirement to persuade a fact finder, such as a judge or jury (often-times, the IRS) of the legitimacy of your claim.

BUSINESS MASTER FILE (BMF): The IRS' internal, computerized record of account for a business tax return, such as Form 1120, corporate return or Form 941, employment tax return. See INDIVIDUAL MASTER FILE.

CHAPTER 7: The chapter of the BANKRUPTCY CODE that provides for a full LIQUIDATION of NON-EXEMPT PROPERTY and DISCHARGE of all dischargeable debts. CHAPTER 7 is sometimes referred to as straight bankruptcy. See EXEMPT PROPERTY.

CHAPTER 13: The chapter of the BANKRUPTCY CODE that provides for partial payment of some debts and partial DISCHARGE some debts. It is known as the WAGE-EARNER'S REPAYMENT PLAN since all creditors must receive a "DIVIDEND."

CHAPTER 20: The process of filing a CHAPTER 7 followed by a CHAPTER 13. This is a not a formal chapter within the BANKRUPTCY CODE but is informally dubbed the CHAPTER 20 by adding the two previous numbers.

COLLECTION APPEAL: The process of making an administrative appeal of IRS collection action. The appeal is directed to the APPEALS OFFICE, which has authority to issue binding recommendations in collection appeal matters.

COLLECTION DIVISION: The division of IRS responsible to collect tax ASSESSMENTS. See REVENUE OFFICER.

COLLECTION STATUTE OF LIMITATIONS: Code section 6503 provides an express limit on the time in which the IRS may collect a tax. Subject to certain acts which extend the collection statute expiration date (CSED), the IRS' right to collect dies after ten years.

COMMUNITY PROPERTY: State law which creates a "community estate" in property acquired during marriage where both husband and wife enjoy a vested, one-half interest in the assets of each, regardless of whose name the property is held in. Community property states include Arizona, California, Idaho, Louisiana, Nevada, New Mexico, Texas, Washington, Wisconsin.

CRIMINAL INVESTIGATION DIVISION (CID): The division of IRS responsible to investigate possible violations of the criminal tax and other related federal laws. See SPECIAL AGENT.

CRIMINAL STATUTE OF LIMITATIONS: The time limit under code section 6531 in which the IRS may charge a crime. Ordinarily, a crime must be brought within six years of the date of filing the return or of the return due date.

CURRENT TAXES: Taxes due for the present year. This also refers to filing the return due for the most recent tax year.

DEBTOR: A person who owes a debt. In the context of the federal bankruptcy laws, it is the person who filed a petition under CHAPTER 7 or CHAPTER 13 of the bankruptcy code.

DEFICIENCY PROCEDURES: The administrative procedures the IRS must follow in order to achieve an ASSESSMENT. See NOTICE OF DEFICIENCY.

DESIGNATED PAYMENT: A voluntary payment in which the citizen specifically instructs the IRS as to the tax year and type of tax to which the payment should be applied. A voluntary payment is one which is not procured through enforcement action, such as levy or seizure of assets.

DISCHARGE: The act or process by which a DEBTOR is relieved of debts pursuant to an order of the federal BANKRUPTCY COURT.

DISCRIMINATE FUNCTION SYSTEM (DIF): The computer program used to select returns for examination.

DISPOSABLE INCOME: When used in connection with the IRS' installment agreement process, it is the amount available to pay a monthly installment payment. See LOCAL STANDARDS and NATIONAL STANDARDS. When used in connection with the BANKRUPTCY CODE, it is the amount available to fund a plan of partial repayment of creditors under a CHAPTER 13 plan.

DISTRICT COUNSEL: The IRS' staff of "in house" lawyers whose job it is to represent the IRS in certain litigation and other legal matters.

DISTRICT COURT: The primary or introductory branch of the federal court system with authority to hear controversies involving the tax laws of the United States.

DIVIDEND: A partial payment. When used in connection with CHAPTER 13, a dividend is a partial payment to a creditor against his claim.

EFFECTIVE TAX RATE: The ultimate rate of tax that is paid after considering all income and tax liabilities, without regard to deductions.

EMPLOYMENT TAXES: Taxes assessed on wages paid to employees. These include social security (FICA) and unemployment (FUTA) taxes. See TRUST TAXES AND NON-TRUST TAXES.

EXAMINATION DIVISION: The IRS division responsible to examine or audit personal and business tax returns. It's primary function is to determine the "correct" tax liability. See REVENUE AGENT.

EXEMPT PROPERTY: When used in connection with the IRS' enforced collection powers, exempt property is that which is legally beyond the IRS' power to seize. Code section 6334. When used in connection with the BANKRUPTCY CODE, it is property which does not become a part of the BANKRUPTCY ESTATE and therefore, is not subject to the TRUSTEE'S power to LIQUIDATE. See NON-EXEMPT PROPERTY.

HARDSHIP: A condition that exists when a person is unable to pay ordinary and necessary living expenses. It is a condition that can lead to serious privation if the IRS' collection actions are carried out. See TAXPAYER ADVOCATE AND TAXPAYER ASSISTANCE ORDER.

INDEPENDENT CONTRACTOR: A self-employed person who makes his services available to businesses on a contract basis.

INDIVIDUAL MASTER FILE (IMF): The IRS' internal, computerized record of account for an individual tax return, Form 1040. See BUSINESS MASTER FILE.

INFORMATION RETURN: A form that transmits information to the IRS. Generally, these include (1) Form W-2, Wage and Tax Statement, showing wages and withholdings to employees, and (2) Form 1099, Non-employee Compensation, showing payments to non-employees, such as INDEPENDENT CONTRACTORS.

INJURED SPOUSE: A spouse who does not owe money to the IRS but whose separate share of a tax refund due on a jointly filed income tax return is seized to pay the separate tax or non-tax debt of her spouse.

INNOCENT SPOUSE: One who files a joint income tax return as a result of which the IRS assesses additional taxes due to either unreported income or bogus deductions attributable to the other spouse.

INTERNAL REVENUE CODE (IRC): The tax laws as written and enacted by Congress. This is the law of the United States with respect to taxation. See UNITED STATES CODE.

INTERNAL REVENUE MANUAL (IRM): The procedural guidebook written by the IRS to guide its agents, officers and employees in the conduct of their official duties. The IRM is not law. See INTERNAL REVENUE CODE.

JEOPARDY: A condition that exists when one is taking steps to place himself or his assets out of the reach of the IRS. See DEFICIENCY PROCEDURES, NOTICE OF DEFICIENCY and ASSESSMENT.

LEVY: The enforced collection process of attaching property such as wages, bank accounts, etc.

LIEN: The enforced collection process of recording a security interest or potential security interest in favor of the IRS in and to real and personal property.

LIQUIDATION: The process of forcibly selling assets, especially real estate. This occurs both by the IRS administratively and by a TRUSTEE in the BANKRUPTCY COURT.

LOCAL STANDARDS (LS): Fixed personal living expenses the IRS has established to standardize the process of negotiating installment agreements. Local standards apply to housing and transportation expenses, including vehicle costs and maintenance. See NATIONAL STANDARDS.

NATIONAL STANDARDS (NS): Fixed personal living expenses the IRS has established to standardize the process of negotiating installment agreements. NATIONAL STANDARDS apply to food, utilities, housekeeping supplies, clothing and clothing services, personal care products and services and miscellaneous items. See LOCAL STANDARDS.

NET PAYROLL: The process of paying employees their net wages, after accounting for all tax withholding requirements, but then not paying the taxes. See EMPLOYMENT TAXES, TRUST TAXES AND NON-TRUST TAXES.

NON-EXEMPT PROPERTY: Property which is not exempt from LEVY or sale by the IRS. When used in connection with the BANKRUPTCY CODE, it is property which becomes property of the ESTATE and is therefore subject to LIQUIDATION.

NON-FILER PROGRAM: The program introduced by former IRS Commissioner Shirley Peterson in which non-filers are offered the opportunity to get back into the system without fear of criminal prosecution.

NON-PRIORITY DEBT: Debts, including federal income tax debts, which are discharged under bankruptcy law if they meet the applicable rules set forth in BANKRUPTCY CODE section 507. See PRIORITY DEBT.

NON-TRUST TAXES: EMPLOYMENT TAXES not withheld from the pay of employees. These include unemployment taxes (FUTA) and matching social security (FICA) taxes. See TRUST TAXES.

OFFER IN COMPROMISE (OIC): Code section 7122. It is the formal process by which one offers the IRS less than full payment when he can show that he is unable to pay the full tax or does not owe the tax.

OFFSET: The process IRS uses to seize refunds due for the current year in order to apply them against outstanding assessments for a prior year.

ONE-YEAR RULE: Provides that citizens who have excessive personal expenses above those authorized by NATIONAL STANDARDS and LOCAL STANDARDS are given one year in which to make adjustments to their lifestyle in order that the excess may be applied to the installment payment amount.

NOTICE OF DEFICIENCY (NOD): The final administrative determination that you owe additional taxes. This is the formal notice that must be mailed before the IRS can assess taxes. It provides ninety days in which to file a petition in the TAX COURT. See DEFICIENCY PROCEDURES.

PRIORITY DEBT: Debts defined under BANKRUPTCY CODE section 507 which are never discharged. Taxes are priority debt only if they do not meet the rules set forth in BANKRUPTCY CODE section 507(a)(7). See NON-PRIORITY DEBT.

PROBLEMS RESOLUTION OFFICE (PRO): PRO functions as a liaison between the IRS and the citizen to assist in solving problems where normal channels have failed. Code section 7811. See HARDSHIP AND TAXPAYER ADVOCATE.

QUIET TITLE ACTION: Title 28, United States Code, section 2410, empowers the federal courts to consider cases in which the United States asserts a claim to real property.

REVENUE AGENT: The IRS employee responsible to determine one's correct liability through the audit process. See EXAMINATION DIVISION.

REVENUE OFFICER: The IRS employee responsible to collect assessed taxes debts. See COLLECTION DIVISION.

SECURED DEBT: BANKRUPTCY CODE section 506 defines a secured debt as one which is perfected by filing the proper documents, such as a mortgage or LIEN, with a public recorder's office. The debt is secured to the extent of the DEBTOR'S equity in such property. Such debts are not DISCHARGED in BANKRUPTCY COURT.

SPECIAL AGENT: The IRS employee responsible for conducting investigations into the possible violations of the tax and other criminal financial laws. See CRIMINAL INVESTIGATION DIVISION.

SPECIAL PROCEDURES STAFF: An adjunct to the COLLECTION DIVISION responsible to handle collection paperwork, such as LIEN releases, etc., and also handles the procedural aspects of tax bankruptcies.

STATUTE: A law of the United States or of a state. See UNITED STATES CODE.

SUBORDINATION: The process by which the IRS places its LIEN in an inferior position to that of another creditor. The priority of the position is generally determined by the timing of filing. For example, if a bank's mortgage lien pre-dates an IRS LIEN, the mortgage lien has priority over the IRS' lien.

SUBSTITUTE FOR RETURN (SFR): A tax return made by the IRS under the authority of code section 6020. This allows the IRS to make a return for a citizen when none has been made by him, or where a false return has been filed.

SUMMONS: An administrative tool used in the investigative process. It commands the production of documents and the testimony of witnesses and is used by all IRS enforcement divisions. Code section 7602.

SUMMONS ENFORCEMENT PROCEEDING: A legal proceeding in the DISTRICT COURT in which the IRS seeks a court order requiring a person to comply with a summons.

UNCOLLECTIBLE STATUS: The process by which the IRS freezes the collection account. This happens when a person's allowable personal living expenses meet or exceed his income, thereby making any payment impossible.

UNITED STATES CODE (USC): The entire body of United States laws. The code is organized by topic, called a title. Each title is dedicated to a specific area of the law and is given a number. For example, Title 26 contains all of the tax law. It is known as the INTERNAL REVENUE CODE. Each title is then broken down into sections, which are also numbered. Each section is one specific law. Thus, reference to Internal Revenue Code section 6331 is to Title 26, United States Code, section 6331.

TAX COLLECTION WAIVER: A voluntary waiver by the citizen of the collection statute of limitations. The waiver is usually accomplished by signing IRS Form 900. See COLLECTION STATUTE OF LIMITATIONS.

TAX COURT: A court of limited authority to resolve disputes between the IRS and a citizen. The court only has the authority to "redetermine" deficiency determinations made by the IRS. See NOTICE OF DEFICIENCY.

TAXPAYER ADVOCATE (TA): The IRS official whose duty is to help citizens resolve disputes with various enforcement divisions. He has the authority to issue a TAXPAYER ASSISTANCE ORDER. See HARDSHIP and PROBLEMS RESOLUTION OFFICE.

TAXPAYER ASSISTANCE ORDER (TAO): An order issued by a TAXPAYER ADVOCATE requiring the IRS to cease action it is taking or to refrain from taking threatened action. See HARDSHIP and PROBLEMS RESOLUTION OFFICE.

TRUSTEE: A person with a fiduciary responsibility over assets. When used in connection with the phrase "TRUST TAXES" it refers to the employer who withheld money from the pay of his employees. When used in connection with the BANKRUPTCY CODE, it refers to the bankruptcy official responsible to administer the ESTATE of the DEBTOR for the benefit of creditors.

TRUST FUND RECOVERY PENALTY: The law allowing the IRS to make a personal ASSESSMENT equal to the TRUST TAXES which were withheld from the pay of employees but were not paid. An ASSESSMENT of the Trust Fund Recovery Penalty cannot lawfully include NON-TRUST tax. Code section 6672. See WILLFULNESS.

TRUST TAXES: Taxes withheld from the pay of employees for their personal income and social security tax debts. See NON-TRUST TAXES.

WAGE-EARNER'S PLAN: A payment plan administered under CHAPTER 13 of the BANKRUPTCY CODE.

WILLFULNESS: When used in connection with the criminal tax laws, it means a voluntary, intentional violation of a known legal duty. It is the opposite of mistake, negligence, inadvertence or misunderstanding. See CRIMINAL INVESTIGATION DIVISION. When used in connection with the TRUST FUND RECOVERY PENALTY, it means simply that a responsible officer paid another creditor at a time when he knew TRUST TAXES were outstanding. In this context, it does not imply a bad purpose of evil motive.

DAN PILLA'S
COMPLETE IRS DEFENSE LIBRARY

41 Ways To Lick the IRS With a Postage Stamp . . .

Contains perhaps the most comprehensive discussion of IRS Penalty Abatement Procedures of any book ever written. You can even abate interest in certain cases where IRS error and delay are the cause of mounting tax bills. It is written for the average taxpayer and includes over 40 sample letters you can use to abate penalties and enforce your rights.

In addition, this book will show you how to audit-proof your tax return using an IRS form they don't publicize. Within this book you will also find sample affidavits and the secrets to using them with the IRS' own audit-proofing forms. Now you can get out of trouble and stay out of trouble with the IRS. This book is proof that the pen is truly mightier than the sword!

. . . $15.95 plus P&H

IRS Taxes and the Beast . . .

In 1984, IRS began to implement its secret "Strategic Plan," the goal of which is to audit every citizen each year. Claiming 80% of citizens cheat on their taxes by underreporting income, IRS relies more and more on computers to monitor all financial transactions. Financial Privacy is about to become something written of only in history books.

As computers scan more and more financial records, more people are sucked into the audit machine, a machine that grinds you up unless you know the IRS' limit of power. This book is a complete audit defense guide designed to help you avoid the pitfalls brought on by ignorance of your rights. It includes dozens of tips and techniques for surviving audits and maintaining a higher level of financial privacy and freedom.

. . .$15.95 plus P&H

Taxpayers' Ultimate Defense Manual . . .

When your rights have been violated and you have already paid taxes you do not owe, you need to call out the biggest defensive weapons we have in our arsenal. Sometimes the best offense is a great defense. This book will provide you with nine different Actions, Petitions, Procedures and even Lawsuits you can use to defend your wealth and your rights! On the next page is a list of all the actions you can take without the high cost of legal assistance.

Actions, Petitions, Procedures and Lawsuits

- **Using Tax Court to Call the Final IRS Bluff**
- **Recover Illegally Seized Property**
- **Make the IRS Pay Your Cost of Fighting When They Lose**
- **Claim a Refund on Past Returns**
- **Protect the Assets of an Innocent Spouse**
- **Punish IRS Agents for Unlawful Collection Activities**
- **Gain Access to Secret IRS Files Kept on You**
- **Protect Your Business . . . and Much More!**

The information you will get from this manual will make you a force to reckon with if the IRS begins to make unjustified demands for more of your money. No taxpayer should be without the knowledge provided in this oversized book that is actually nine books in one!

. . .$39.95 plus P&H

PILLA TALKS TAXES
A Monthly Newsletter & Consultation Service

Pilla Talks Taxes is a monthly tax expose'. Keeping a constant vigil over lawmakers in Washington, Dan reports the behind-the-scenes truth about pending legislation and changes in tax law. Rarely do we get the whole truth about changes which are supposed to simplify your tax life or lower your taxes. Without *Pilla Talks Taxes* you could find out too late you were sold a bill of goods instead of a Bill of Rights.

This newsletter is small in circulation but powerful in its effect on lawmakers and the laws they pass. This newsletter is read by key members of the media and members of Congress. This provides a national platform on which many obscure bits of tax legislation can be exposed to and discussed by the national public.

For example, this newsletter contributed to the much publicized discussion over the proposed version of the *Taxpayers' Bill of Rights Act*. *Pilla Talks Taxes* played a key role in defeating that first version of the bill, a version proven by Dan Pilla to take away rights rather than provide new ones. Subsequent to its defeat, a new version of the bill was proposed and passed—one that actually provided taxpayers with new rights.

The dischargeability of taxes in bankruptcy was another issue that exploded into the national media through this newsletter. The results were an admission by the IRS that taxes were indeed dischargeable. This led to the installation of tax amnesty programs which the IRS still tries to hide but nonetheless exist for those who know their rights.

SPECIAL BONUS

Subscribe now to Pilla Talks Taxes and get a <u>Free</u> copy of Dan Pilla's Special Report . . .

How The IRS Tries To Make You Die Poor
&
What You Can Do About It

As a subscriber to this newsletter you are also granted special privileges. It has always been the purpose of Dan Pilla and Dave Engstrom, President of WINNING Publications, Inc., to provide citizens with affordable solutions to devastating tax problems. That's why subscribers to PTT get . . .

<u>ONE HOUR FREE</u> OF PERSONAL CONSULTATION

With a value greater than the cost of a one year subscription, this personal consultation with Dan Pilla makes this newsletter one of the best informational values on the market today.

If you wish to subscribe to *Pilla Talks Taxes* or purchase any of our WINNING Publications, call the toll-free number listed below and ask if there are any special subscriber offers or package price opportunities on our complete line of IRS Defense Publications. You can also visit our website for the latest and greatest information.

1-800-34-NO-TAX

WINNING Publications, Inc.
2372 Leibel Street
White Bear Lake, MN 55110
www.taxhelponline.com